From Broncs to Bronzes

From Broncs ❧ ❧ to Bronzes

The Life and Work of Grant Speed

By DON HEDGPETH *with a Foreword by William E. Burford*

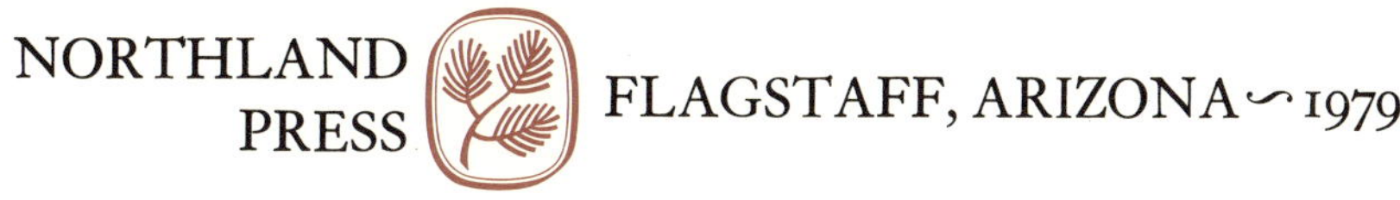

NORTHLAND PRESS FLAGSTAFF, ARIZONA ~ 1979

Contents

Foreword

BRONZE AS AN ART MEDIUM GOES BACK INTO ANTIQUITY. *As early as 5,000 B.C. the Chinese were casting, incising, and molding decorative vessels and tools from bronze with such technical skill and consummate creativity as to remove their creations above and beyond purely utilitarian purposes, achieving works of "art for art's sake."*

The medium has great durability, enhancing the created subject with an aura of immortality. Bronze has mass and substance, enforcing the reality of the artist's dream. It has tactile intrigue, drawing the viewer into personal contact. But it makes special inherent demands upon artists who choose to use it for the vehicle of their inspiration. It must have a unity of design as well as of the theme or intent of the creator. Its values and intensities must be achieved through more limited means than those available to the painter in oils or watercolors.

Many artists of the contemporary scene take great pride and satisfaction in working toward the mastery of different media. They switch back and forth among oils, watercolors, charcoal and pencil, and sculpture, finding that the variety enhances their own enthusiasm for creative effort. And so it is interesting to find an artist who from the beginning of his career has had such singleness of purpose, such satisfaction in his medium as has Grant Speed. It is through the medium of bronze, and working much in the same manner and with the same techniques as did artists several thousand years ago, that Speed has achieved his position in the field of western American art.

It was natural, coming from a "cowboying" youth, that Speed would use a rodeo theme for his early sculptures. He knew rodeo life personally, was alive to the actions of both man and animal under the tensions of a ten-second ride. But early in his career he produced a sculpture embodying a fresh approach in design, yet thoroughly researched for its historical accuracy. The piece, Scouting the War Party, *was a new concept in modeling. And Speed has continued through the years to create sculptures that are unique in their conceptual patterns. His* Ridin' Point *was the first to include a bronze vignette to expand and enforce the statement the artist was making about the life and times of the man portrayed. In addition, Speed has been one of very few Cowboy Artists who have chosen to use women for their sculptural themes. His prize-winning bronze,* The Half-Breed, *makes a sensitive and poignant statement, one far removed from the hackneyed concept of a cowboy on a bucking horse.*

Many sculptors dream of the opportunity to break out of the economically-feasible size model and do something great — something bigger than lifesize, a sculpture of commanding presence. Few are ever so honored by such a commission. Grant Speed has recently capped his career with an assignment to create a heroic-sized statue of Charles Goodnight, the legendary cattleman of the Texas Panhandle. The bronze will be placed at the entrance of the Mesa Petroleum Company in Amarillo, Texas.

We feel that it is possible to make some assessment about the inherent nature of an artist through his created works. Grant Speed's sculptures are invested with his own innate honesty and his sincere striving for universal understanding of the lives of the people and animals he portrays. The growth of the man has been reflected in the development of his artistic ideas.

WILLIAM E. BURFORD
President
Texas Art Gallery, Dallas

Introduction

From the days of prehistoric clay models in Babylon, of the Sphinx and the mysterious figures of Easter Island, of the carvings in the Mayan jungles and the perfections of Phideas, the sculptor has added something special of his own to the likenesses of men and animals he has fashioned. Always he has been enthralled by horses and by men on horseback. This has carried forward to our own day. The sculptured cowboy on a horse is a lineal descendant of Egyptian, Byzantine, Greek and Roman forebears.

Nearly every Western painter of the last one hundred years has felt at some time the urge to sculpt, to by-pass the intervening brush or palette knife, and by the direct and elemental use of the tactile faculty to feel, by actual touch of the fingers, the emerging image (Ed Ainsworth, The Cowboy in Art *[World Publishing Company, 1968], page 161).*

The first distinguishable American trend in sculpture came in the nineteenth century as sculptors developed the themes of Indian and animal life of the West. Many sculptors in the United States, as well as eminent European masters, found the "noble savage" a particularly appealing subject for idealization in bronze.

In fact, sculpture using western subjects enjoys a broader, less regional reputation than do oil paintings and watercolors that depict the same kind of subjects. Cyrus Dallin's heroic *Appeal to the Great Spirit* is installed prominently in front of the Museum of Fine Arts in Boston. This artist's rugged sculptures of western subjects are also displayed in other non-western cities such as Philadelphia and Hanover, Pennsylvania.

Among the outstanding American sculptors of the nineteenth and twentieth centuries are several native sons of the West. Classical educations in sculpture at such art meccas as the Académie Julian and the Ecole des Beaux-Arts provided these men with the technical means to convey their impressions of the western scene.

James Earle Fraser, the creator of a number of America's most well known sculptures, was raised on the Dakota prairies. Dallin was born in Utah, as was Salon Borghum, who worked as a cowhand in his youth. Remington and Russell, though both essentially self-taught in the medium of sculpture, equaled and in some instances even surpassed as sculptors their better-known efforts as painters.

The history of the American West is replete with heroic themes and individuals ideally suited to representation in bronze. What has been accomplished in this medium thus far is one of the strongest artistic testimonies to patriotism and the American character.

In the present generation, Grant Speed carries on the tradition of sculpture that is rooted in western inspiration. Grant's life in general, and his art career in particular, is a reflection of the qualities that have always exemplified the best in western life. It is a story of determination, hard work, discipline, independence, sensitivity to one's heritage, and a strong belief in God.

Grant's own story is as interesting and as full of genuine western flavor as are his bronzes. On a remote west Texas ranch, along the banks of the Pecos River, Grant made the transition from child to cowboy. He drew a cowboy's wages on ranches all over west Texas and in Wyoming. But more important than the scant pay he received were the horseback experiences and memories he acquired. To own a ranch became his dream.

The harsh economic realities of west Texas cowboy life finally brought Grant to the realization that he was never going to be able to afford his own cow outfit. He traded in his saddle and spurs for school supplies and went after a college degree in animal husbandry. As it turned out, he was soon cowboying again — in the rodeo arena. While at Brigham Young University he majored in agriculture, with an unofficial minor in bronc riding.

A college degree and rodeo trophy buckles did not seem to help Grant get any closer to his dream of owning a ranch. But he did begin to lose some of the rough edges of a cowboy and to show signs of settling down. There were two things that changed Grant's life during his college days. First, he met and married Sue Collins; second, he decided to stay in Utah instead of going back to Texas. He began a career as a schoolteacher but never really found what he was looking for in the classroom.

Finally, in 1964, as a complete surprise to everyone who knew him, he made up his mind to be an artist — specifically, a sculptor. With unfaltering dedication and plenty of hard work he began to pursue a career in western art.

Grant's success as an artist is a matter of record. The initial stage of his career coincided with the emergence of the group known as the Cowboy Artists of America. This group, and individual members like Grant Speed, were the prime movers in establishing a valid, creditable reputation for contemporary western art. The momentum has never leveled off, and Grant's career has been steadily marked by popular acceptance and critical acclaim.

The term "cowboy artist" is subject to all sorts of applications and interpretations in the present generation of western art. Originally, the term was used in association with Charles M. Russell, who had been a horse wrangler in Montana's Judith Basin country and then had gone on to a career in fine arts. Grant Speed fits the cowboy artist designation in the same way Russell did. They were both genuine cowboys — and they both became genuine artists. More loosely drawn interpretations of the term have allowed its application to almost anyone who uses western subject matter in his art. But it is appropriate and legitimate to consider Grant a cowboy artist in the strictest sense of the term.

And there is significance in this consideration. The fact that he lived the life of a cowboy gave Grant an intimate and privileged perspective of the very thing he would portray in his art. It is a perspective that can never be obtained from library research or visits to a ranch. Grant's bronzes of western life are never superficial representations of simply the way things *look*. They contain the actual essence of the subject: that quality that is discernable only to someone who is himself a product of the cowboy environment and life.

Through study, discipline, and hard work Grant has achieved the technical ability to produce sculpture. But his own background and experience in ranch country have given an additional and invaluable dimension to his art. It is one thing to create art from a perspective of objective reality. It is something infinitely better to create a work of art in which the artist uses not only his eye and his hand, but his heart as well. This involves the same kind of distinction between a journalist and a poet.

Any close observer of the contemporary western art scene will readily agree that Grant Speed is one of the leading talents in the area of sculpture. Of particular significance are the six "heads" (*Ridin' Point, Free Spirit, The Squaw Man, The Half-Breed, Almost Home from the War,* and *One Who Lived to Tell It*), which many feel to be some of the most outstanding accomplishments associated with this generation of western art. These six bronzes are ample evidence to support the widely held opinion that Grant Speed is one of a very small handful of sculptors who have contributed significant quality, depth, and substance to contemporary western art.

The fact that Grant's pieces are included in museum and institutional permanent collections, such as that of the Whitney Gallery of Western Art, lends special credence to his reputation. Such endorsements are not influenced by promotion-minded commercial dealers or by the whims of fad-oriented collectors.

One does not have to speculate that, perhaps, Grant Speed's work will be remembered a generation hence. It will be. It will be recognized, as it is today, as an important contribution, both artistically and historically, to the field of western American art.

Grant is still a long way from reaching the point where an artist exhausts his creativity and inspiration. His work is still fresh and original, and he is even more dedicated today to making meaningful and worthwhile statements in his sculpture. It is a safe bet that his most important artistic triumphs are still to come. But even if he never completed another piece, he has already left an indelible mark of accomplishment on western art.

There are many artists who have no real substance to them beyond their art. Grant Speed is a man who would be worth knowing even if he had never picked up a lump of sculptor's wax. He is still a Texas cowboy to the core, and that's a kind of creature that is something of an endangered species. His most impressionable years were spent around cowboys, in bunkhouses and cow camps from the Concho and the Pecos country of west Texas to the Laramie plains of Wyoming.

No one can ever know about cowboys like another cowboy, and Grant knows them well. In addition to having the skills necessary to hold the jobs he did on several big cow outfits, Grant also had a good reputation for being able to make usable cow horses out of just about anybody's broncs. His ability to handle ranch colts and spoiled horses always added to his usefulness at whatever ranch he worked for. This faculty made him a natural when he discovered rodeo while in college. The fact that he made the National Intercollegiate Rodeo Association's national finals the first year he competed is a pretty fair indication of how good he really was.

In the style of all genuinely good cowboys, Grant is a modest man. He is proud, but never boastful, about the wild cattle he has roped and the broncs he has ridden. Those years spent as a working cowpuncher and bronc rider allowed Grant to test and measure himself and develop a caliber of confidence that most modern men do not have.

Grant believes strongly in self-reliance — in doing for himself. His art career is a dramatic reflection of this kind of personal trait. And in Grant's case, they are facets of character that were forged in a cowboy context, rather than in the art world.

A major part of Grant's life revolves around his family. If there has ever been a cowboy who has finally amounted to something, it has usually been because of the healthy influences of a woman. Grant's wife Sue has had much to do with his success in art. Her support, encouragement, faith, patience, and love enabled Grant to risk a career in art, and it is Sue and those same virtues that sustain him today.

Cowboys usually do not take domestication as well as Grant has. In addition to being a good husband to Sue, he is also a great father to his children. Their first daughter, Peggy Sue, who died during childhood, and their other daughter Samantha and son Boone have always been more important to Grant than his cowboy memories or his art.

He has a good grasp on his life and a keen sense of his priorities. The first priority will always be his family. Grant is also a deeply religious person, a member of the Mormon church. His active, day-to-day faith in God has allowed him to handle the highs and the lows of life with steady perseverance.

Although he has achieved success in the art world, Grant will always be more relaxed and at ease among plain country folks and cowboys. The pressures of the art world have not affected his natural easygoing manner. His dramatic success as a sculptor has never once altered his way of life. He would still rather be at home with Sue and the kids than at a prestigious gallery opening. He has not allowed his life to become unmanageably complicated. And this is what keeps his art fresh and exciting. Despite his established success, he still approaches each new sculpture like he would a bronc. He knows he could get thrown, that it will demand all of his abilities and resources; but he has the certainty of a top hand, "that there never was a horse that couldn't be rode."

From Broncs to Bronzes

CHAPTER ONE

Ten Years of Cowboyin'

There is a distinct sense of confidence observable in the majority of men who are born in Texas. I realize that this comment will be considered by many to be just another timeworn Texas brag. But I believe that there is ample evidence to support it. The traditions of a frontier heritage remain a relevant part of life in the Lone Star State.

Other states pay lip service to their heritage but have gone on to other preoccupations in modern times. Texas remains a sanctuary for the flavor, tempo, and values that are uniquely western.

Out in west Texas, particularly, the sparsely vegetated range and the endless cycle of drought and dust have produced generations of men whose hardy character and self-reliance are etched in the lines of their weathered faces. The common denominator of life in west Texas is the range cattle industry, and the cowman in this dry, dusty region has never had the upper hand on nature. Over the years, this has produced a man who is endowed with an element of toughness, a large measure of pride in "doing for himself," an abundance of optimism, and a sustaining belief in God.

West Texas boys inherit these characteristics from their fathers and grandfathers. Heredity for west Texans involves more than just hair and eye color. These are men who come ready to handle whatever is thrown at them by life. It is an asset not possessed by those born in the more sophisticated and urban regions of America.

Grant Speed is a product of this healthy and vigorous heritage. The Speeds originally came from England. They were in South Carolina in the 1700s, making a life on America's earliest frontier. One of Grant's ancestors farmed a piece of land where Clemson University is located today.

From the Carolinas, Grant can trace his people to Mississippi and a little settlement called Speedtown. Grant's father came to Texas in 1914 with a brother who was suffering from tuberculosis. The two brothers settled in the San Angelo country. This part of Texas had a frontier heritage that was still very much alive. Nature continually challenged men to make a living in the dry and dust-blown region. And the battle for a cowman's survival there continues in the present day.

Grant's mother's family was already in Texas in the 1800s. They were farmers and stockmen and early settlers of Van Zandt County. Grant's great-grandmother remembered the night the party of men who had rescued the Comanche captive, Cynthia Ann Parker, spent the night at the Norton farm on their way back to the settlements. Grant's mother, Opal Rainey, came from Van Zandt County to San Angelo country and then on to Coke County by covered wagon in 1901.

Grant's mother and his father, George Franklin Speed, met at a country dance at Carlsbad, Texas in 1922. Grant's mother and some other girls had come to the dance in a Model T. Grant's dad walked up to the car and announced, "I want the prettiest girl in this bunch." The spark struck, and they began to go together to the little country dances and picnics around the San Angelo country.

Before long the young couple had a serious "falling out," and Opal left home for a remote hill-country ranch where her brother was cowboying. George set out to find her and patch things up. After talking to her family, he was finally able to get directions to the ranch. Opal was sitting at the kitchen table writing to him when he walked in the door. Needless to say, they ironed out their differences. They came back to San Angelo together and were married on April 14, 1923.

In June of 1924, the Speeds had a daughter, Mary Jo, and three years later, a son, George Franklin, Jr. By this time the young family had a little homeplace just north of San Angelo. Grant's parents still live there today.

The year 1930 was ushered into west Texas by a record-busting "blue norther." Stock tanks and windmill pumps froze up all over the region, and the country was in the grip of frigid storms sweeping down from the Panhandle. On January 6, Opal Speed presented her family with a new baby boy, Ulysses Grant.

Grant maintains, with all the proud conviction of a native southerner, that he was not named after the Yankee general and president. He says that Ulysses and Grant were two separate names decided upon by his parents from their own family trees. Nevertheless, it made it tough for a boy growing up in what had once been Confederate territory to have to carry the name of someone so conspicuous on the Union side.

San Angelo in 1930 was still a trading center for the ranching country that stretched on out to the west. Grant's first vivid memories are of cow people. Most prominent among them were his uncles, Boone and Sheridan Rainey. Both men were cowpunchers, and whenever they came to San Angelo on cow business, they always stopped for a visit at the Speed's place. These hard-bitten Texas cowmen made a dramatic impression on the Speed children. The way they dressed and talked and the stories they told set the youngsters' imaginations on fire. In 1932, Grant's younger brother, Rainey, was born, and then in 1936, a younger sister, Virgie.

Since the range country extended right up to the city limits of San Angelo, it was not at all unusual in the years before World War II to see men on horseback close to town. The old Nolke ranch was close to the Speed's property. The color and excitement of spring and fall cow work was practically right in their own backyard.

In the mind of the little boy named Ulysses Grant there was no doubt about what he wanted to do when he got big enough. He was going to be a cowboy.

It was probably Uncle Boone who had the strongest influence on the young boy. He represented to Grant the ultimate cowboy, and still does. He was an outstanding bronc rider and horse trainer and was also a superior roper. He was good at "cowboy arithmetic" and could tally cattle in the middle of a dust storm without missing a head. Boone Rainey's abilities with cattle were widely known. It was said that "he could talk a cow out of her calf." He knew what cattle and horses were thinking. This ability was particularly apparent in his work with horses.

For years it seemed that every spoiled bronc and full-grown outlaw horse from throughout west Texas wound up at Boone's place on the Pecos River. Broncs just can't earn their keep on a working cow ranch, and it was well known that Boone Rainey could make a tough, mean outlaw into a usable cow horse in short order. Boone was a complete cowboy; he could do it all. It is the figure of Uncle Boone that looms largest in Grant's memory of his earliest years.

Grant's dad wasn't a rancher or a cowboy. He worked for the county and kept only a few milk cows and other farm animals at the homeplace. The young Grant could not see the romance in that kind of a livestock operation. If he couldn't be out on horseback among big steer herds, at least he could daydream about it. Consequently, he turned out to be a pretty poor hand when it came to doing his share of the chores around home.

"I wasn't worth ten cents in Mexican money," Grant recalls. "I had a bad reputation for being lazy, and folks began to say that my first initial 'U.' was for 'Useless.'"

It wasn't that Grant couldn't get "stirred up" — he could, and did, about cowboys and beef cattle; but not about farmhands and dairy cows.

On top of his natural reluctance to do anything that didn't smell of cowboy, the boy also had a health problem. He was born with a bad stomach and had a bad bout with pneumonia right about the time he started to school. With the stomach problem, he was always "just nearly sick."

But Grant was artistically inclined right from the beginning. He liked to make things with his hands, and he liked to draw. He began to develop this inclination when he began the first grade at the little country school on the Nolke ranch in 1935. He didn't care much for school but remembers that he "was good at art and playing."

Aside from the periodic visits of his Uncle Boone, there were only a couple of incidents that really caught Grant's attention during his days in primary school. The first was the time in 1936 when it rained nearly sixteen inches during a twenty-four hour period and flooded the San Angelo country. Given the aridity of the region, a rain like that would make a lasting impression on an entire generation of people who were more used to drought conditions. Another incident recalled clearly was when his teacher took all the students from the little school to her home to listen to the radio as Congress declared war on Japan.

In the spring of 1942 Grant finished the sixth grade and figured he was big enough to make a hand on anybody's ranch. He was twelve years old and ready for some relief from the monotony of home life. About this time, Uncle Boone stopped by on his way back to the Pecos country. Grant's folks agreed to let him go out to Boone's ranch for a couple of weeks. "I wasn't much use around home anyway," he recalls.

That summer was of major importance in Grant's life. It reinforced his affection for the cowboy life and settled his goals and priorities on living that life himself. His impressions of that summer are still vivid nearly forty years later.

We hit the Pecos River just a little before sundown, just east of Sheffield. It had come a little rain and the purple sage was blooming. We turned off the highway on the road to the ranch and I just couldn't believe the difference in the country. It looked wild, and I loved it. We got to the ranch just at dark. The little house was about one hundred and fifty yards from the Pecos, and as soon as I had helped Uncle Boone unload the truck, I took off for the river. I had seen the river for years in my imagination, and when I finally stood on the bluff looking at it, I figured it must be the neatest place on earth.

The little cabin that Uncle Boone and his wife, "Aunt Bill," lived in was a source of fascination for the boy. There were stacks of old "Cattlemen" magazines and a radio that ran off a car battery. Since there was no electricity on the banks of the Pecos, the old coal-oil lanterns were lit every evening. There was a single-shot .22 rifle for Grant to use, and an abundance of jackrabbits to satisfy any young Davy Crockett. The smells of juniper and salt cedar were wonderfully new and exciting. And there was the river right at hand for fishing and swimming.

From the first morning, Grant learned how to be a cowboy. He learned to know all the horses on the place and to know about horse nature in general. He had a great teacher. On the first morning when they ran the horses into the corrals, Uncle Boone cut out an old, steady cow horse named Tanglefoot for Grant to ride while he was on the place.

"I was tickled to death," Grant says. He quickly disproved his parents' judgment of him being lazy. He just couldn't get enough of ranch work. It was hard, to be sure, but to him it was fun. Pecos country cowpunching had San Angelo dairy cow work beat a million ways to the mind of this twelve-year-old boy.

Grant wrangled the horses every morning on foot.

This saved the necessity of keeping up and feeding a night horse. Grant felt he learned more that summer than he had in six years of school. He and Uncle Boone were out in the pastures all day, just about every day. Before long, Boone was sending Grant out alone.

Finally, Boone began to get up the range colts to break. That was, to the mind of a boy, what cowboying really was. The first bronc Grant went on that summer was a bay filly called Sister. "She wasn't bad to buck," Grant says, "but she bucked me off over her head when Uncle Boone jumped out and spooked her. But I got back up and got on her again. I was scared, but I got over it. I didn't want my uncle to be disappointed in me."

Pretty soon Grant was riding colts that were about half bronc every day as he went about his chores. Uncle Boone kept up a steady tutoring session on horse handling, and it soaked in and stayed with the boy.

What was supposed to have been a two-week visit turned into an entire summer. Grant met a lot of other cowboys during that summer, including a brother of Ben Kilpatrick, who had been one of Butch Cassidy's "Wild Bunch." It was a summer that would have turned any boy's head around. Grant would never again be a candidate for town life until he got cowpunching out of his system.

Much too soon to suit him, it was time for school to start, and Grant had to go home. But he wasn't the same boy. He watched the Nolke ranch cowboys riding past the school house and he wanted to be with them.

As soon as school was out the next year, Grant packed his bag and headed for Pecos. He traveled by bus this time, arriving in the little town of Sheffield after dark. He had just a little change in his Levi's, but he was sure hungry. Entering a small café, he looked over the menu and ordered the cheapest thing, a short stack of pancakes. Because of the bad stomach he had had since birth, Grant never could eat sweets. So he couldn't put syrup on them. The waitress hadn't given him any water and was pretty tight with the butter, too. When he got a big mouthful of the dry pancakes he began to chew…and chew…and he realized he was in trouble. He tried to swallow, but couldn't. A big lump of it was stuck in his throat and wouldn't go down. His eyes were watering and he was gasping for air when the waitress finally put a glass of water in front of him. It was a narrow escape. From the café he went back out on the street and bedded down on a bench in front of a store. Before daylight he started out for the ranch on foot and arrived just as Uncle Boone and Aunt Bill were eating breakfast. He was glad to be there. Being out on your own was not always that much fun. It was good to be back among folks you knew.

This year he knew a lot more to begin with and Uncle Boone gave him more responsibility. At thirteen he was doing a grown cowboy's job.

The first morning on the ranch that summer, Grant and his uncle rode out to find a mare that was due to foal. They found her tracks and those of her new colt. They heard brush popping ahead of them and set out in a high lope after the noise. As they tore through the brush, Boone hollered to watch for a fence that was in the vicinity. At just about that moment Boone's horse, Blackjack, hit the fence at full speed. Wire screeched and popped, and Blackjack was thrown straight up to come down with Boone in a cloud of dust and a big tangle of wire, horse, and man. It was a genuine cowboy wreck, and it set the tone for Grant's second summer of cowpunching.

That summer Grant was loaned out to neighboring

outfits for cow work and also began to learn how to ride broncs the right way. But there was time to watch the coyotes and wild turkeys, to go fishing in the Pecos, and to slide down mud banks into a swimming hole.

Too soon again, summer was over, and it was back to San Angelo and school. In school it was becoming more apparent that Grant did have a natural talent for art. But it was not something that a young cowboy would take seriously.

And so it went during the rest of his school years. Grant would "put up" with school and look forward with relish to summers, when he could strap on his spurs. But he didn't go back to the Pecos, although it remained a special place to him. During his fifteenth summer he was making a hand on a ranch near Paint Rock, to the east of San Angelo, and earning a grown man's wages for a grown man's work.

"By then," Grant says, "I felt like I could handle just about anything." His sixteenth summer Grant worked with his older brother on the Nolke ranch near the Speed home. "The Nolkes were the kind of ranchers that made hard labor out of many things," Grant says. It fit the old cowboy description, "Sell your bed and buy a lantern." By now Grant was making fifty dollars a month, living in the bunkhouse, and could hold his own with any cowboy. It was at the Nolke's that Grant met and worked with Alton Howard, "the only man I ever saw," Grant says, "who could set flat on his rear end in the saddle and rope really well without standing up in his stirrups."

The next spring Grant graduated from high school in San Angelo. He was seventeen, and there was no question in his mind about which career to pursue. Before the ink was dry on the diploma, he was on his way to the Pecos country. He worked full-time for Uncle Boone for the next ten months. During this period he learned all Boone could teach him about breaking horses — and that was a lot. There were long days of riding broncs, chasing horses, and doctoring wormy cattle and sheep, and he relished it all. There was little doubt but that he had found the life that suited him.

The Pecos River country is a rough, barren range. It has never supported large numbers of cattle. Boone ran mostly sheep and goats and, of course, his horses. By March 1948, Grant was ready to pack his war bag and find work with a big cow outfit. He headed for Midland and signed on with Foy Proctor's outfit. Proctor was one of the original, hard-twist cowmen of the Midland area. Grant unrolled his bed in the bunkhouse of the NA ranch, one hundred and ten sections that Proctor had leased. Callie Hirst was the boss at the NA's. He and his wife, Madge, were nice to the young cowboy, and he still remembers their kindness. Grant started cowboying from the first day, and he earned his wages.

There was a small corner of Grant's mind that was preoccupied with art. All through school he had been interested in the art classes, and it was obvious that he did have a natural talent. That first season at his uncle's place, after graduation, he spent some time drawing bucking horse pictures. Grant was already aware of Charlie Russell, and he was collecting Russell reproductions that he cut out of western magazines like "Hoofs and Horns." He did some drawing at the NA's, but it had never become anything very important.

The summer of 1948, Grant worked through the roundup with the NA's, then worked through on the C ranch, which Proctor also leased, then went on out to Arizona to work Proctor's outfit near Willcox. Grant met a lot of good cowboys, rode a lot of broncs, and roped a lot of cattle. By then Grant could do just about anything he wanted to on a bronc. His bosses always noticed this special knack and gave him more than his share of "green" colts to ride.

By the time the season's work was over, Grant was face to face with the U.S. Selective Service. He had the option of joining up for a year and then going in the inactive reserve, or he could be drafted for two years. He decided to get it over with and volunteered for the Air Force. He joined up in San Angelo and was sent directly to San Antonio to be put into an aircraft mechanics school. He enjoyed getting the chance to fly around the country, and he also liked San Antonio. There were plenty of idle hours, and Grant began to spend more time drawing. He liked to do a Will James kind of picture of bucking horses.

Grant was discharged in December of 1949 and, once again, he headed for Uncle Boone's outfit. By the late '40s, all of west Texas was in the grip of a prolonged and severe drought. Many cowmen never recovered from its ravages. Boone Rainey had been forced out of his Pecos River place and had relocated in central Texas, near the small town of Hico. It just wasn't real ranching country, though, and Grant soon got tired of building fence.

He packed his gear before long and hauled out for west Texas. John Scott's forty-five sections near Mertzon were a genuine cow outfit, and they could use an all-around hand who could also do a good job breaking colts. Scott had three sons, who were all top cowboys. Grant felt at home.

It has always been part of a cowboy's makeup that he just can't stay too long in any one place. It has something to do with the anticipation of seeing new country and expanding his knowledge of people and places and cow work. The freedom to roll your bed, sack your saddle, and go see what's over the next hill will always be a constant feature of the genuine cowpuncher.

Things were going well at the Scott's, but when Grant heard from his sister, who was married and living in Wyoming, he once again set out "to see what he could see." He had always heard exciting stories about that state and that it was genuine cow country.

After visiting for a while with his sister and her husband at Laramie, Grant went into Cheyenne to find a riding job. He found work on the historic old Van Tassel ranch, replacing a cowboy who had just been struck and killed by lightning. The cowboy's widow was the cook for the outfit. As it turned out, Grant was the only cowboy on this thirty-section division of the ranch. Except for the general manager, who lived in Cheyenne, he had the day-to-day responsibility for the whole place. Grant was twenty years old that summer of 1950, and he was equipped to handle the job.

The manager could have had some reservations about leaving this young Texan in charge of the ranch. Not long after Grant started to work, the old man told him to deliver a bunch of bulls to another division of the ranch the next day. Grant was working by himself. He got up the next morning long before daylight, brought in the bulls, loaded as many as he could in the bobtail truck, and had them delivered and was back at the ranch before daylight. He was sitting down to breakfast when the manager drove up. "I could tell by the look on his face," Grant says, "that he thought I was getting a late start. He thought I had just gotten up, but he didn't say anything. We walked out to the corrals and he asked, 'Where's the rest of those bulls?' I told him I'd already hauled half of them over to the other place. He said, 'This morning?', like he didn't believe it. Then he remarked that cowboys sure must get up early in Texas."

From then on the manager had no doubts about Grant's ability to do his job or to handle responsibility. Before long he gave him another place to look after. It was a season of long, hard days and short nights. He was drawing top hand wages, one hundred and twenty-five dollars a month plus room and board.

There was a bronc rider living on the second place Grant had to take care of. This boy had been in jail and was pretty much an outlaw. As it turned out, he had several men staying with him, including some Army deserters. They would hide out in the brush when Grant was around. The manager noticed how big the grocery bill was running for that one bronc rider, and he began to question Grant about it. By this time Grant knew something shady was going on, but in true cowboy style he minded his own business. Finally it came to a night when the sheriff from Cheyenne threatened to throw Grant in jail unless he told what he knew about this bunch of hard-cases. But Grant told him he wasn't going to tell him anything. He was tending to his own business, and this situation was none of his affair. Grant had learned more about cowboying than just riding broncs and roping cattle. The ranch manager finally was able to convince the sheriff that Grant was a good man and not hooked up with the outlaw bunch. But Grant remembers that this incident came awfully close to handcuffs and windows with bars before it was settled.

Once again, the itchy feet that are a cowboy's constant affliction began to bother Grant. From the Van Tassel's he moved to the Getz ranch out west and south of Laramie. It was summer, and the new job involved a lot of haying. Although he didn't care much for that kind of work, Grant guessed he could stick it out until the fall roundup began.

Cowboys have never paid much attention to what

is going on in the world outside the boundaries of the ranch for which they work. A cowboy discussion of "current events" will generally concentrate on such subjects as the condition of the pastures and of the cattle, what colts they're riding, and what they did the last time they spent a Saturday night in town. Broader considerations of national or international matters hold little interest for a cowboy. But all of a sudden world affairs confronted Grant in the form of a recall from the Air Force. The Korean situation was heating up at this time and many inactive reserve units were being called up.

Airman Speed found himself back in uniform and in Roswell, New Mexico. The year he had spent previously in the service had been something of an adventure, but this time his mind was not with it at all. He was flattered when on the basis of test scores he was offered an appointment to West Point, but he wasn't tempted a bit. By now, cowboying was too much in his blood. During the year he was back on active duty, Grant spent three months in England. He said, "That's one place that may have Texas beat on strange weather. I saw it hail, rain, snow, and then the sun shine all within a fifteen-minute period." He had a harrowing experience aboard a burning B-29 and nearly had to bail out. It was one thing to buck off a horse and hit the ground, but this was an entirely different matter. He enjoyed the passes into London and also remembers how Paris looked from the tail of a B-29 at night. But there were no earthshaking episodes during the year, and he was glad to get back into Levi's and boots.

After being discharged, Grant visited his folks at San Angelo and then spent a few days with Uncle Boone at Hico. All of his life Grant had heard stories about the big cow outfits in Old Mexico. Now he decided to head south and see what he could learn from

the *vaqueros*. He bought a 1935 Chevrolet coupe for $115 in Meridian, Texas, threw in his saddle and bed, and started for the Rio Grande. Heading out to the Big Bend area of far west Texas, he slept alongside of the road for several nights. He reached the border at Ojinaga. A kindly customs service officer asked Grant if he knew exactly where he was going and how to get there. When Grant said he didn't, the customs officer said that he knew the country and he wouldn't think about striking out alone in that old car. He went on to tell Grant about the very real dangers that were waiting south of the river for a gringo traveling alone and without a gun. Finally it sunk in, and Grant turned his old jalopy around, deciding to leave Mexico to the Mexicans.

He pulled in to Marfa and stopped at a saddle shop to inquire about prospects for a riding job. It was the fall of 1951, and the roundup season was just beginning. The man in the saddle shop said he had heard that the X's were putting on men for the fall work, and he gave Grant directions. The boss, Ralph Boone, hired Grant at the Rincon headquarters of the X ranch, and the twenty-one-year-old cowboy unrolled his bed in the bunkhouse. Grant has good memories about the cowboys and the country of the X's. "I never enjoyed a place more in my life," he remembers. "It was a six-hundred-section operation and a pure, straight cow outfit. The cowboys were all good hands, and the country was beautiful to see. Most any of the horses would pitch if they got the chance. I loved it."

Grant stayed on at the X's through the roundup and on into the winter. He chased some of the wildest cattle he'd ever seen during those months. "We lost a whole herd of six hundred head one time trying to pen them. They were two year olds and they spooked as we crowded them toward the pens. There was just no way on earth to stop them once they turned back on us."

The country was rocky, with pretty good-sized mountains for Texas and cut up with deep canyons and arroyos. Twenty-five years before Grant got there they had begun trying to gather all of an old herd of black Angus cattle off the place. Twenty-five years later, remnants of that Angus blood were still apparent in the X cattle. Cowboys will understand this in relation to how rough and rugged the country was.

Among the horses in Grant's string was an old cow pony named Blue Goose:

"He was more than half bronc, and sure not any fancy cutting horse, but you could get a job done on him most of the time. He had a mean streak and would always duck out from under you when you went to get on him. He didn't want any petting, he just wanted to be left alone. One day we were making a big gather in the roughest part of the ranch. It was called Phillip's Canyon. The cattle were wild and the country was rocky and bad. The foreman told the boys to let the cows go if they had to, but to be sure and catch all the calves. A cow and calf broke out past me, and I grabbed my rope and took after the calf. I roped it just right, but Blue Goose blew up just then and stampeded past the calf, and when the slack played out the rope broke. Blue Goose went all to pieces and had a wild fit. He bucked all over the country before I was finally able to get him settled again. He knew he had me at a bad place and just took advantage of it. After the storm, I tried to get him to buck when I was ready, but he wouldn't do it. It sure made me mad."

In the spring of 1952, Grant's older brother wrote that he saw the opportunity to make some real money on some cotton land leases. Grant had never felt more in his element than at the X's, but for quite a while he had been wanting to put together enough of a stake to lease some land and buy some cattle for himself. He had decided that it was never going to happen on a cowboy's wages. His brother believed that if they farmed this cotton land for a year, they just might make enough money to get in the cattle business.

But as it turned out, the cotton farming proposition wasn't a good deal, and Grant went back to the X's for a while. From there he worked on three or four outfits back in the San Angelo area, around Mertzon and Water Valley. It became more obvious to him all the time that he was going to have to do something else if he was ever going to get enough money together to get into the cattle business. This was on his mind a lot now, and he stayed with an outfit for shorter periods of time before moving on. West Texas was several years into the worst drought in its history. The sight of starving stock also took a lot of the charm out of the work. It was depressing, day after day, to tend to thirsty, starving cattle. This period broke a lot of men who had been in the business all their life.

While breaking colts for the Boatright ranch, Grant came up against the toughest bucking horse he had ever met. It was a four-year-old bay and plenty stout. He was a good-looking horse and seemed to be really easy to get along with at first. One of the things Uncle Boone had taught Grant was to get a horse used to a rope right from the first saddle.

On this particular morning, Grant was riding the colt and roping bushes, uprooting them, and pulling them up all over the horse. The horse seemed to be calm and taking it all in stride. They were getting along fine. As Grant turned back toward the corrals, he roped a small stump and dragged it up to the horse and let it bump along at the colt's heels. At the corral gate, Grant jerked on the rope, and the stump swung around and hit the horse in the shoulder. Grant remembers what happened next: "I have been on a lot of bucking horses, but I have never felt a horse strain under me like that one did and try so hard to buck a man off. The horse was terrified. He went all to pieces, jumped as high as he could, wheeled, and kicked at the stump." The rope was tied hard and fast to the saddle horn, and, as the colt continued to buck, the stump swung in wide arcs all around. Grant was trying to stay on the horse and at the same time attempting to dodge the flying stump. Grant lost both stirrups, and the colt was jumping harder and higher all the time. They bucked clear over the top of some feed troughs and headed straight for a four-strand barbed wire fence.

The stump was still swinging through the air just past Grant's hat brim. Just as the colt touched the wire, he stopped, turned, and started bucking off down through a hackberry thicket. He was beginning to get winded, quit bucking, and started running away. Grant and the colt finally came to ground in a little clearing. The colt was wide-eyed and blowing and snorting something fierce.

About that time, Mr. Boatright and Uncle Boone drove up. The horse was beginning to calm down. Boone read the story right away and asked Grant, "Why don't you pull that little-bitty stump up on the horse?" Grant tugged on the rope ever so slightly, and the colt started the whole show again. Finally things settled down again. Boone said, "Boy, that pony sure did buck!" And Grant replied, "You didn't see anything. You should have been here before he got tired."

In the fall of 1952, Grant was working for T. Wayne Harris near Water Valley, Texas, not far from San Angelo. The drought still had a firm hold on the coun-

try. The cattle and sheep were down to eating prickly pear. The thorns cut their mouths, and screwworms were taking a terrible toll in livestock. It seemed like the country would never be green again.

One Sunday afternoon, Grant was lying out in the bunkhouse alone, thinking about his future. "I was twenty-two years old. And I didn't seem to be getting any closer to having a place of my own. It hit me that I'd better change my plans." He got up and drove in to San Angelo to figure out a new course for his life.

He decided that it might make sense to go to college and get a degree in animal husbandry. A degree, along with his practical knowledge of ranching, just might increase his opportunities. Grant's family were all Mormons, and it was decided that, with the help of the GI Bill and the money he had saved from cowboying, he would try to get into Brigham Young University in Utah. He had to come to grips with the dilemma that has faced hundreds of young men who want to own their own ranch: you just can't pay off a ranch mortgage on the profits from a cattle operation. It's a modern day fact in the cow country that there are only two ways a young man can get his own outfit. He has to either marry into it or inherit it.

At the age of twenty-two, Grant already had nearly ten years of cowboying under his belt. He would have been a top hand on anybody's outfit, but there was something in him that made him want to amount to more than just a cowboy working for wages. He had seen many old cowboys who had ended up not being able to find a job. They had little to show for their horseback experience except a measure of old aches and pains from too many bad broncs and some worn-out memories that no one wanted to hear about.

So, in the fall of 1952, with a hope and a prayer, Grant set his sights on Utah and college.

Classrooms and Rodeos

It is a long-established fact that native sons of the Lone Star State do not transplant well into other regions. Men who grow up in Texas are usually content to stay there. Most of those who leave become discontented and start looking for a way to get home. An old cowboy song from the late 1800s expresses the yearnings of a Lone Star cowpuncher who had gone to work in Montana: "I'd like to be in Texas when they roundup in the spring." But, by the same token, Texans are always excited by the prospect of at least seeing new country. Maybe it's just that it make them appreciate their own state more. To paraphrase an old axiom, "You can take the cowboy out of Texas, but you can't take Texas out of the cowboy."

These feelings are felt the strongest in men who have spent most of their time outside, rather than in a city or town. Grant had come to know a wide measure of Texas range country. It was a country that he had deep attachment for, despite the long drought. And not only was he going to a new country, he was also exchanging his rope and spurs for school books. He knew he could hold his own with a roundup, but he knew that a college classroom was a far different situation. But once Grant had made up his mind, his well-developed determination to "make a go of it" took over, and there was no turning back. He had never backed away from a ranch bronc, either, and determination had become a part of his character.

Grant responded well to the Utah country. It presented a marked contrast to the west Texas range country he had come to know so well over the past several years. The scenic beauty of the Utah mountains appealed to him, as did the forest. Trees were a genuine novelty in west Texas. He liked his new surroundings with all the enthusiasm of a cowboy seeing new ranges for the first time.

But Grant was in Utah to go to school, of course, and not just to enjoy the scenery. He had never really worked up any appetite for classroom experience during his twelve years of public school back in San Angelo. This same "ho-hum" attitude surfaces again when Grant talks about his studies at Brigham Young University. He studied, did his class work, made his grades, and ultimately received a degree, but it was not education that held his interest during this period. It was something entirely apart from campus life and something still closely akin to his background with ranch work. It was rodeo.

The National Intercollegiate Rodeo Association (N.I.R.A.) was still a relatively new organization in 1952. It began in Texas and spread quickly throughout the western states. The states were divided into regions, with each participating college or university fielding a rodeo team to compete against other teams in their region. Individual event winners and top teams from each region competed against each other in a National Finals rodeo at the end of the season.

Grant had never competed in a rodeo arena before coming to Utah. During the years he was working as a cowboy, there just wasn't the opportunity to take off and go to town for a rodeo. Then, too, rodeo cowboys were somewhat frowned upon by cowmen as something more like circus performers than genuine cowpunchers. A rancher wanted men to get their work done with just as little spurring of the horses and roping of the cattle as possible.

But all those lessons learned from Uncle Boone and all those colts he had broken had more than adequately prepared Grant to feel comfortable around bucking chutes and full-grown outlaw stock. It was in the arena, rather than the classroom, where Grant distinguished himself during his college days.

He was a natural bronc rider. Fitting a stylish ride on a bareback horse or a saddle bronc came easier to Grant than to other boys who had not put in the time he had with wild ranch colts — and it was fun. In between rodeos, and in the off-season, Grant and his buddies scoured the countryside looking for horses that might buck. They went to rendering plants and borrowed wild horses that were destined for slaughter. Before long, ranchers all around the Provo country were bringing in their spoiled horses for the boys to

try. Although Grant rode bareback horses, bulls, and "dogged" steers, it was saddle bronc riding that suited him best.

Grant and four or five other cowboy-students lived together in a little off-campus duplex. One night while they were right in the middle of eating supper, two loose horses came trotting down the road in front of the house. The boys jumped up from the meal, as if by reflex, and went out to catch the horses. They penned them in a little grassy trap, stuck a bareback rigging on them, and used a lariat for a flank strap.

That little incident is just an example of the extent to which rodeo gets into a boy's blood. It is tough to match the exhilaration that comes from climbing down on a bucking horse and then pitting your ability against his raw power. And when you have ridden him, there's a sense of pride and of accomplishment that is in proportion to the risk. Winning a game of checkers, golf, or tennis could never produce the high that comes with a successful ride on a bronc that weighs a half ton. Once you have done it, you will never be the same again. Rodeo is one of the few, the very few, environments in which modern man can come to grips with such a high degree of personal danger. During the process of riding broncs, men find out what sort of stuff they are really made of. Most men go through life never really knowing the things about themselves that an eight-second ride on a bull or a bronc will reveal. But it becomes an addiction and can often overshadow other priorities in one's life. And it's a habit that is tough to kick.

The first year that Grant rodeoed at Brigham Young he won regularly. Rodeo is the only officially sanctioned collegiate sport that pays money to its winners. Grant found this to be a great way to make money and do something he enjoyed completely, all at the same time.

wasn't much in being a ranch cowboy."

Grant had a social life in college, too. He had never had much time for dating when he was out on a ranch, but now, the same boys he rodeoed with were also "chasing" girls together.

At the end of the first year at Brigham Young, Grant came back to San Angelo. He got a job driving a truck and spent each weekend traveling to every little rodeo he could get to. He knew that if he got a job on a ranch he wouldn't be able to rodeo, and he was too far gone by now to give it up willingly.

In the fall of 1953 he was back in school at B.Y.U., learning what he could about academic agriculture and working on perfecting his "spurring lick." The next

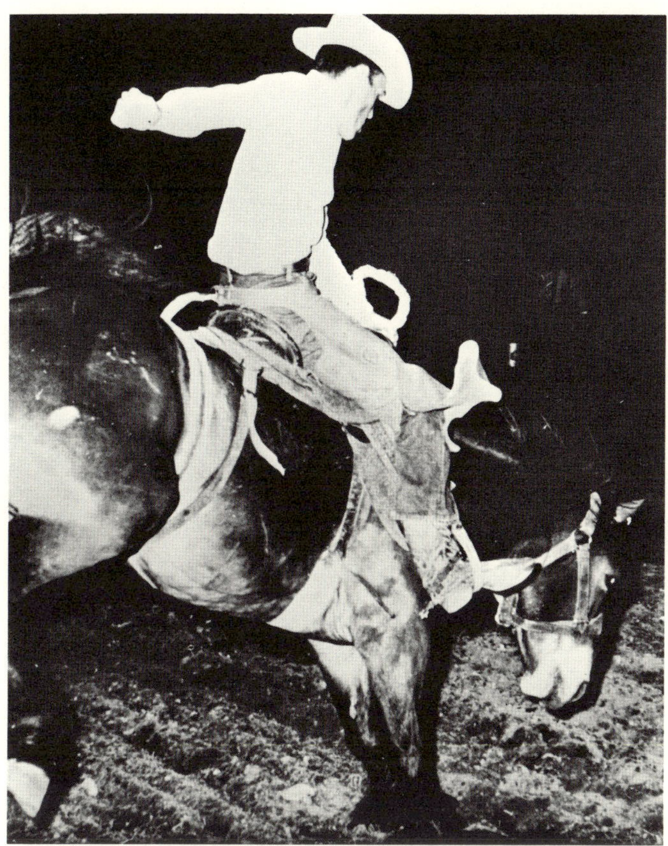

Grant on Indian Boy at Kennewick, Washington, 1954

By the end of the first season he had qualified for the N.I.R.A. National Finals. He was hooked.

Consideration of this new period in Grant's life brings the conclusion that he had given up being a ranch cowboy and had become, instead, a rodeo cowboy. The role of college student seemed to figure in his life much less prominently than did the role of bronc rider. Grant says: "If the rodeo hadn't been there, I guess I would have seen it on through with the studying and stuff. I knew I was old enough that I had to think about the future and that there just

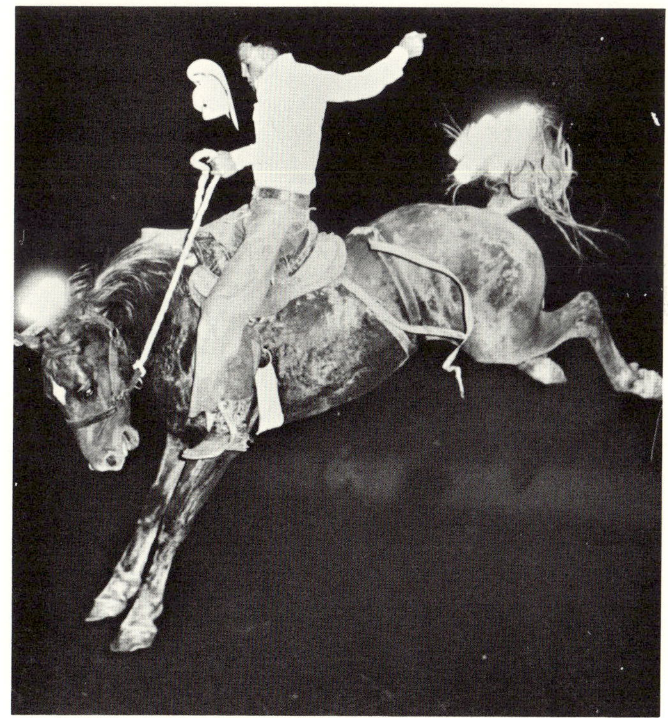

Grant Speed on Big Piney, Logan, Utah, 1954

summer he stayed in Utah to rodeo throughout the Rocky Mountain area. At Logan, Utah, that summer, he drew a bronc called Big Piney. "He came out bucking so wild that after about six seconds he missed the ground altogether and fell with me. Then he rolled over the top of me and broke my ankle."

Grant spent some time back with his Uncle Boone in Texas while his ankle was knitting. He had a walking cast on his leg but could get around well enough to build fence and do other odd jobs. Boone had a drought-starved Hereford bull on the place and challenged the "rodeo star" to ride him. Over a period of days, Grant tried the bull twenty-one times, and he figures he made maybe two rides that were qualified.

At this stage, the Mormon church asked Grant to go on a mission for two and a half years. All young Mormon men who take their church as seriously as Grant did are required to perform missionary work. He spent the period working among the Mexicans in south Texas and New Mexico. It strengthened his own faith and also increased his recognition of the responsibilities that come with maturity.

He completed his mission for the church in May of 1957 and headed back to Utah for the summer rodeo circuit. It didn't take long to realize that he had lost a lot of his polish as a rough stock rider during the two and a half years he had been away. Early into the summer, Grant entered a small Idaho rodeo. He drew a horse called Reno. About the second jump out of the chute, the horse fell with Grant and wrecked his right knee. He laid off a couple of weeks until he was able to get some movement back in the knee, then tried it again. But there just was not enough strength in the right leg to really get good spurring action during a ride. He tried to spur twice as fancy with his left leg and keep his right side away from the arena judges.

That trick wouldn't win him any money, though.

That fall the sore-legged bronc rider was back in school in Provo and pretty well disgusted with himself. But he guessed his luck had changed when he met a pretty coed named Sue Collins. Grant stayed around campus during the Christmas vacation in 1957, and he and Sue went out often.

After a career as a working cowboy, and another as a rodeo hand, Grant had pretty well gotten most of the foolishness out of his system. Ever since he had finished the church mission he had been aware of the fact that it was time to start thinking about something past the next rodeo. Sue intensified these feelings, and Grant began to consider settling down. On June 6, 1958, Grant and Sue were married. The cow ranges and rodeo arenas were no longer as important to him as they had been. He was still a cowboy to the core and always would be, but now there was more to his life than spurs and worn-out saddles.

Following their marriage in June, Grant took Sue to Texas for the summer. He had fun showing her all his old stomping grounds, and she was excited about coming to know the people and the country where her new husband had grown up. Grant worked during the week as an interpreter with the *Bracero* program at Lamesa. This was a government-sanctioned program where Mexican nationals did farm work on contract with American farmers' cooperative organizations. On the weekends, the newlyweds spent a lot of time traveling to rodeos all over west Texas as Grant tried to pick up extra money for his last year at B.Y.U.

They were back in school at Provo in the fall of 1958. Grant would receive his degree in animal husbandry the following spring. Like a lot of cowboys who get married, Grant discovered quickly that it takes more money to get a family's bills paid than it

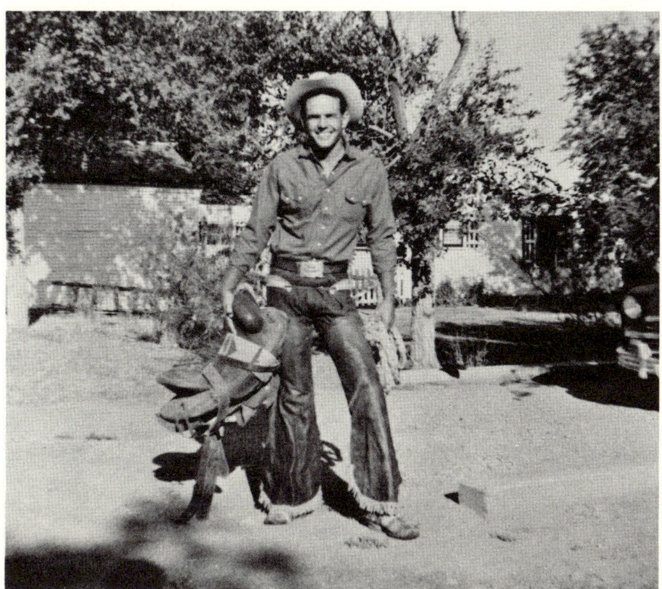

*Grant with the official Rodeo Cowboy Association saddle
for riding broncs, 1958*

did to pay bills when he was single and living with a bunch of rodeo buddies who pooled their winnings. He took a job with a steel plant during that last school year to supplement his summer job and rodeo savings.

Grant had never given up on his ambition to get in the livestock business. But a college degree did not prove to be the key to his dream that he had hoped. Now, with a wife to support, and their first child on the way, a ranch seemed to be an even more remote possibility with each passing day. "I was looking for any place on earth where a man with no money could maybe try to get a toehold." But such an opportunity was not to be found, and with college behind him, Grant still had no concrete plans for the future. He accepted the hard fact that he just wasn't going to be a rancher and turned his attention to more immediate problems. He continued to work at the steel plant.

Sue gave birth to a daughter, Peggy Sue, in the fall of 1959. Their joy as new parents was tempered by Peggy's frail health from birth. She had a heart defect that required continual attention. It was a bleak time for the little family, but their love and their steady faith sustained them.

Grant got an offer to teach school on a temporary permit out in the Uinta Basin at the town of Roosevelt. He figured that maybe they could get by if he taught school for nine months and then did rodeo during the summer.

Things were hectic, to say the least, the autumn day that they moved into a little rented house in Neola, outside Roosevelt. Cardboard boxes full of pots and pans, piles of clothes and bedding, and a jumble of assorted household things were heaped all over the front yard. Sue was struggling to get things sorted out, watching the baby, and telling Grant what to put where.

About this time, a pickup full of local cowboys pulled up in front and started sizing up Grant. It's an old western tradition that whenever a cowboy moves onto a new range he has got to establish his credentials and show what he's made of. Grant, of course, had always worn boots and a hat. He was also wearing one of his rodeo trophy buckles on this day. The local boys stood around watching him carrying things into the house and remarking that they had some real bad horses in this country, probably a lot tougher than he was used to. Before long, Grant was challenged outright to prove he could ride a bronc. With Sue right in the middle of the moving mess and practically in tears, Grant said he would go down to the local arena and try one of their old ponies.

By the time they got to the arena, word had spread, and a pretty good crowd had gathered to see this "college cowboy" bite the dust. All the local boys were laughing up their sleeves, and Grant knew that if he didn't ride their bronc he would never be able to live in this town and hold his head up. A big sorrel horse was put in the chute for him, and he could guess that they'd picked their worst bronc. Grant got his saddle set, adjusted a borrowed rein, pulled his hat down, called for him, and mounted. The bronc broke out and immediately dodged to the left, clear through two catch-pen gates that had been left open, nearly tearing Grant's knee off as they went through. Grant got off on the fence and hobbled and limped around for a while until he got some feeling back in his knee. Everyone apologized about the open gate, and asked if he was up to trying the horse again. It was still a case of "do or die," so they again rigged the horse in the chute and Grant got down on him. This time the gates were all shut, and the horse bucked straight out into the arena. He bucked well, and Grant sat right in the middle and got his spurring lick going just right. After the ride, everyone gathered around to shake his hand. He made some friends that day. In ranch country no one is automatically entitled to respect. You've got to earn it. There are all kinds of ways to do it; Grant had passed his test on the back of a saddle bronc, the best way he knew how.

That winter, Grant taught fourth grade at the little Roosevelt school. Teaching school seemed to be as good a way as any to spend the fall and winter. Unlike other jobs, it kept the summers free for rodeo. So Grant and Sue decided that he should go back to B.Y.U. the next year and take the courses necessary to receive a teaching certificate.

Back in Provo, Peggy could be nearer her doctors. She was a constant delight and, at the same time, a constant concern to her parents. Grant got a job as a postal employee and went to school part-time to take required education courses.

By 1962, Grant was a qualified school teacher and began teaching in Salt Lake City. This job lasted for seven long years. After a few years, Grant could already tell that he just wasn't cut out to be a schoolteacher for the rest of his life. He was nearly thirty-five years old now, and it didn't seem like he was getting anywhere.

He knew that he couldn't go back to cowboying for wages and ever hope to support his family. He had given up rodeo as a cumulative result of the knocks and falls he had taken over the years. In fact, he never again got on a bronc, on purpose, after that afternoon in Neola. The chances of owning his own ranch were even more slim now than they had ever been. He, Sue, and Peggy were happy with each other, although there was the ever-present problem of Peggy's heart defect. But, in his own mind, Grant could just not accept his lot as a career teacher. He needed something that would give him the same kind of feeling about himself that he'd had when he was working as a cowboy for the old X ranch, or when he had ridden a tough bronc and won top money. It had to do with his own pride in himself and his sense of self-esteem. There just had to be something else he could do.

In 1964 Grant wrote down three ideas on a piece of paper. Each of these ideas had to do with a possible career. They were all of a self-employed nature and would succeed or fail based in large measure on Grant's own initiative. To this day, Grant will not disclose what the second two plans were, but the first one was art. "I knew that if things were ever going to change that it would have to be the result of something coming out of me. I couldn't count on anybody else making it happen. I didn't have any other choice. It would have to be something that I could, with blood and sweat and tears, develop on my own. So I decided, very seriously, that I was going to give art everything I had in me and see if it would amount to anything."

This decision surprised just about everyone. Grant had always kept his interest in art pretty much to himself. He had drawn a lot as a kid and messed around with it during slack times on the ranches and while he was in the service. But neither he nor his family and friends had any reason to think that it was a serious inclination.

The first attempt Grant made at sculpture was, of course, a cowboy on a bucking horse. It was modeled with Peggy Sue's kids' clay. She was delighted with her daddy's work. Grant realized that if he were going to give art a fair chance, he would have to do a lot of studying. Unlike many contemporary western artists, he believed that a natural talent can only be worthwhile if it is developed, channeled, and matured through study and dedicated application.

For a straight three-month period he spent almost all night, every night, pouring over anatomy books. He was a frequent visitor to local libraries and carried home armloads of books on art and anatomy. He bought clay and wax and began to work every chance he could.

During the fall of 1964, Grant visited several art galleries in Jackson Hole, Wyoming. At Dick Flood's Trailside Gallery he marveled at the bronzes of his idol, Charlie Russell. This experience fired his determination to stick with it. "The Russell bronzes really did something to me," Grant remembers.

Russell's bronzes had a power and a message for Grant. They had a quality that he didn't see in other sculpture he had studied. When he looked at a Russell piece, he felt like he was studying the heart of the original cowboy artist himself. He saw power and beauty and, most of all, he saw a basic honesty and a sympathy for the West. It was just as if Russell were there talking to him.

The first man to have a profound influence on Grant was his uncle, Boone Rainey. The second was a Montana cowboy-turned-artist who had died in 1926, Charles M. Russell. As Grant worked with his wax models, he continually reached for those qualities of power, beauty, and honesty that Russell had commanded. He was not trying to imitate Russell's idea — only his force and feeling. After all, the two men had a lot in common. Most significantly they shared a reverence for the land and the heritage of the West.

Grant went about his art work very quietly. Even Sue didn't know about the three ideas he had written down. If visitors came by while he was working on a model, Grant would scurry around hiding all of his materials. He was not yet ready to stick his chin out all the way. After all, why would a man of his age just begin to get serious about a career in art, of all things? It could be a hobby, perhaps, but surely he couldn't be serious about making a living at it.

At least he had found something to take the edge off the boredom of teaching school. He taught all day, then spent his nights and weekends learning about and working with his secret ambition. He would model and tear up and model again, striving for the qualities that made the Russell pieces come alive for him.

The first serious piece he finished was called *End of a Short Acquaintance*. Right after that one came a bareback bronc piece. It seems only natural that rodeo provided the inspiration for his initial attempts. He knew things about this subject matter that he could never learn in an art book.

In the summer of 1965, Grant took these first two pieces, still in wax, back to Jackson Hole to show to

Dick Flood. The waxes were on display at Flood's gallery that summer, and, to Grant's amazement, orders were taken for several to be cast in bronze. Grant has always been grateful to Dick Flood for his encouragement, advice, and support at this critical point. It was Flood's confidence in the young, unknown sculptor that opened some early and important doors.

That fall Grant went back to teaching. In addition to modeling on his own, he also enrolled for sculpture classes at B.Y.U.

"It didn't seem like there was hardly any time to sleep." But he was moving in the direction that he wanted to go, and he was seeing positive results.

Near the end of the year, in November, 1965, Peggy Sue died from the heart problems she had had since birth. It completely devastated Grant and Sue. And although things would never be the same again, they had to accept it and go on somehow. By this time their son Boone had been born, and he filled up a lot of the empty space in their hearts.

In April 1966 Grant cast his first piece in bronze as part of his classwork. It was a tangible and permanent symbol of his own unfaltering dedication to a new course in his life. He presented the first bronze casting of *End of a Short Acquaintance* to Sue. Although he had learned the technical process involved in bronze casting, there was just too much else going on for him to really get into the foundry business. He was still teaching, taking art classes, and modeling at home in the evenings.

Dick Flood wanted to handle Grant's work for the next summer tourist season in Jackson Hole. He suggested that Grant get his pieces cast at Classic Bronze in California. But this didn't work out well. It was a hassle taking the waxes to California and then going back to pick up the finished bronzes a few at a time.

Grant started scouting around and found Hughes Curtis, a barber who had an old foundry at Springville, Utah. Together he, Hughes, and Hughes' wife Cecile rejuvenated the foundry and began to produce Grant's bronzes. There was another whole set of challenges and problems in learning the highly sophisticated techniques involved in casting. Grant read everything he could find about chemistry, physics, and other related fields that were integral to the process of casting bronze.

There must have been moments during this time when Grant remembered his cowboying days on the Nolke ranch near San Angelo, where it was said that "you could sell your bed and buy a lantern." He never seemed to have enough time to get everything done. But it is different when you are expending the effort for yourself. Before long Grant and Hughes had the kinks worked out and were achieving excellent results with their castings.

The family was able to get along on Grant's salary from teaching, and this allowed him to plow back everything from the sale of his bronzes into the foundry.

The mid-1960s marked a significant point in the development of western art. The paintings of the Russell and Remington era reached six-figure values in the old-line New York galleries. New institutions such as the Montana Historical Society, the Gilcrease Institute, the National Cowboy Hall of Fame, and the Whitney Gallery of Western Art based their reputations on traditional western art.

These factors created a new and fairly wide public awareness of western art and a potential market for contemporary sculptors and painters of western subject matter. Then in the summer of 1965, the first clearly identifiable contemporary western art movement was begun in Sedona, Arizona, when four men organized the Cowboy Artists of America.

The founders of the Cowboy Artists of America were George Phippen, Charlie Dye, Joe Beeler, and John Hampton. These four men were individually responsible for an important measure of the limited reputation that contemporary western art had by 1965. All four had established individual reputations and were finding an audience for their work. Their attachment to the western country and its people was genuine, and it was a dominant factor in their art.

About this time, Grant saw a magazine article about the men who had gotten together to organize the Cowboy Artists of America. Grant had not yet felt entirely comfortable about being an artist. He knew what kind of prejudices existed in the cow camps and rodeo arenas where he had spent so much of his life. To cowboys, an artist was bound to be some kind of a sissy. This is why Grant had been so uncomfortable for so long about letting anyone know how serious he was about his goal of a career in art. But here was a bunch of guys who were calling themselves "cowboy artists." It seemed almost a paradox, but it gave him hope that maybe there were others like himself who could have a foot in two worlds — who could be comfortable doing both cow work and art work. Of course, Charlie Russell had done it, but he was long gone.

The magazine article Grant read said that John Hampton, one of the four founders of the Cowboy Artists of America, lived in Cave Creek, Arizona. With the same kind of nerve that he had always mustered when he climbed down on a bronc, Grant called Hampton to inquire about membership in the Cowboy Artists. He wanted to ask if he could bring down a few pieces of sculpture for Hampton to look at. Hampton couldn't have been nicer or more encouraging to Grant when they visited over the phone.

In short order, Grant and Sue were headed for Arizona. It was the summer of 1966 and hot as the blazes. They had one bronze and two waxes in the non-air-conditioned Volkswagen and had to keep sprinkling water on the wax models to keep them from melting. They met Hampton at Cave Creek, and he not only liked Grant but was also delighted with his sculpture. He suggested that Grant and Sue stop off in Sedona on their way home. Joe Beeler and Charlie Dye both lived there, and that would allow three of the four founders to consider his work.

Grant and Sue were hot and thirsty by the time they arrived in Sedona. The Oak Creek Tavern was the place where the Cowboy Artists had been founded, and this was the Speeds' first stop. The man behind the bar took pity on the two overheated travelers and offered them ice-cold drinks of the only thing he had for Mormons — water. This revived them, and Grant proceeded to introduce himself and Sue and to state his business. There were paintings by Dye, Phippen, Hampton, and Beeler hanging in the tavern, and Grant was amazed to realize that this quality of western art was being produced in modern times — that it hadn't all ended when Charlie Russell died. And that it was being created by artists who were not limp-wristed sissies, but who, like himself, wore a hat and boots and were at ease around ranch people. Until this moment Grant had felt pretty much alone, but now he was encouraged as never before. He saw that it was actually possible for a cowboy to be an artist, and that maybe it was even possible for such a man to be taken seriously. All four of the Cowboy Artists founders had successful independent careers and were making a living from their art. The prospect staggered Grant. For the first time he began to think that maybe all the work, long hours, and anguish of pursuing an art career had really been worth it.

Both Dye and Beeler were out of town on that day in Sedona. But Mr. John Vaughn, a Sedona area cowman and an early patron of cowboy art, stopped by at the tavern. He bought one of Grant's pieces and said that he would see to it that Dye and Beeler got to look at it when they returned.

Grant and Sue headed back north for Utah, but now they were glowing from newfound encouragement and optimism, as well as from the Arizona heat.

Before long a letter arrived from Hampton. It included congratulations on being accepted as a new member in the Cowboy Artists of America and went on to talk about details for an exhibition in the fall at the National Cowboy Hall of Fame.

Grant and Sue both felt at least ten feet tall. It was hard for them to believe that everything had come together so perfectly. And it is difficult to overemphasize the significance of this point in Grant's life. Had it not been for the Cowboy Artists and their annual show, he would have no doubt gone on to develop a regional reputation as a sculptor. But he would probably have had to stay at his teaching job for a long time to come. With the vehicle of the Cowboy Artists, he started out his art career with a bang. The show at a nationally known institution such as the Cowboy Hall of Fame, the association with artists who already had creditable reputations, the publicity, and the potential for meeting collectors and art dealers — all of these and other positive considerations blended into a package that held nothing but promise. Even Russell himself had not had such an opportunity right in the beginning to get a serious audience for his work.

The sparks began to fly fast and furiously around the little foundry in Springville as Grant prepared for the show at the Cowboy Hall of Fame in Oklahoma City. The show was set to open in September of 1966. Once again, Grant experienced those feelings in the pit of his stomach that he had learned to live with ever since Uncle Boone put him on his first green colt out in the Pecos River country. He had also known the feeling every time he set his saddle on a rodeo bronc. It was a feeling of apprehension, of anxiety, and of a special kind of fear: the fear of not doing his best, of being embarrassed in front of people who mattered. But the feeling was tempered with a determination that had gotten him through tight spots before.

Grant was not alone in his sense of apprehension. None of those who were among the first group to exhibit as members of the Cowboy Artists of America had any idea of how they would be received. In addition to the founders — Phippen, Beeler, Dye, and Hampton — that first group in 1966 included Fred Harman, Darol Dickinson, Wayne Hunt, Harvey Johnson, John Kittelson, George Marks, "Shorty" Shope, Gordon Snidow, Byron Wolfe, and an ex-bronc rider from Utah by way of Texas, Ulysses Grant Speed.

CHAPTER THREE

Portraits of the West

The first Cowboy Artists of America exhibition opened in Oklahoma City at the National Cowboy Hall of Fame on September 9, 1966. Up to the time of the first show, the group held no real promise of power or influence. It was just an informally organized group of western artists who were looking for the company of their own kind. But a group exhibition at a major new museum did offer the promise of some relief from the obscurity that plagued the field of contemporary western art.

Luck and timing played a big part in the subsequent achievements of the Cowboy Artists. The Cowboy Hall of Fame was a new institution that needed events to generate public relations, and the Cowboy Artists was a new organization that needed the sponsorship of a major institution. Both organizations served the needs of each other. This is an important point to recognize in considering the trouble that later developed between the two organizations.

It is not an oversimplification to say that Grant Speed's career in art began with that first Cowboy Artists show and that his reputation has developed in direct proportion to the development of the reputation of the Cowboy Artists group. If it had not been for the Cowboy Artists, Grant would have gone ahead with his sculpture. But he would most likely have developed only a regional reputation. The vehicle of the annual Cowboy Artists show at the Cowboy Hall of Fame gave both him and his work a degree of exposure that no commercial gallery nor his own efforts could have matched. Grant's emergence as a professional artist is tied solidly to the beginning of the Cowboy Artists of America.

The little four-page brochure that was printed for the first exhibition contains a picture of Grant's bronze, *The Bull Rider,* and the following statement: "U. Grant Speed — a Texan by birth (San Angelo, 1930) — now resides with his wife Sue and son Boone in Provo, Utah. He has spent a lifetime getting the education of a cowhand in Texas, Arizona, Wyoming, and Utah. Grant's a real cowboy; he was a member of the Brigham Young University rodeo team, then later toured the circuit as a professional. Finally turning to sculpture, he was able to draw on his knowledge and experience to dramatize in beautiful and convincing fashion the exciting events of the rodeo arena." An interesting footnote to Cowboy Artists history is that James Boren, Art Director at the Cowboy Hall of Fame, wrote the copy for the brochure for the first exhibition.

That first year in Oklahoma City was an exciting experience for the young sculptor. He met and talked with men who were *the* names in contemporary western art — men like Charlie Dye, who freely offered advice and encouragement. He also met artists who were only getting started, just like himself, and who shared his own feelings and concerns. He no longer felt completely alone.

It was also something close to a religious experience to see the original art in the permanent collection of the Cowboy Hall of Fame. Here, for the first time, he could study major works by Charles Russell, who had for so long been a primary source of his inspiration.

To top it all off, the museum also had a rodeo section that displayed the saddles, spurs, and other items of the men who were legends in the history of rodeo. For Grant there was something very special about seeing Bob Crosby's battered old black hat and Fritz Truan's buck rein. Overall, the first Cowboy Artists show was an experience unlike any he had ever known.

As Grant and Sue headed back for Utah from Oklahoma City, he was bubbling over with enthusiasm and anticipation. For the first time he was able to quell the doubts he had had about his art. The first Cowboy Artists show had given him the confidence and the determination to "hang and rattle." Western art was just like a bronc, and now Grant believed he could ride it.

One immediate result of the Oklahoma City show came when the Rodeo Cowboys' Association contacted Grant about using one of his bronzes that had been in the show as their Todd Whatley Memorial Award, which would be presented to the world champion All-Around Cowboy. The fact that he could be an artist and still do something that would appeal to rodeo people also boosted his confidence. One thing was for certain: Grant would never deny his background. He would be a cowboy first, last, and always.

Back in Utah, Grant plunged into sculpting and casting with all the inspiration and energy he had. He was still teaching school, but it was art that was foremost in his mind now that he saw the opportunity to really make it a career.

Response to the first show was so unexpectedly strong that the Cowboy Hall of Fame rescheduled and extended the period of the show for the second year. The first show, in 1966, had only run from September 9 through October 16. In 1967, the show ran from May 27 through September 9. This took in the summer months, the peak of the tourist season when attendance at the museum was at its best. The success of the second show was obvious from the opening gun. This was no "flash in the pan" art; contemporary western art had come of age. And those who set the patterns were the members of the Cowboy Artists of America.

The impact of the Cowboy Artists' successes on contemporary western art is distinct. This organization, through its annual show, has exerted the single strongest influence on the development of a market for all contemporary western art and has provided the basis for its credibility and reputation as a legitimate movement in American art.

The influence of the Cowboy Artists has been felt a long way beyond the annual show. Old-line New York galleries have marveled at the sales performance of the organization and are regularly represented at the annual shows.

Many collectors today who are seeking out the classic western art of a generation or two ago received their first exposure and initial impulse to collect through the excitement of the Cowboy Artists exhibitions and acquisitions made there. Established eastern galleries have developed a new and substantial western clientele for old western art among those who have developed interests through their Cowboy Artists experiences.

There can be little doubt that the Cowboy Artists have created in their wake an appetite for contemporary western painting and sculpture that cannot be completely satisfied at their annual show. The members of the organization now have a potential for a year-round market. A market has also been created for contemporary western art other than that produced by Cowboy Artists members. The traditional circle of art collectors has expanded into a context much broader than has ever been observed in western art. The Cowboy Artists have brought art to the people.

An entire industry of commercial retail galleries dealing in both original and graphic contemporary western art has developed on a broad regional basis as an indirect result of the success of the Cowboy Artists effort. New galleries have sprung up in both western and eastern cities with a major emphasis on Cowboy Artists' work. A considerable number of commercial galleries have begun operation since the beginning of the Cowboy Artists. It is not an overstatement to say that these new openings have been motivated primarily because of buying interests whetted each year at the Cowboy Artists show. Many contemporary western painters and sculptors have found a market for their work where none existed before as a result of interest developed and encouraged by the Cowboy Artists movement.

It is also worth noting that Cowboy Artists members were among the first in the history of western art to have their work not only exhibited but also acquired by major institutions during their own lifetime.

There is virtually no facet of the western art scene that has not been affected to some extent by the influence of the Cowboy Artists of America in the years since 1966. Those first Cowboy Artists members, such as Grant Speed, have individually and collectively brought contemporary western art from obscurity to dramatic prominence in slightly more than a decade. It would be impossible to discuss any aspect of contemporary western art without considering the Cowboy Artists' influence. It is also a major thread throughout the professional career of Grant Speed. As an original member, and as an officer and director of the organization, Grant's career cannot be considered apart from the organization.

In 1968, the first book to take contemporary western art seriously was published. It was Ed Ainsworth's *The Cowboy in Art*. The publication of this book marked the first time that any contemporary western artist had received recognition in print beyond commercial gallery, public-relations-oriented material. Since Ainsworth's book was the first in a line of many contemporary western art books to follow, it occupies something of a singular character in the development of cowboy art.

Ainsworth devoted significant space in his book to the young sculptor from Utah:

When Big Piney started to fall, Grant Speed knew he was in trouble and a lot of thoughts flashed through his mind in the split second before he and the rodeo bucking horse hit the ground. When the dust cleared, Grant Speed was suffering from a broken ankle and, although he may not have known it for sure at the moment, he was headed for a new line of work. Up to the time of this rodeo at Logan,

Utah, where Big Piney — one of the champs among bucking horses — fell with him, Speed had been a rodeo rider for several years. While his ankle was healing he did a lot of thinking about getting into some other occupation besides the hazardous one in which he had won many awards. The net result of the accident was that Grant Speed became a sculptor.

His background had prepared him for this new effort. In his classes at Utah State University at Provo, he had been taking animal husbandy while aiming at a ranching life. This was in keeping with his early training, because this Texan, born in San Angelo, had gone to work when he was only twelve in neighboring ranches and had begun to break horses.

After the Big Piney incident, he decided that rodeoing was becoming a little too rough, and he began teaching as a career. Then he became interested in sculpting, but he had misgivings about his ability.

"Russell and Remington were so great in their sculpting of horses, cowboys and cattle that I was afraid I might be tempted to model my stuff after theirs," he confesses. "So from the start I have avoided copying like the plague."

When he did begin sculpting, he built into his models some of his own experience — as indicated by the titles, *The End of a Short Acquaintance* and *Doubtful Outcome*. These depictions of bucking horses were linked with his own memories of some of the great outlaws he had tried to ride in his rodeo days.

Artists generally struggle for years to achieve any sort of recognition. In the first two years of Grant's art career he had exhibited in a museum of national prominence, was represented in a few good commercial galleries, and had appeared in the first book to deal with contemporary western art. All of this initial success only increased his determination to work even harder.

After 1966, Grant's success as an artist was assured. He continued to sell his work through the Trailside Gallery in Jackson Hole where he had begun, and he also began to handle inquiries direct from collectors as a result of his participation in the Cowboy Artists show. In more recent years, Texas Art Gallery in Dallas has accounted for a majority of Grant's sales during the year between Cowboy Artists shows.

At the Fifth Annual Exhibit, in 1970, Grant accomplished a singular achievement. The entire edition of his *Ridin' Point* was sold out completely on the opening night of the exhibition. No other western sculptor had ever known such an immediate response to one of his works.

Ridin' Point marks the place in Grant's career where he has achieved an obvious level of artistic maturity. To the strength of a traditional bust, Grant added a sculptured vignette in reduced scale. *Ridin' Point* brought a new and exciting dimension to traditional patterns of western sculpture. It was the freshest and most creative innovation in the present generation of western art. *Ridin' Point* and the five subsequent bronzes that also use the same design concept constitute some of the most distinguished contributions to the reputation of all contemporary western art.

In the summer issue (volume I, number 4) of the Cowboy Hall of Fame's quarterly, "Persimmon Hill," Grant was quoted about his feelings for the West as a subject matter for his art: "My life and interests have revolved around the West, and I feel very fortunate to be able to spend my time re-creating it in my art work. There is no other place on earth that has had as dynamic a history as the western part of the United States. It has attracted and held the interest of people all over the world."

Grant has never been content to relax in his art just because of commercial success. He has continued to study and to reach down inside himself and his heritage for fresh inspiration. He is most concerned in capturing the spirit of the subjects he sculpts. Literal representations are not as important to him as is this quality of spirit. This is the quality that attracted him to Russell's work in sculpture, and it remains his primary concern in his own work. He reaches for a feeling in each of his pieces rather than a perfection of line or form. Grant is an impressionist at heart.

During these years, Grant was not only growing in his art, but was also elected president of the Cowboy Artists of America for 1972. The responsibilities associated with this position can distract an artist from his creative work in the best of years, and during Grant's term the office took on an awesome dimension.

Following the close of the annual exhibition at the Cowboy Hall of Fame early in the fall of 1972, several Cowboy Artists members agreed to participate in an exhibition at Post, Texas, at Jim Prather's OS Ranch. The art show was to be held in connection with a steer roping, and proceeds were to benefit the West Texas Boys Ranch at San Angelo. The idea of combining western art with the atmosphere of a ranch house setting for exhibition and with a cowboy weekend of steer roping appealed to several of the Cowboy Artists. And it was also for a worthwhile cause.

Just as the exhibit was set to open, the Cowboy Hall of Fame notified Grant, as C.A.A. president, that participation by Cowboy Artists in the OS Ranch show violated the agreement between the Cowboy Hall of

Fame and the C.A.A. and that the Cowboy Hall of Fame would no longer host the annual C.A.A. exhibition. The full weight of this fell directly on Grant as the group's president. Under Grant's capable leadership, the organization weathered what could have been a disaster for the group and went on to bigger and more dramatic successes at the Phoenix Art Museum beginning in 1973.

It was a difficult period, not only for the Cowboy Artists but specifically for Grant. At a time when he was really hitting his stride in his art, he was swamped with the problems of finding a direction for the organization independent of the Cowboy Hall of Fame. All of the distress and pressures were compensated for by several positive factors. First, Sue gave birth to a new baby daughter, Samantha, on October 23, 1973. In addition, Grant's career was attracting more and more attention from the western art critics and collectors. In the catalog of the OS Ranch show, the following was written:

I have never found out what the U. is for in U. Grant Speed's name, but I've seen him horseback and I'm sure it isn't for Useless. Grant was a kid in the San Angelo country during the late forties and early fifties when a bunch of old reprobate cowmen were praying to the Lord for rain and to the banker for another loan extension. He made a pretty fair saddle bronc rider while in college and wound up teaching school in Utah. Grant, as an artist, concentrates exclusively on sculpture. His work is authentic in every detail and highly individual in design. In a couple of his most recent pieces he has produced fine portraits in bronze, a feat not frequently seen in contemporary art, and hardly ever in western art. The idea and execution for his *Free Spirit* and *Ridin'*

Point are unique and have attracted considerable critical acclaim. Grant makes his home in Utah and gave up schoolteaching a while back to spend all of his time in telling good stories of the West in bronze.

It is difficult for most artists to explain their feelings about what they do, their motivations and sense of commitment. Grant is no exception, but as president of the Cowboy Artists of America, he wrote some of his thoughts down for the introduction to the exhibition catalog for 1973:

> Several years ago I was talking with an old man who had been a cowboy all his life. In spite of his age, he still made a good hand, and I asked him, "If you could do anything in the world, what would you do?"
>
> "I'm doing it," was his quick reply.
>
> There is a mystique about the West that has captured not only the working cowboy of today, but people in all walks of life in countries throughout the world. A western movie with Japanese actors plays in a downtown Tokyo theater; men and women wearing cowboy boots and Indian jewelry walk along the Champs d'Élysées; in a back street in Rome, Italian children play "cowboys and Indians." And, of course, in the United States there are movies, television shows, rodeos, books, magazines and fine art all depicting the West. Not all of these presentations portray the West accurately, but the demand for them remains strong.
>
> In the midst of this worldwide enthusiasm for the West there is growing interest in western art. Since the founding of the Cowboy Artists of America in 1966, our membership has more than doubled, and our work has become widely accepted.
>
> This past year has been the best and worst of years for the C.A.A. The interest in Western art is greater than ever. However, a saddening note was the passing of two of our members who had exhibited with us in each of our first seven annual shows. Charlie Dye and Byron Wolfe were men the C.A.A. will miss greatly, and those who love the West will miss them too. The legacy of their art is a rich one, and knowing them was an experience not to be forgotten.
>
> Our contribution to the heritage of the West is still to be measured in the coming years, but if anyone were to ask one of our members, "If you could do anything in the world, what would you do?" I'm sure the answer would be, "I'm doin' it."

That article says a lot about the sincerity and sensitivity of Grant, as an artist as well as a man.

It is a genuine mark of distinction when a contemporary artist is invited to display his work in a prestigious institution. Most artists never have this opportunity during their lifetime. In 1975, several of Grant's bronzes were included in a special exhibition at the Whitney Gallery of Western Art in Cody, Wyoming. The exhibit included sculpture by such classical western artists as Russell, Remington, and Borglum. In reference to Grant's work, the exhibition catalog said:

> Grant Speed is himself a ranch country product. He carries on the cowboy artist tradition begun by Russell. His bronzes are clear evidence of his knowledge of cow country subject matter. Speed's sculpture includes the whole spectrum of range life, from the wild action of a bronc, to the quiet, reflective moments of a cowboy who realizes his is a fast fading way of life.

In 1976, Grant created a sculpture that hit the annual Cowboy Artists show like a bombshell. The piece was entitled *The Half-Breed*. Like *Ridin' Point,* it sold out opening night. But, more than that, this piece represented a degree of artistic achievement that went far beyond the boundaries of traditional western art considerations.

One of the jurists at the 1976 Cowboy Artists show wrote:

I was pleased to be a judge at the 1976 C.A.A. exhibition when *Half-Breed* won the first, and long overdue, gold medal for the sculpture of Grant Speed. In addition to suiting my prejudices for Texans, cowboys and ex-rodeo hands, Grant is also an accomplished sculptor who had not, up until this point, received the degree of recognition to which his work entitled him.

Half-Breed is a sculptured accomplishment that represents a dramatic high point in the artistic development of C.A.A. art. It is a piece which would attract attention and acclaim at anyone's art show, western or otherwise. The delicately sculptured face and the sensitive posturing of the head gives the *Half-Breed* an aura of classic art. It is a piece which has brought new and enthusiastic interest in Grant's work, and one which portends subsequent awards for the artist.

Grant has been known for quite awhile as a pretty good cowboy sculptor. The *Half-Breed* and others of his most recent works have signaled his artistic maturity and insured his reputation as a major force in contemporary western art.

With *The Half-Breed,* Grant made an indelible mark on contemporary western art. This piece provided potent ammunition for those who have tried to develop the argument for western art as *art,* rather than as mere historical illustration.

The year 1976 was the tenth anniversary for the Cowboy Artists of America. It was also the tenth year of Grant's professional career. The organization and Grant had both grown and developed beyond what anyone could have imagined back in 1966.

Ten Years with the Cowboy Artists of America, by Jim Howard, was published to commemorate the first decade of the group's existence. In the portion of the book that dealt with Grant, Howard wrote:

Grant Speed is the stereotyped image of the cowboy. He is tall, lean, handsome and reticent — a Gary Cooper of the seventies. His background would seem to support the image he creates when you meet him face to face.

On January 6, 1930, he was born in San Angelo, Texas. Growing up during the bleakest years of the Depression left its brand on this quiet, earnest cowboy. There is no extravagance in the man. There is a deep-seated belief that problems can be solved by hard work and that there are no easy answers. He is a humble man, and one who is not ashamed or uneasy to address people he meets as "Sir" or "Ma'm"....

Even with a proven track record of supporting his family for six years as a full-time western artist and ten years' membership in the C.A.A., he doesn't see himself as a guaranteed success in the future: "I'll be a student all my life and hope to get better as long as my physical capabilities permit. I do hope to create work that will be of lasting value, appreciated one hundred years from now as good art. It is my intent to develop a distinctive style which will set my work apart from others and permit it to stand alone."

As the Cowboy Artists of America and Grant Speed entered their second decade in the field of contemporary western art, the prognosis was for continued success. Grant has never backed away from his dedication to improve his work and to strive for quality and originality. He has not become complacent with the success and recognition he has achieved. This dedication, along with the promotional efforts of western art dealers like Bill Burford, Candy Bedner, Dick Flood III, and Jim Clark and the Tivoli Gallery have given Grant's work a unique acceptance among collectors of contemporary western art. Grant has regularly sold out complete editions of some of his pieces, a feat only dreamed of by most western sculptors.

As he entered this second decade, Grant had occasion to make the following observations:

Like other artists, I've learned from many sources. I've always enjoyed reading, especially about the West. When I was younger, punching cows around the country, I'd often find dusty old magazines and books around the bunkhouse, and it was always tough to get up at 4:30 the next morning after having read late into the night. I still can't seem to spend enough time browsing in a library or bookstore. Of all the kinds of books, I find biography the most rewarding. Reading what some artists achieved in spite of the hardships they faced has proven one thing to me: the major ingredient for success in this business is plain hard work.

But probably the most important area of study has been nature itself. There is no better textbook anywhere. With all the moods, impressions, color, drama, and conflicts that are always at work, any artist has to feel humbled. The harshness, the brutality, and the reality of it all is infinitely well-balanced with its beauty, gentleness, and sensitivity. All the principles of the best art are there, if we can only complete the near impossible task of catching them. With everything we have learned, all the art principles we've been taught, we can't really get close. But, it's a heck of a lot of fun to try. My home and studio are set at the foot of 12,000 foot Mount Timpanogos in Lindon, Utah. Every day it's hard not to be awed by what's going on up on those crags and peaks above us.

Those thoughts are the reflections of obvious maturity. Grant had developed a sense of responsibility long before he turned to art. His background and his inclinations were in the direction of hard work. The curious thing about the success he has known in his art is that it has resulted in more and more effort on his part each year. Rather than accepting success and easing up, Grant has applied himself to each new idea for a bronze with renewed intensity and vigor. He feels very deeply about his responsibility to the collectors. He will not compromise his own definition of artistic quality. Each new bronze has at least as much thought and work in it as the previous piece, and probably more.

The challenge to conceive fresh, new ideas, to execute them in the studio, to work with the foundry to insure the integrity of the finished bronze, to meet the ever-increasing demand for delivery of his pieces, and to make exhibition deadlines are all factors that demand more and more of his time each year. But Grant has never once thought that it wasn't worth it.

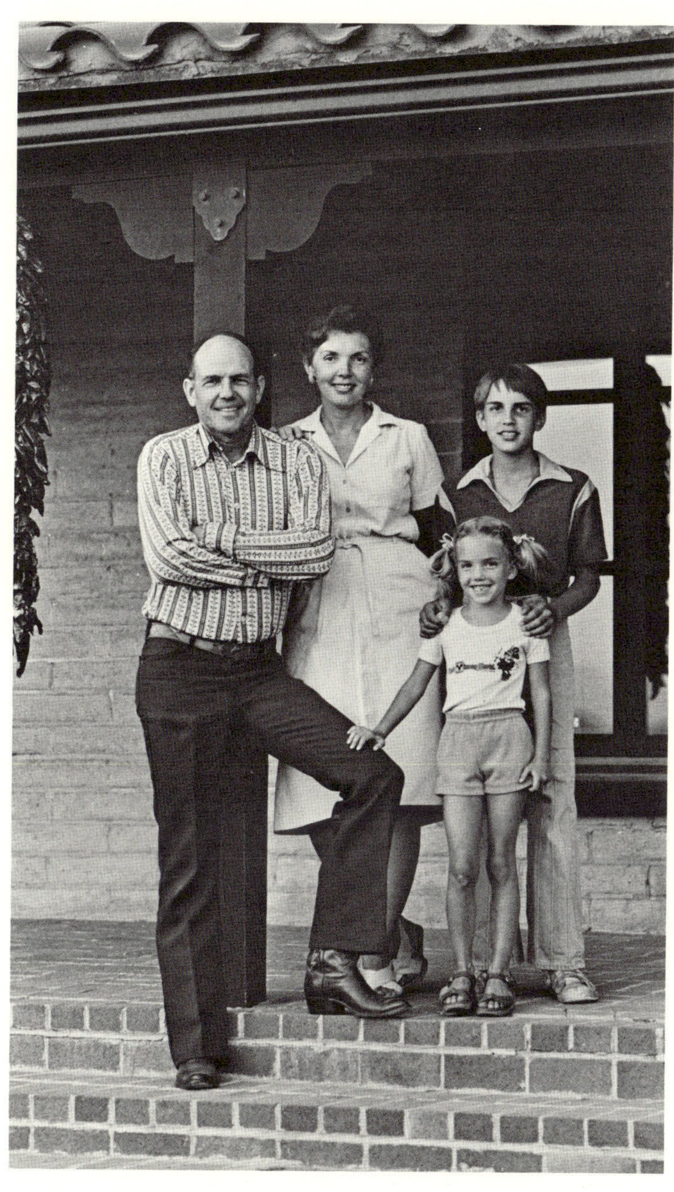

Grant Speed, Sue, Boone, and Samantha

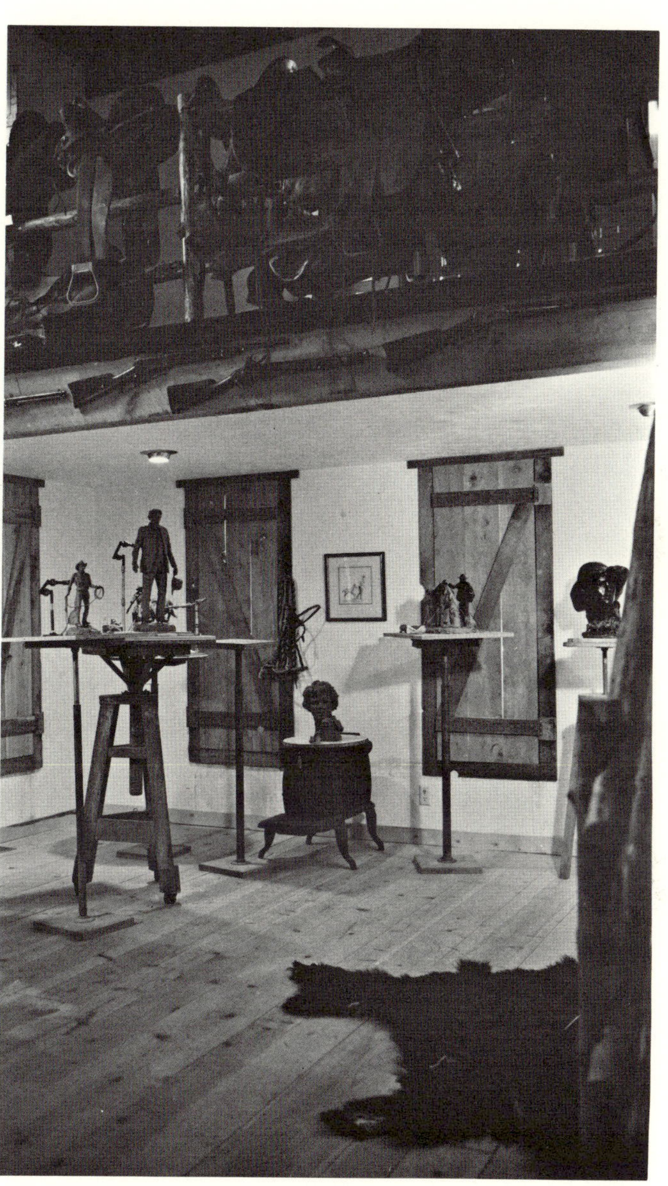

Grant's studio

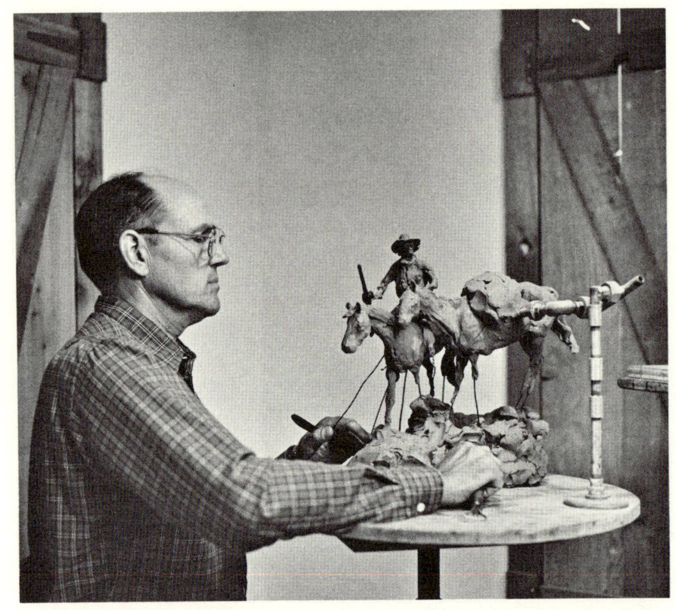

Working on The Law Man

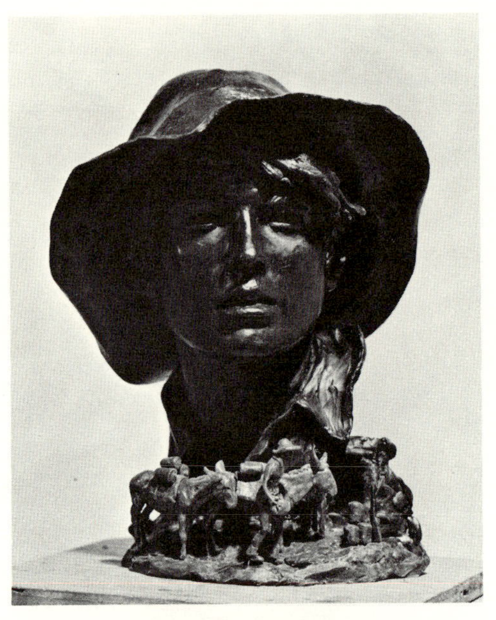

The Powder Monkey

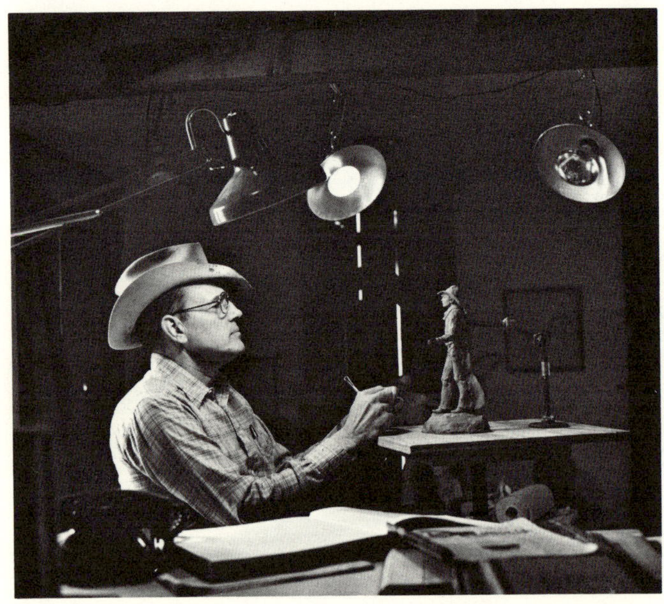

Working on The Bronc Rider

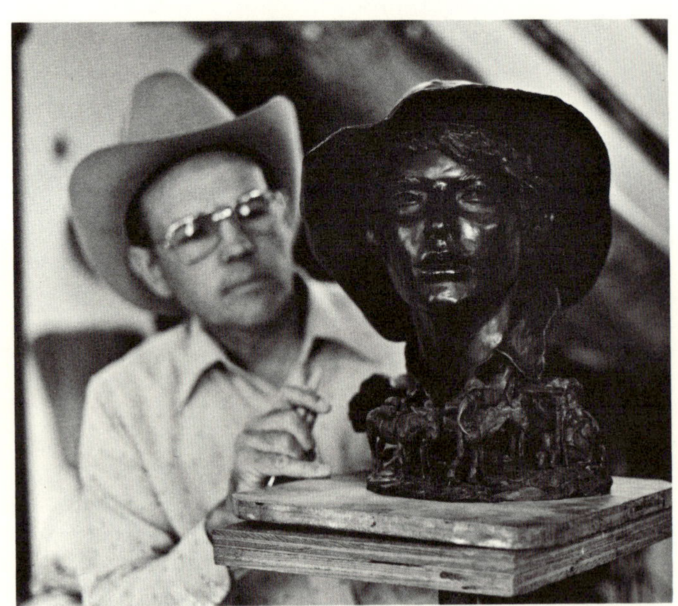

With The Powder Monkey

CHAPTER FOUR

The Technique of Casting

The technical aspects of sculpture are more varied and complex than those involved in painting. An understanding of the physical elements involved in modeling and casting can enhance one's appreciation for the finished artwork.

There are obvious differences between painting and sculpture. A painting is two-dimensional and emphasizes color. Form and space are only suggested or implied. Sculpture is three-dimensional and has actual form and space. Sculptors have an inherent challenge that painters are not faced with: they must plan their composition so that it can be viewed from all sides, whereas paintings are only looked at from the front.

When Grant decided in 1964 to pursue a career in sculpture, he did not have the educational background to prepare him for the technical complexities of sculpture. But he did have a head and a heart full of ideas and inspiration. If he could translate these ideas into art, he felt certain that they would be accepted. It became clear to him very quickly that coming up with a good idea for a sculpture was the easy part. Carrying the creative process through to a finished bronze was something infinitely more complicated.

He studied and worked and studied some more before he began to feel comfortable with his medium. Today he is still a student of sculpture and continues to strive for a more complete grasp of the elements involved in his art.

The element of sculpture that he had the least problem with was style. While he has always admired the basic honesty of Russell's work, he did not want to copy him. Often an artist becomes so intent on discovering his own personal style that he ignores the value of what he, himself, can bring to his work. This includes not only whatever he knows about art, but his total background, his life, beliefs, observations, experiences, attitudes, memories, customs, and imagination. All of these factors combine to become the way in which he sees the world. And these factors translate, through his modeling, into his own personal artistic style.

Grant sees the world as a westerner. He is straightforward and honest both in his life and in his art. The matter of style and of inspiration is of supreme importance in Grant's work. In spite of all the technical aspects, sculpture is not primarily a technical process.

Technique — command of the physical process — only enables the sculptor to say what he wants to say with his art. When he has mastered technique well enough to be comfortable with it, then his creativity and imagination can take over.

Through a long and disciplined regimen of study and work, Grant mastered the techniques of not only modeling, but the casting process as well. He learned the conceptual tools of schematics, proportion, and anatomy — all basic and fundamental in the translation of his ideas into sculpture. He learned to work with clay and wax — the nature of the material and the tools for working with them. He learned the value of "sketching" in wax and how to model on the armature, or "skeleton," of his pieces. And he learned the highly sophisticated procedures involved in lost wax, or *cire perdue,* bronze casting.

At first, Grant finished his waxes and took them to California to be cast in bronze. But this required a lot of time for travel and proved to be an unsatisfactory arrangement. Grant was then more or less forced to get into the foundry business himself. This is when he and Hughes Curtis renovated the old foundry at Springville, Utah. During this period he learned all he could about the casting process. After many more hours of study and work, Grant was finally able to produce excellent results. Along the way he picked up a pretty extensive education in chemistry and physics, as they are major considerations in the technical process involved in casting bronze.

It usually comes as a surprise to art collectors to realize the complex problems involved between the time the sculptor gets an idea for a piece and the time when the finished bronze is ready for exhibition. It is also a fact that this matter of modeling and casting accounts for a major portion of the artist's time and effort. It is every sculptor's lament that he never has enough time to think about new ideas and subjects because he is bogged down in the technical process of foundry work.

Sculpture has never been an occupation to be undertaken lightly. Anyone can pick up a set of paints and a couple of brushes and try their hand at painting. But to even experiment with sculpture is a much more ambitious undertaking. But so is bronc riding — and Grant stuck with the problems and obstacles of sculpture just as he had stuck with riding bucking horses.

Since the early 1970s, Grant has finally eased some of the pressures in connection with foundry work. His friend, Neal Hadlock, has developed a foundry close to Grant's home and is able to perform many of the physical steps that Grant used to have to do himself. This has allowed Grant more freedom to reach down inside himself for fresh ideas and to be out on horseback every so often to recharge his inspiration.

One of the results of Grant finally becoming at ease with the physical steps involved in his work is that it has allowed him to concentrate more on original concepts in his subject matter. Another fairly recent development in his work is the appearance of a subtle touch of impressionism. This was first apparent in his 1974 piece, *Mustang Mare.* Here the emphasis was on artistic form rather than historical storytelling.

This departure from the minutely detailed, literal representation to a more loosely-executed model has been the key to something Grant has been striving for throughout his career — to highlight the spirit or mood of a particular subject. This faculty is what attracted him in the first place to the bronzes of Russell. Now it has become obvious that what he feels about a subject, and the objective of sharing that feeling with those who see the sculpture, is more important than taking care to see that every specific, painstaking detail is correct. The attitude and posture of a figure such as *Bought 'Em for Two and Sold 'Em for One* is much more revealing than the precise crease in the cowboy's hat or the kind of heels on his boots.

This kind of subjective and interpretive approach to his work is what really sets Grant apart from most of the other contemporary western sculptors. He is telling us through his art not only what his subject looks like but, more significantly, about its associated mood and spirit.

The great southwestern writer J. Frank Dobie, in praising Charlie Russell's work as a sculptor, hit upon the qualities that attracted Grant to Russell's bronzes. These same qualities are what Grant tries to get into his pieces.

In nearly all of Russell's bronzes he shows that easy intimacy with life characteristic of his best drawings, watercolors, and paintings. I cannot speak of his technical qualities as a sculptor, but in effect, the process of sculpturing seems to have been as natural to him as the relationship between a mother bear and her cub is in one of his most delightful bronzes.

If Russell had not been more than a "Western" artist, he would not be the artist of the West that he is. That quality of being delightful lifts him above the plane of action — supposed by the ignorant to compass the Old West. Russell's bronzes have a lower proportion of action than his paintings — a good many of which were produced for calendar consumption. The bronzes express a free play of imagination and a spiritual quality often not found in his big canvasses. Consider, for example, *Secrets of the Night,* in which an owl and an Indian, with wonderfully expressive face, communicate, the Indian hearing because he understands. In *Spirit of Winter,* as stark as the Blackfeet legend of human desolation on which it is based, Russell seems to me to have reached the climax of his creative genius.

Russell didn't just show us an image in his sculpture — he talked to us. Grant has spent his art career developing this same quality in his work. It is what will set him apart from the majority of other contemporary western artists.

Grant's larger than life bronze of Charles Goodnight represents much more than a statue of a cowman of the late 1800s. In the face and hands and in the stoop of the shoulders are eloquent reflections of the entire pageant of western range cattle heritage. One is much more aware of the essence of the big ranch and trail driving era by absorbing the subtleties of this bronze than by reading a whole list of books on the subject. Western history books are most often literal and objective. Grant's bronzes are symbols of the western experience, full of vitality and emotion. Our western heritage is worth remembering, and sculpture like Grant Speed's is a major contribution toward that end.

My purpose here is not to go into elaborate detail about modeling and casting, but to provide some basic information to the beginner.

I don't recommend that young sculptors concern themselves with the casting process in the beginning. Their time would be better spent on studying the creative aspects of sculpting, rather than the mechanical details of casting. I also recommend professional instruction from competent teachers whenever possible. This eliminates a lot of trial and error in the development of their talent and ability.

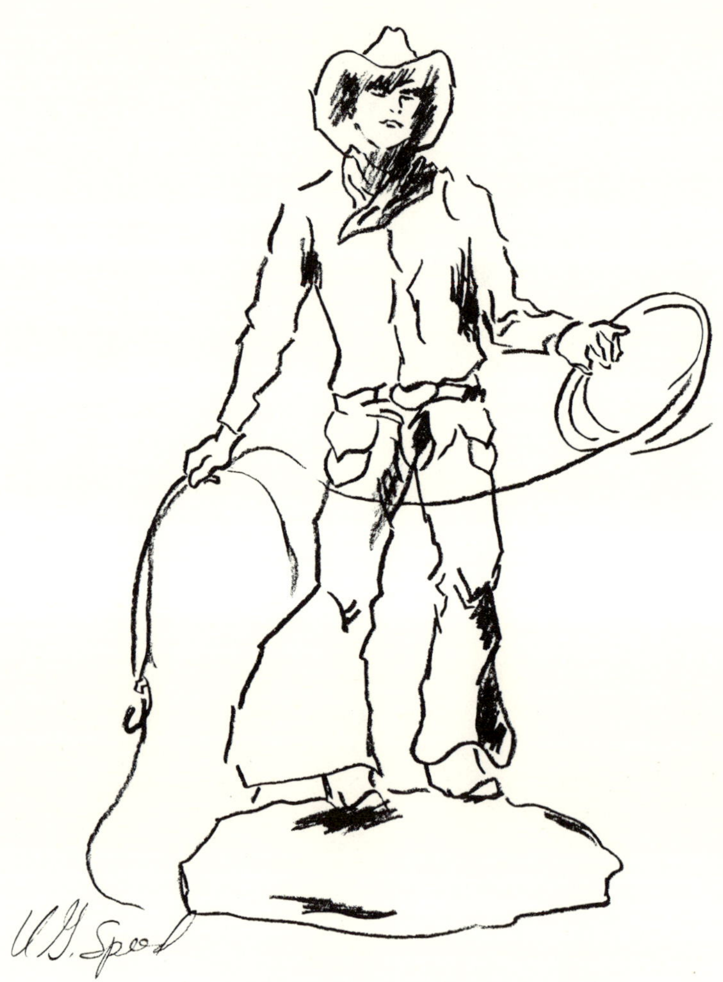

Preliminary sketch for *The Bronc Rider*

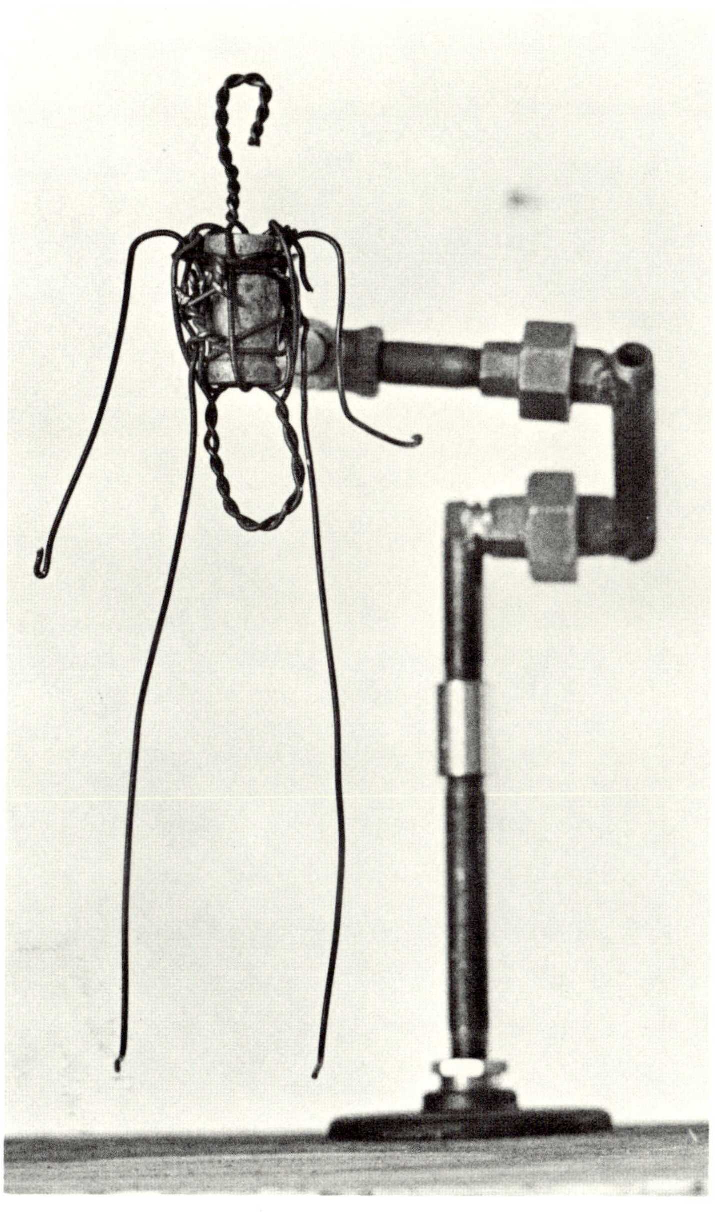 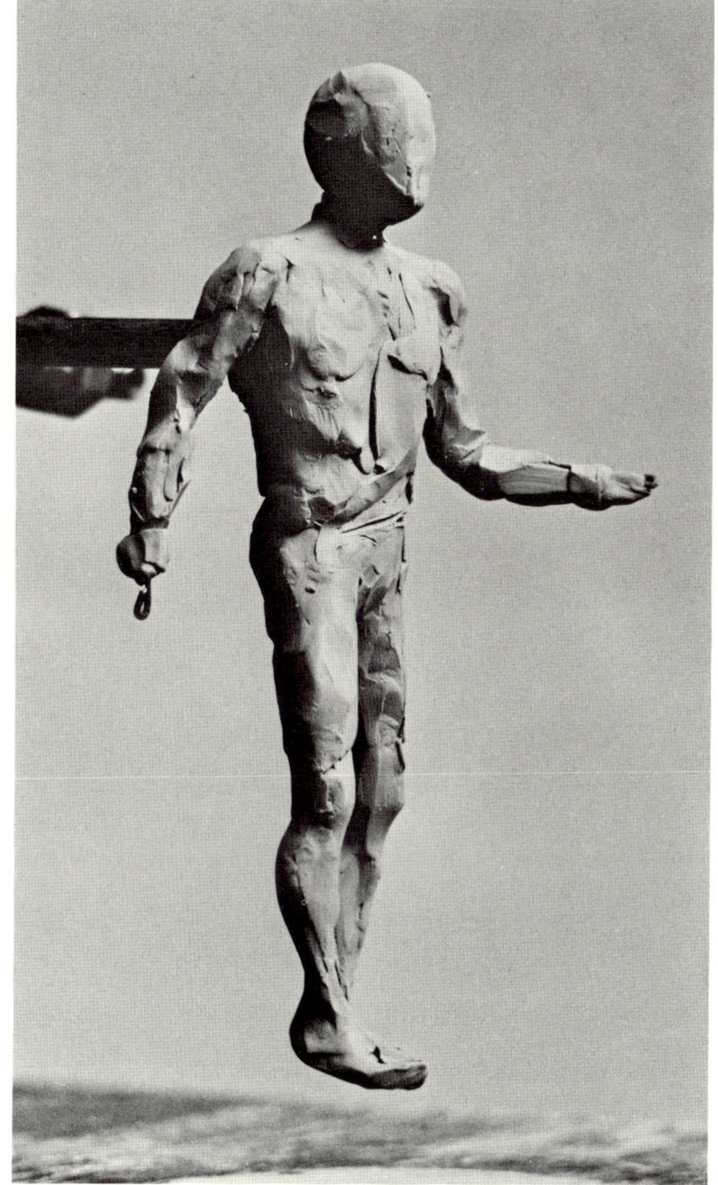

The armature is the framework or "skeleton" upon which the clay will be applied in modeling. The construction of an armature is very important. It must be strong enough to support the weight of the clay and, at the same time, flexible enough to allow for implied action and movement in the design of the model.

In the next step, clay is applied and built up on the armature. The sculptor must have a clear idea of how he wants the finished model to look. From the very beginning he works to incorporate the attitude, action, shape, and form that he wants to see in the finished sculpture.

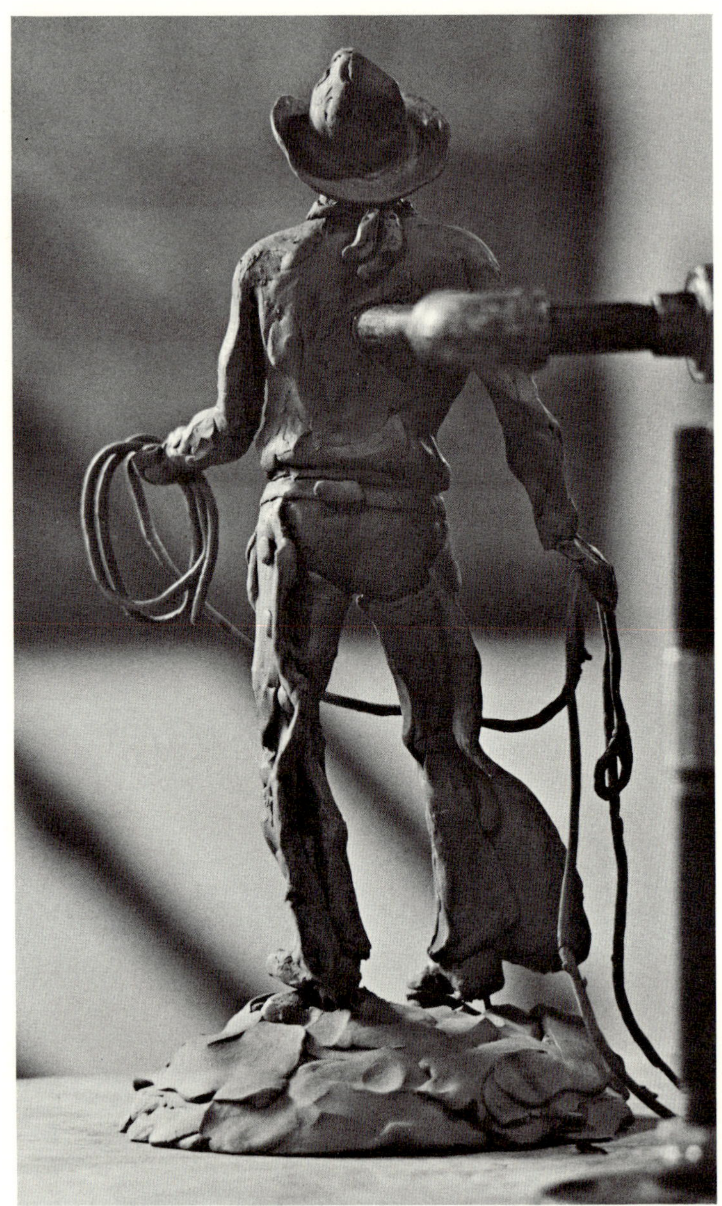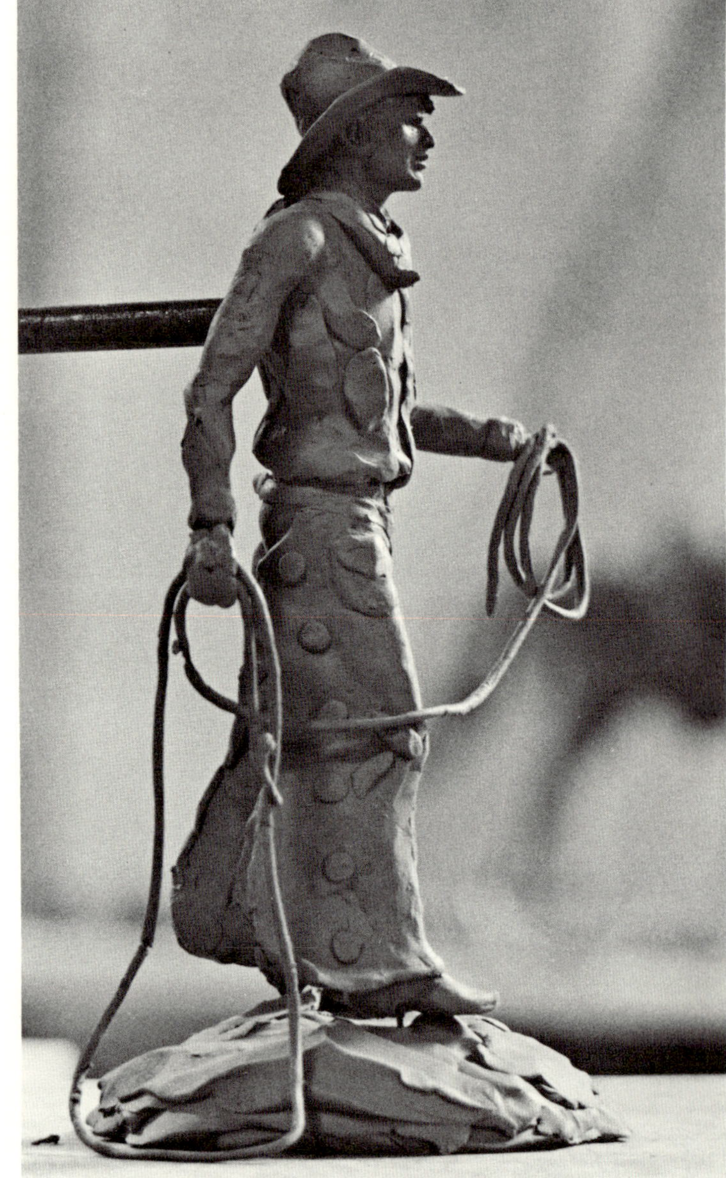

In the early stages of modeling, small detail work is not yet important. But by now the sculptor should be able to decide if the model is going to look like the idea he had when he began the piece. If so, he can begin to work on the details such as the face and clothes in this particular model. Adding accessories like ropes or reins will give a better idea of the look of the finished design.

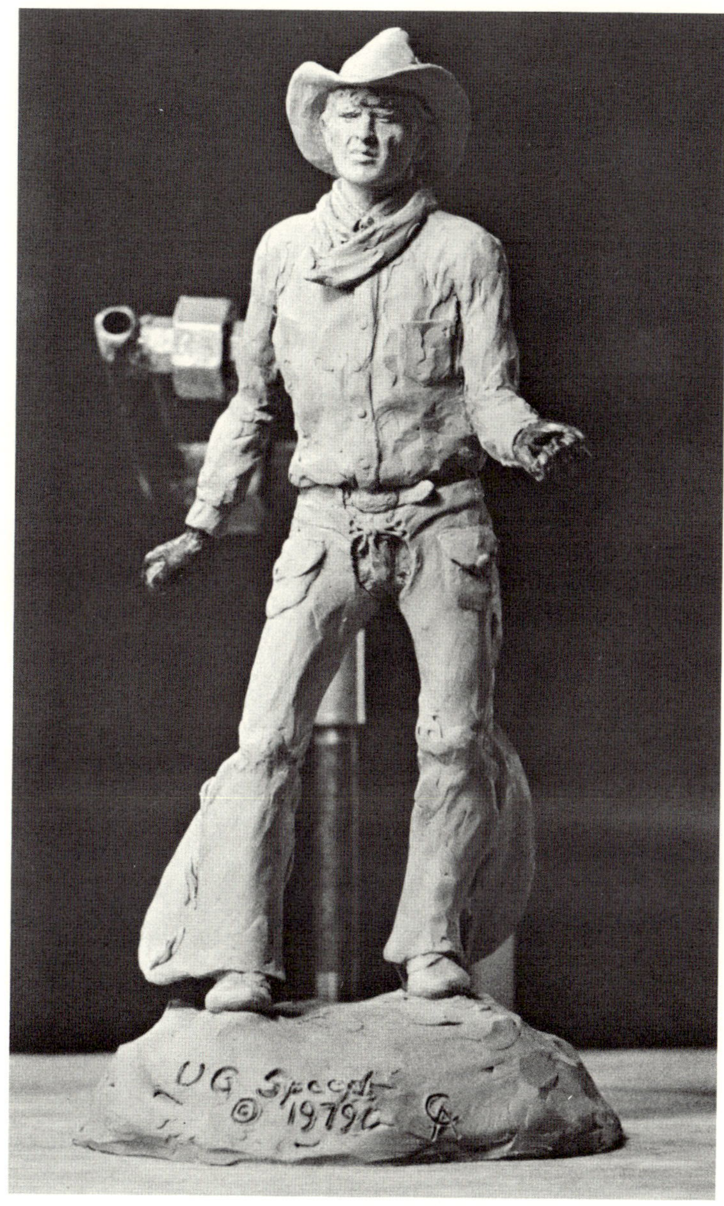 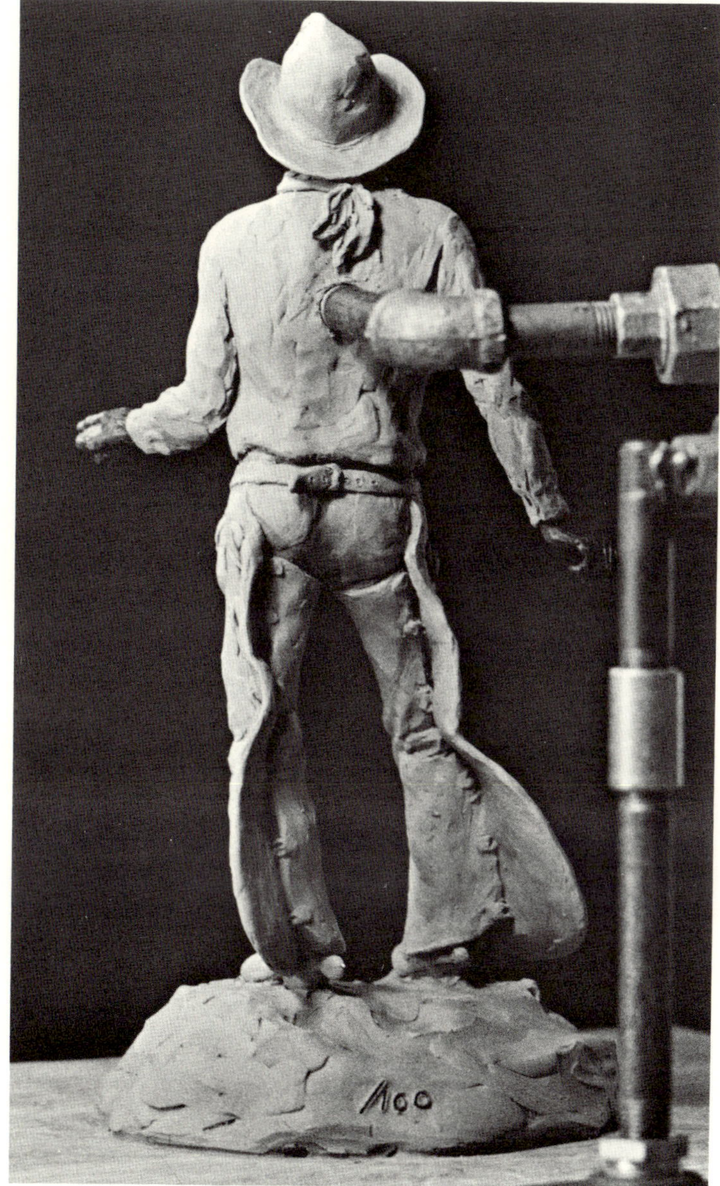

The finished clay model should look exactly like the sculptor wants the finished bronze to appear. Sometimes he may use wax instead of clay on small details such as the model's hands. The wax is stronger than clay and will hold its definition better during the mold-building process. Sometimes a coat of clear shellac is applied to the completed model for added strength.

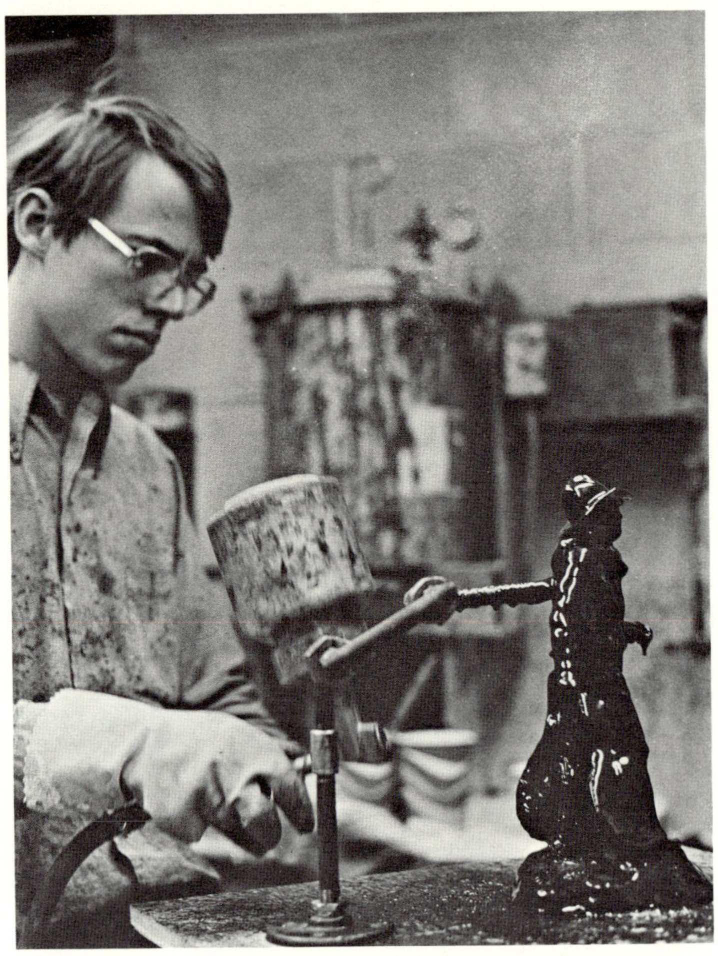

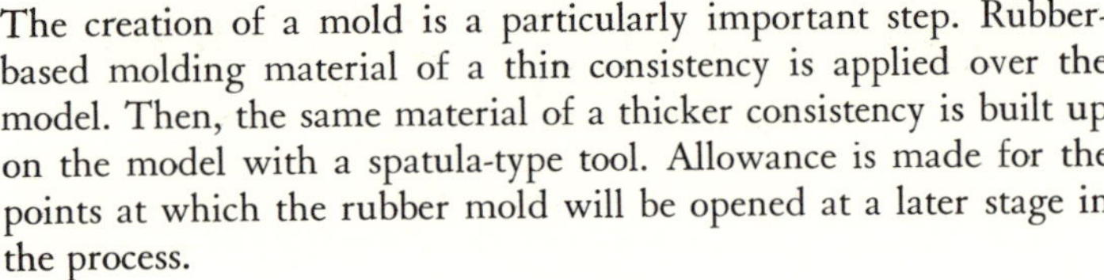

The creation of a mold is a particularly important step. Rubber-based molding material of a thin consistency is applied over the model. Then, the same material of a thicker consistency is built up on the model with a spatula-type tool. Allowance is made for the points at which the rubber mold will be opened at a later stage in the process.

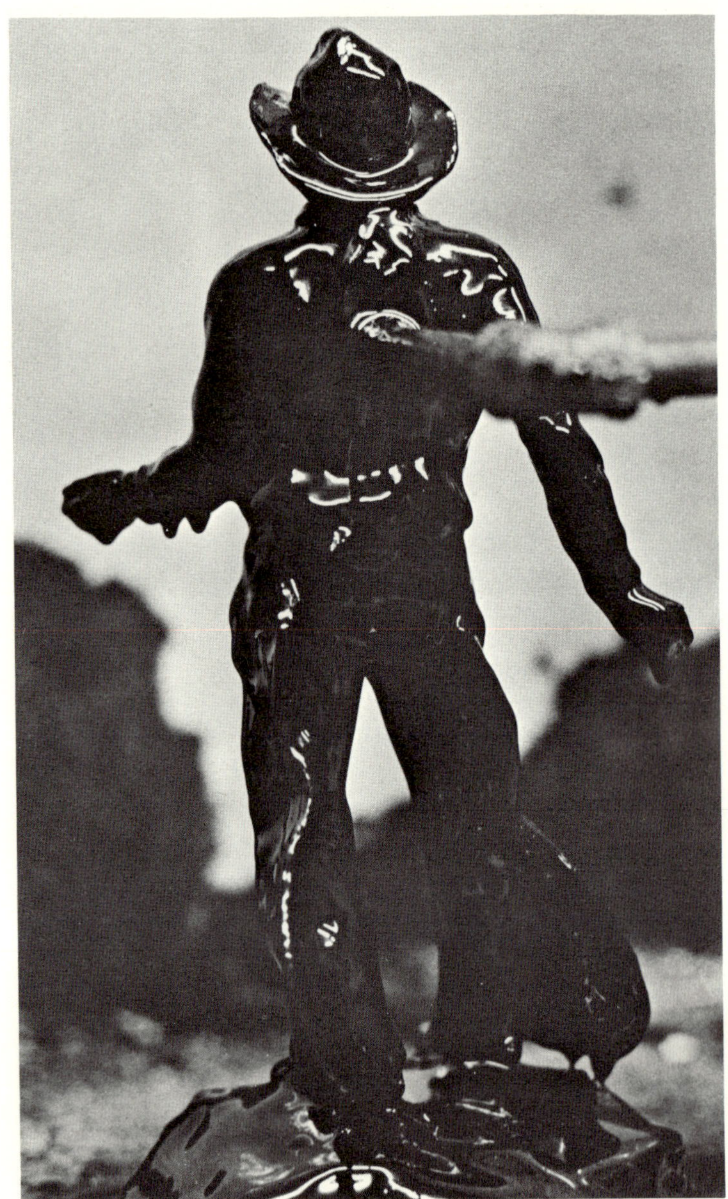

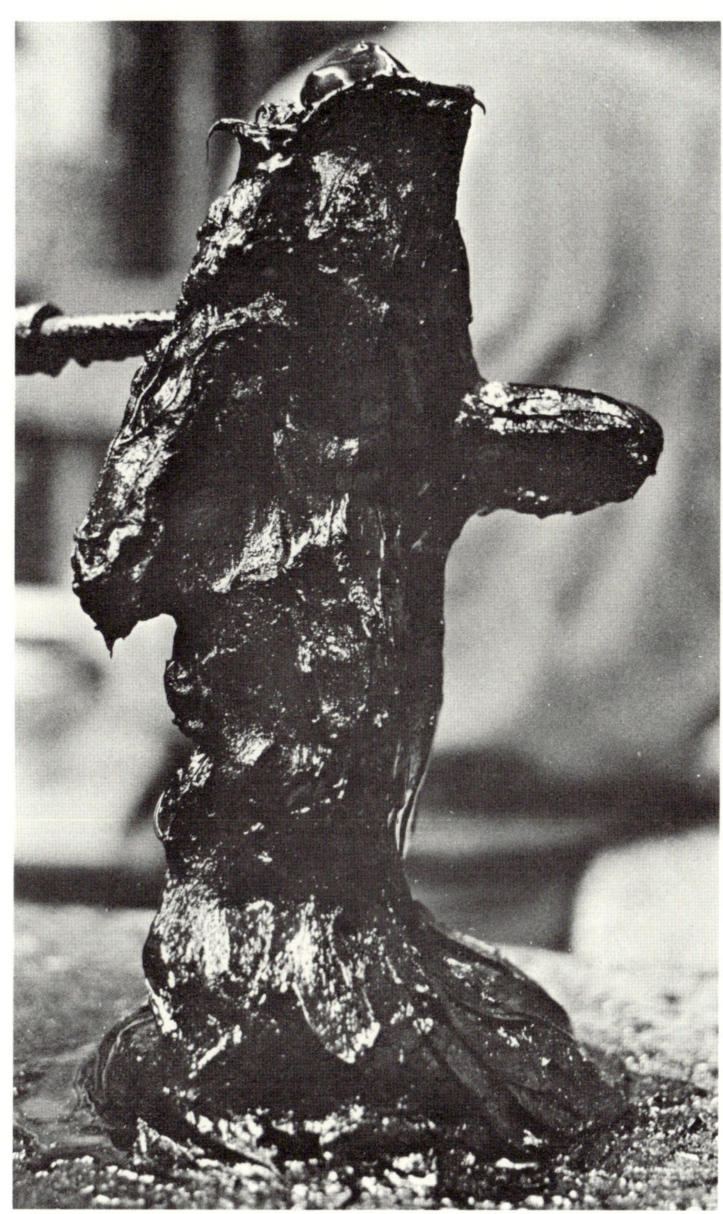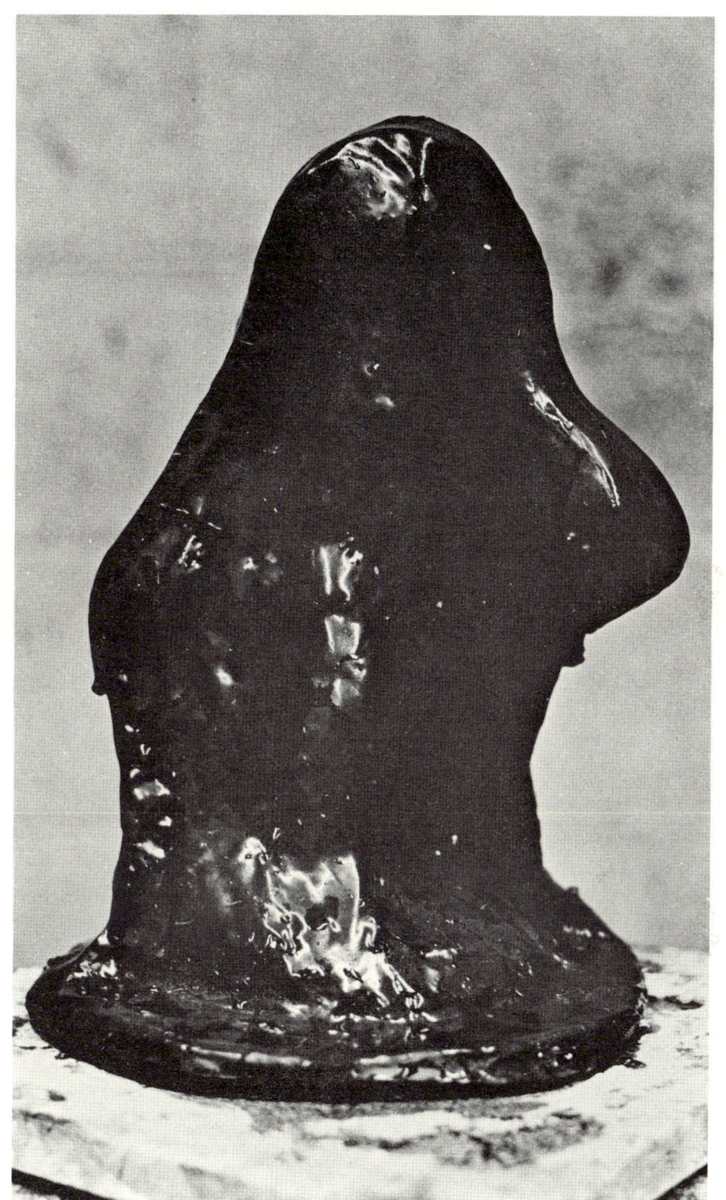

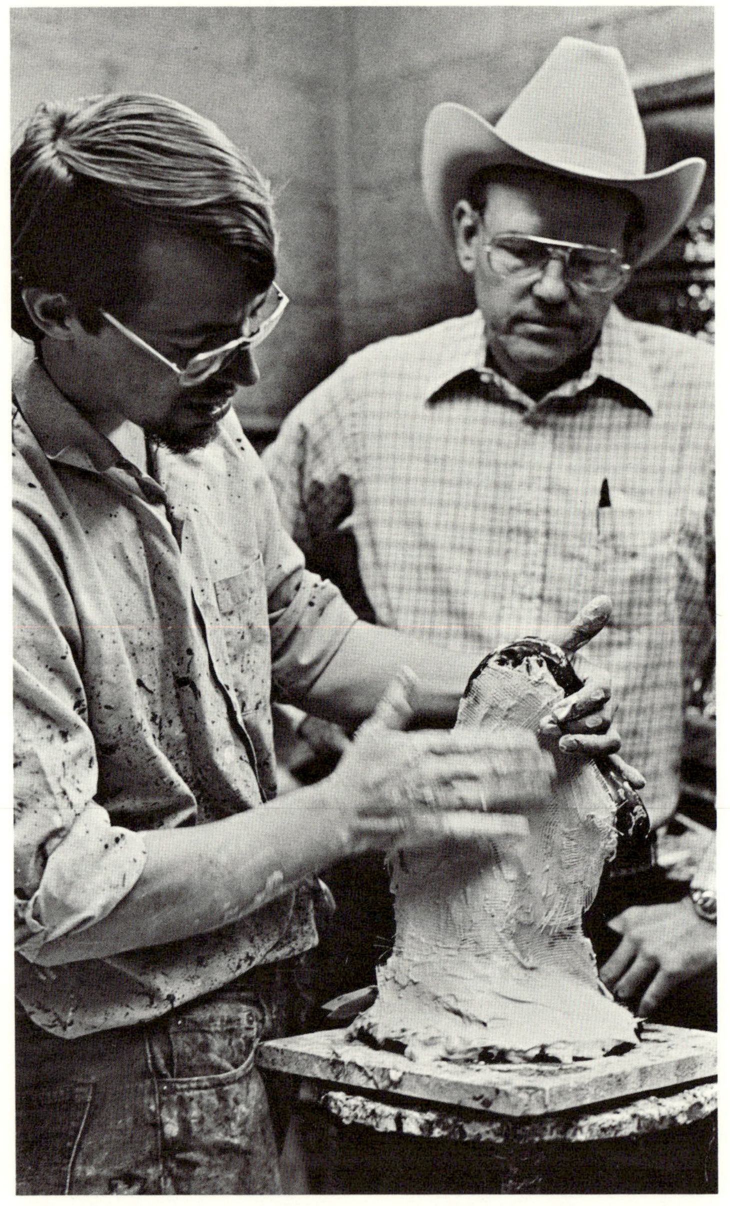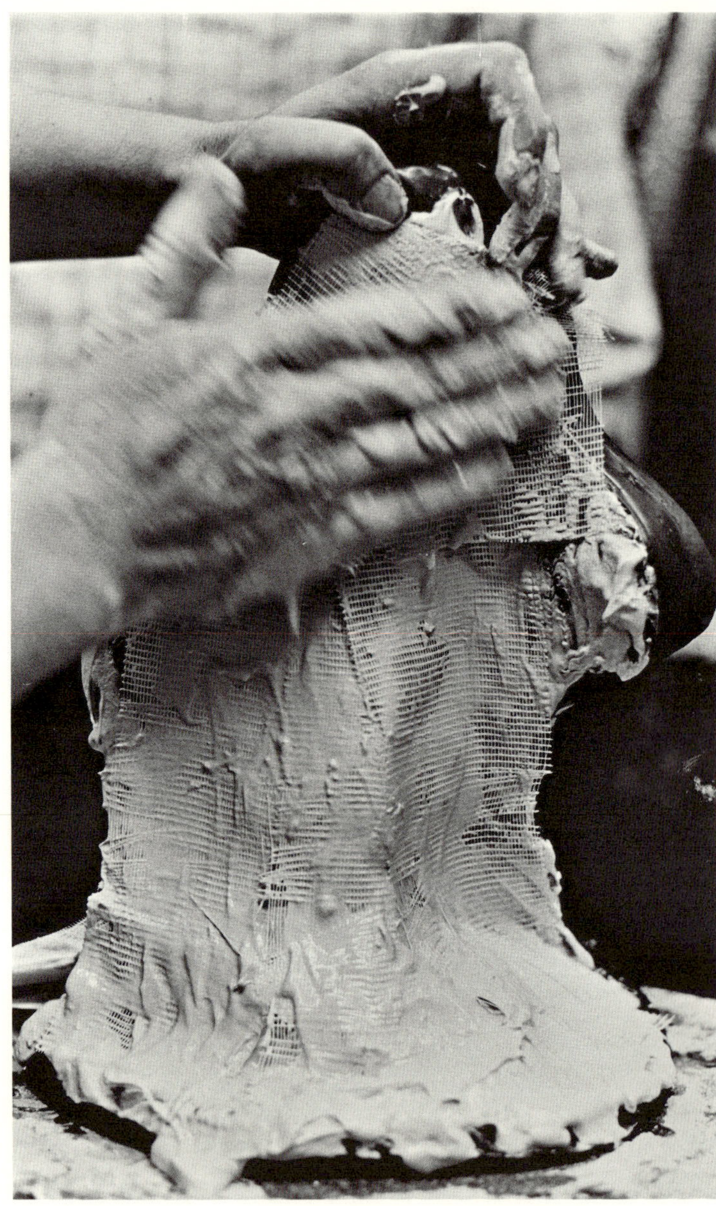

Plaster is used in creating the "mother mold." Hemp or other strong fiber is mixed with the plaster to decrease the weight of the mold without lessening its overall strength. When completed, the mother mold will cover the rubber mold, which in turn covers the clay model.

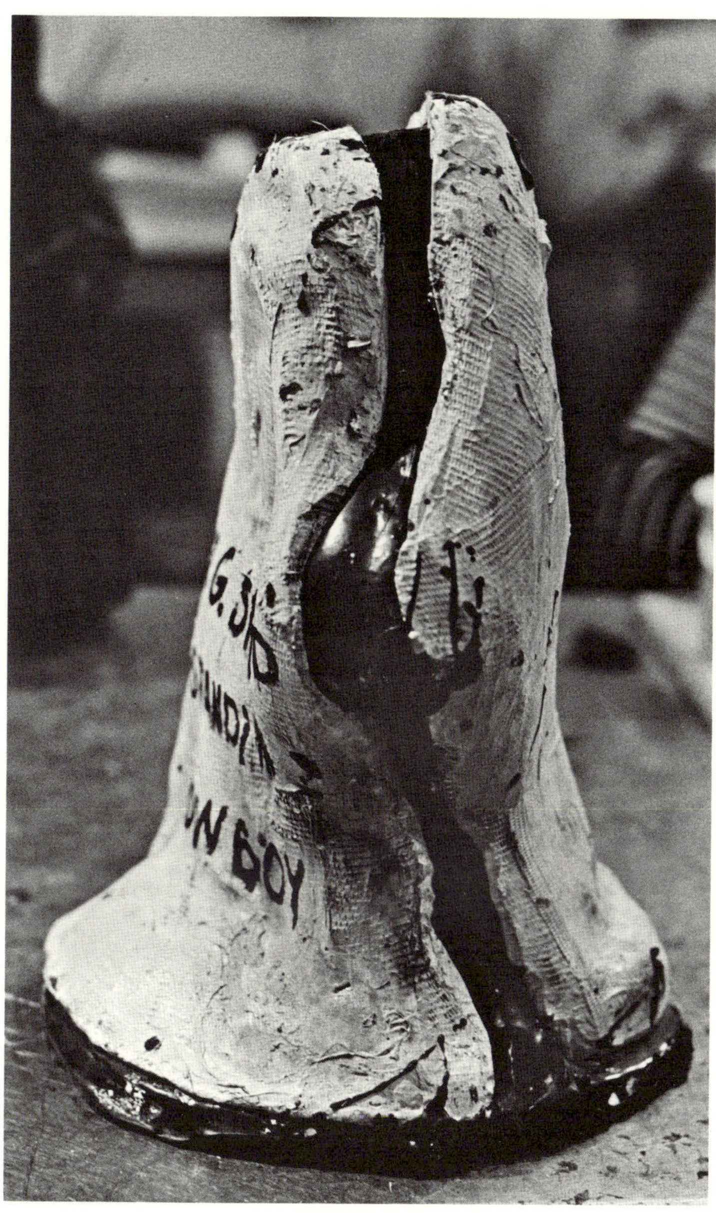
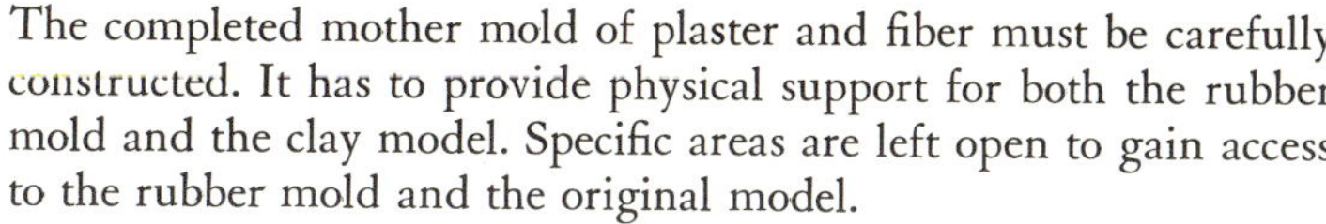

The completed mother mold of plaster and fiber must be carefully constructed. It has to provide physical support for both the rubber mold and the clay model. Specific areas are left open to gain access to the rubber mold and the original model.

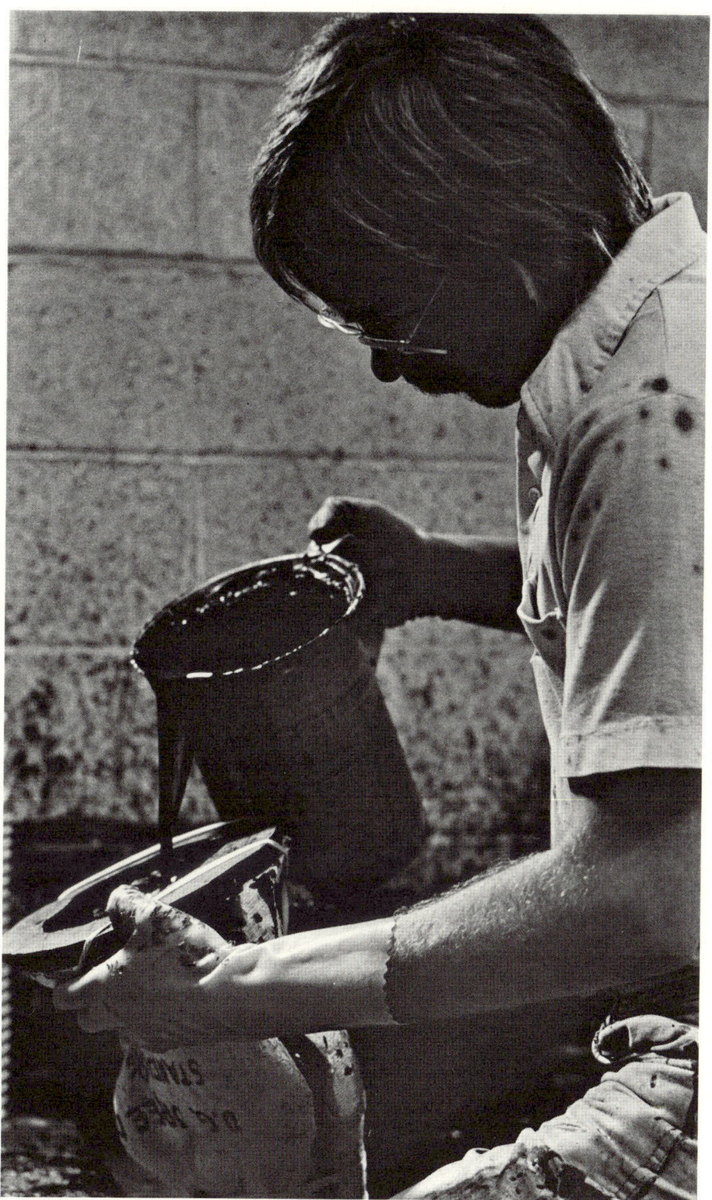

At this point the rubber mold is cut into and the clay of the original model is removed. The rubber mold retains all of the details of the model. Hot wax is poured into the hollow mold to form a thin wax shell within the mold.

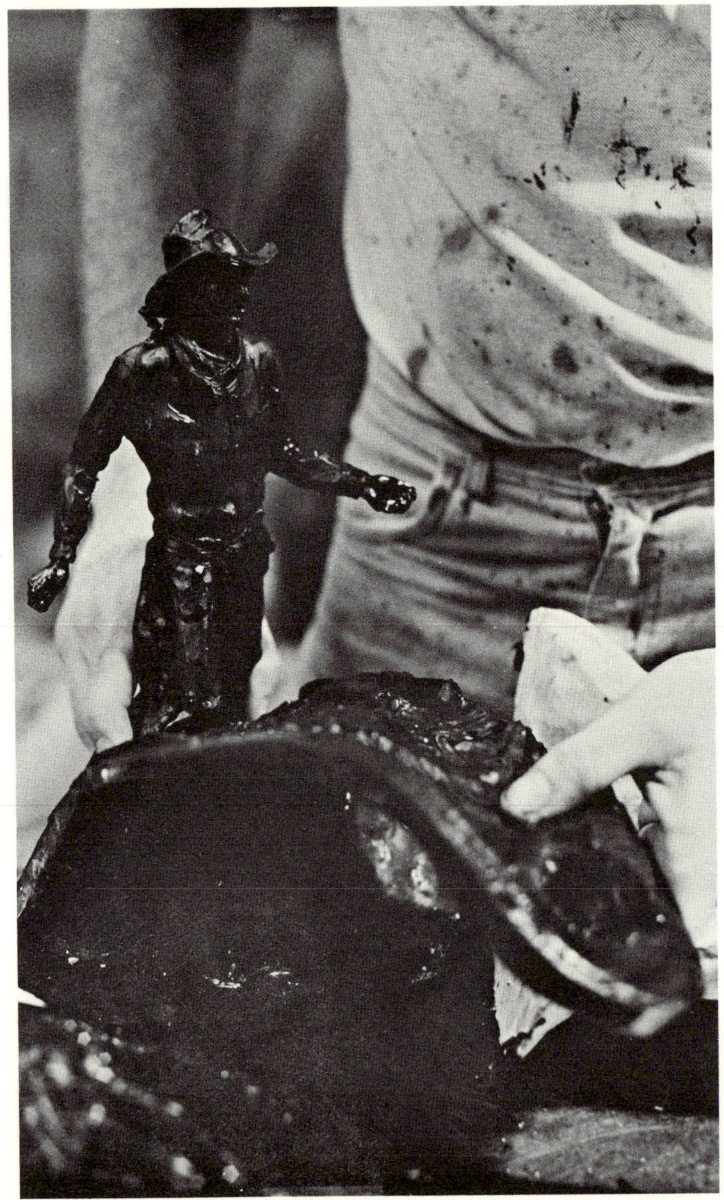

After the wax has cooled, the mother mold is separated, along with the rubber mold, and the wax shell is removed. It is hollow and appears an exact duplication of the original clay model. The wax is only about one-quarter inch thick.

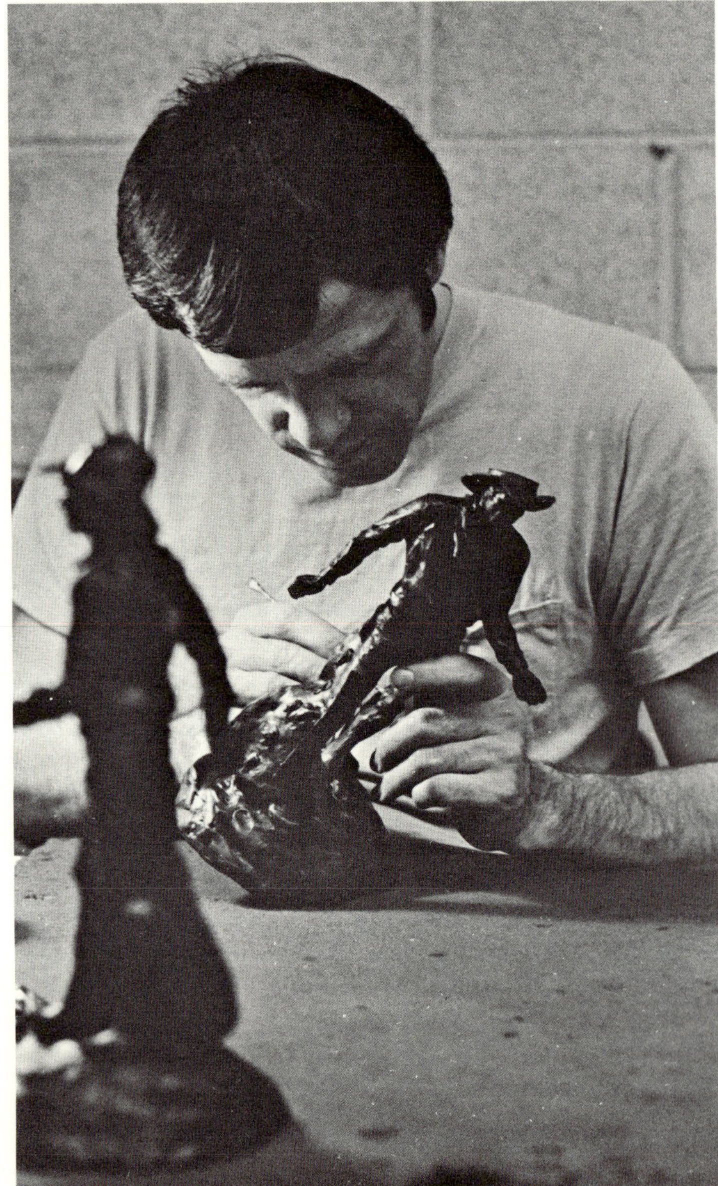

Imperfections in the wax are touched up by the foundry worker. These include the seams left by the rubber mold, as well as points at which air bubbles developed during the pouring of the hot wax.

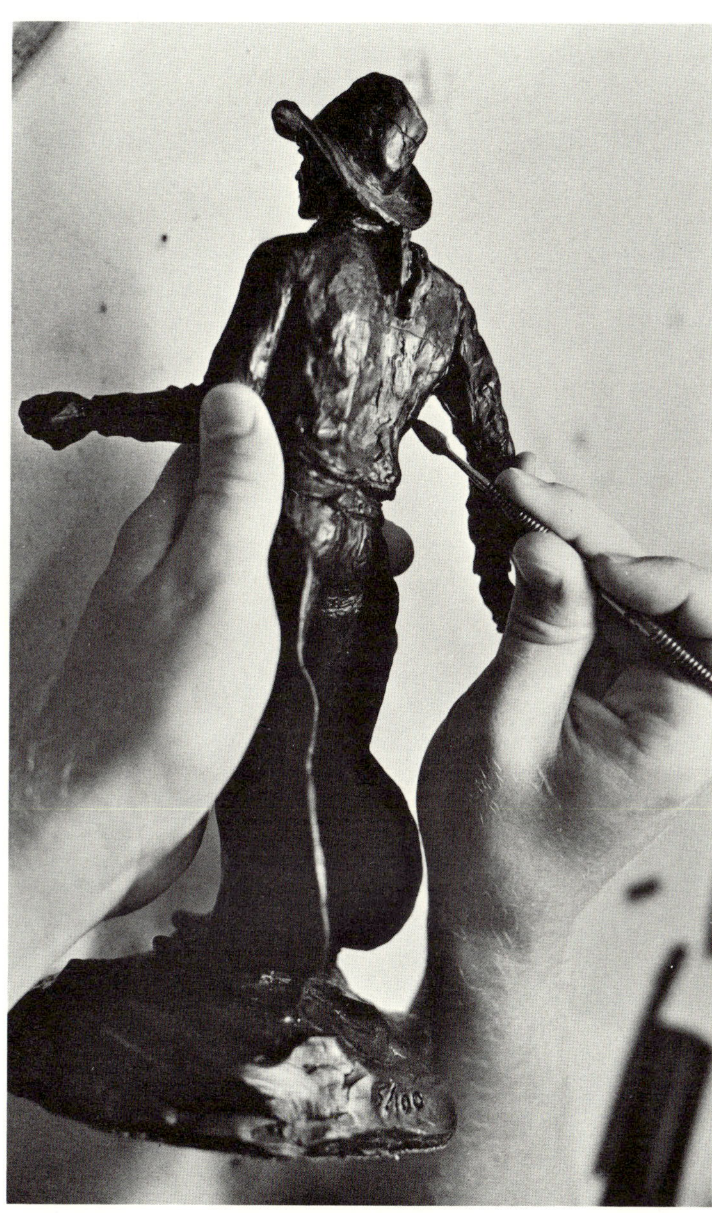
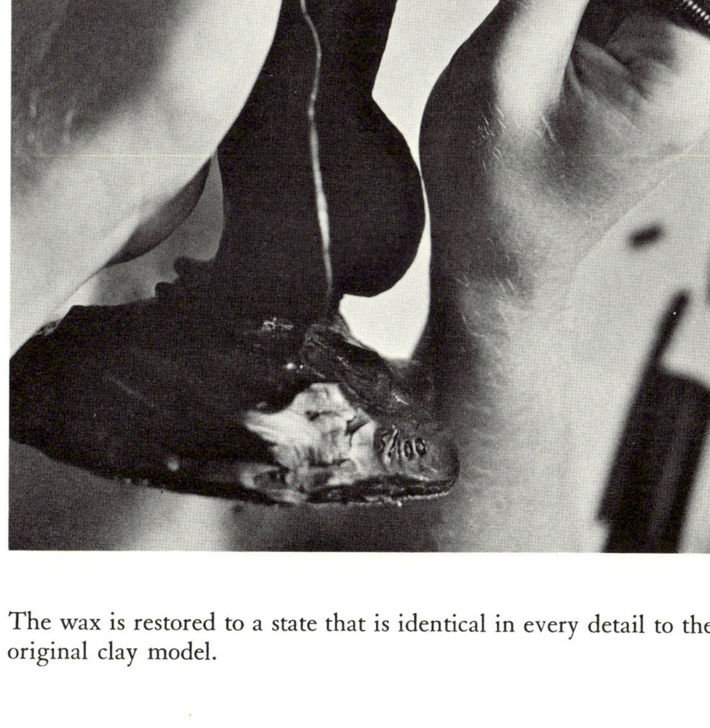

The wax is restored to a state that is identical in every detail to the original clay model.

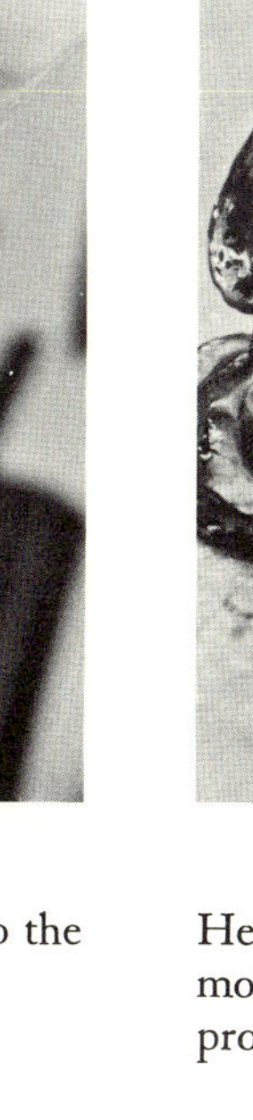

Here is the finished wax shown next to its mother mold. The mother mold, which still encloses the rubber mold, is used repeatedly to produce additional waxes for the number of bronzes that will be cast.

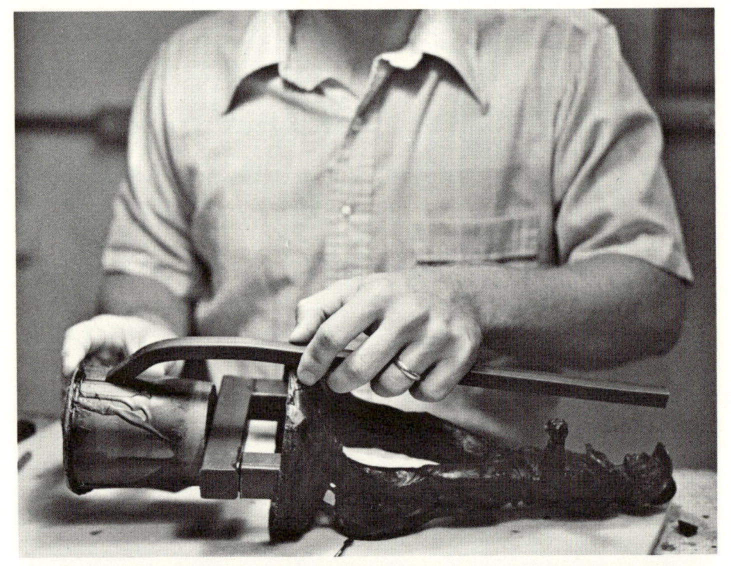
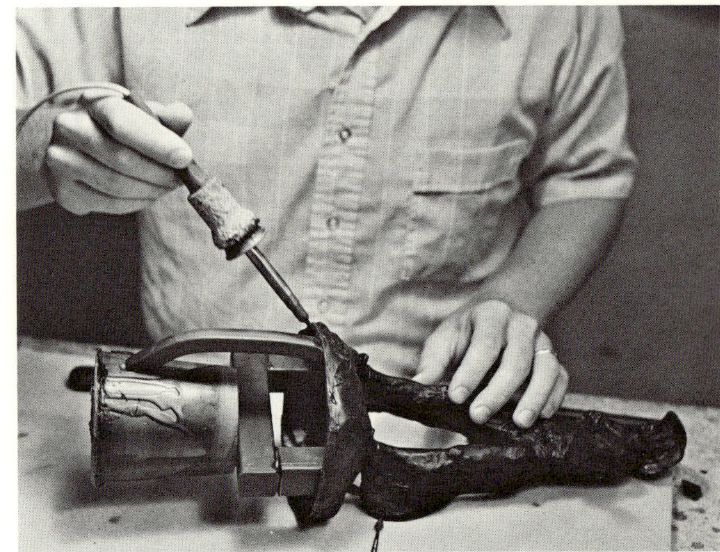
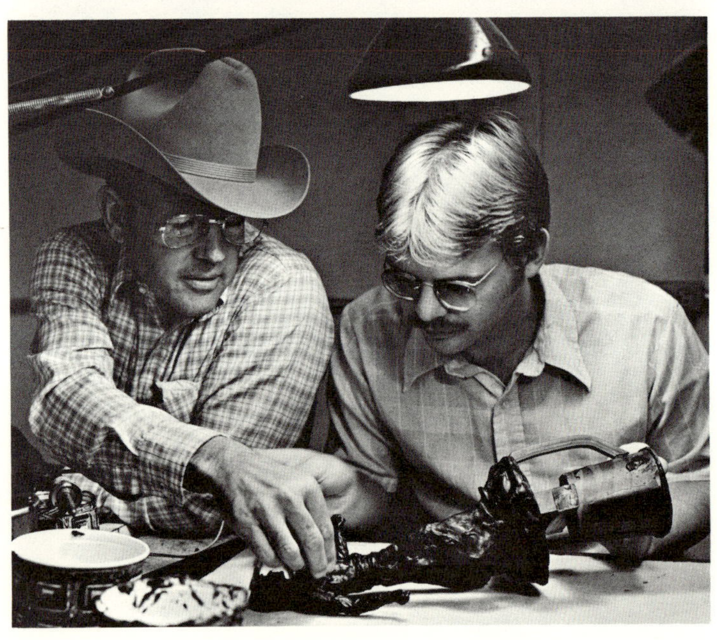
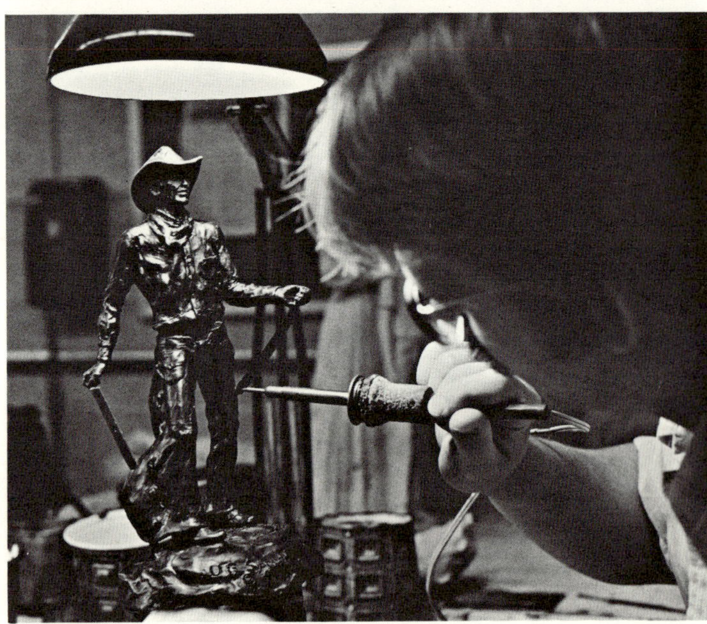

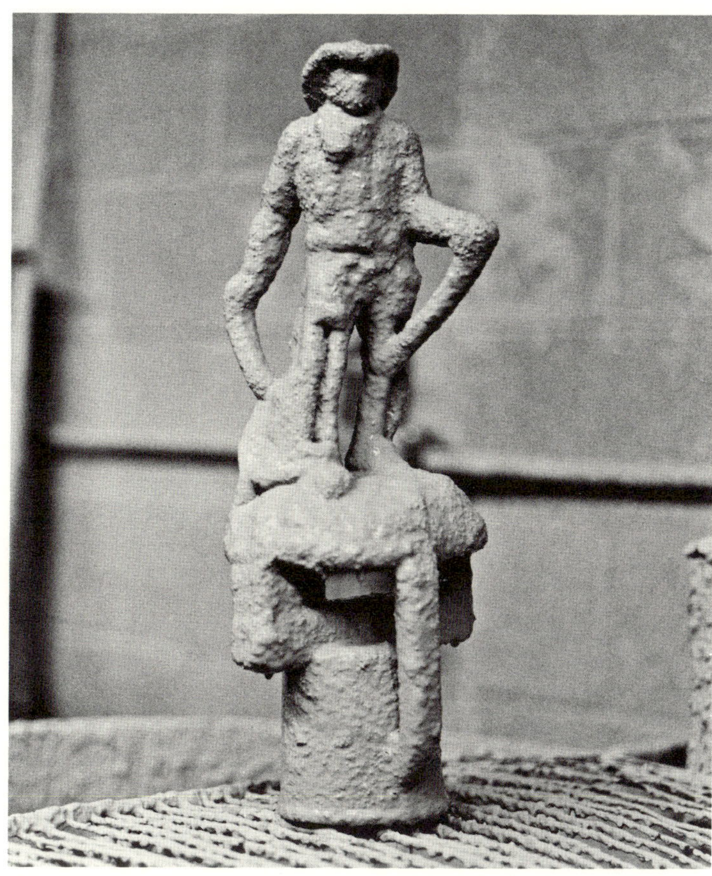

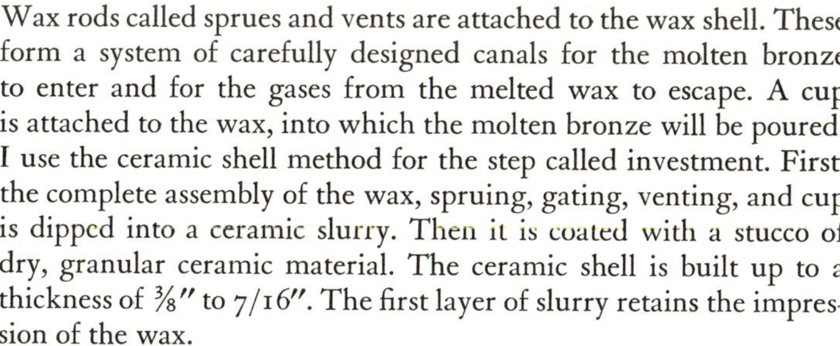

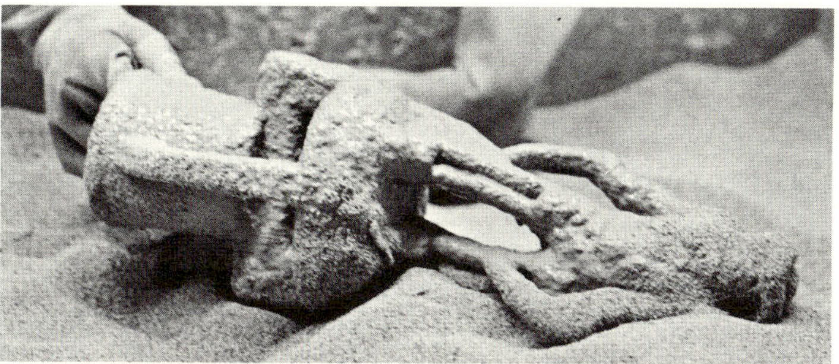

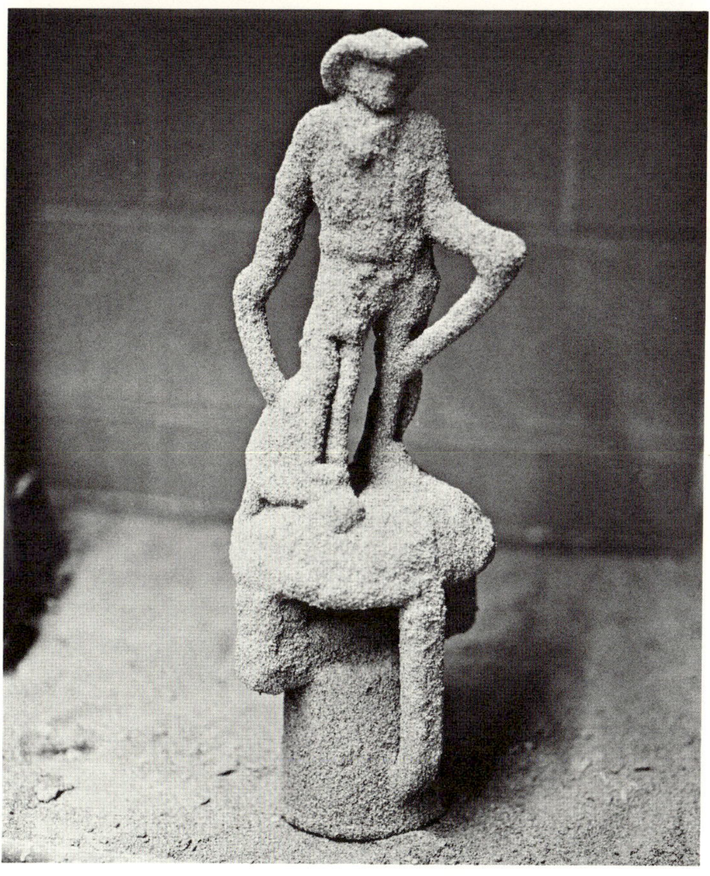

Wax rods called sprues and vents are attached to the wax shell. These form a system of carefully designed canals for the molten bronze to enter and for the gases from the melted wax to escape. A cup is attached to the wax, into which the molten bronze will be poured. I use the ceramic shell method for the step called investment. First, the complete assembly of the wax, spruing, gating, venting, and cup is dipped into a ceramic slurry. Then it is coated with a stucco of dry, granular ceramic material. The ceramic shell is built up to a thickness of ⅜″ to 7/16″. The first layer of slurry retains the impression of the wax.

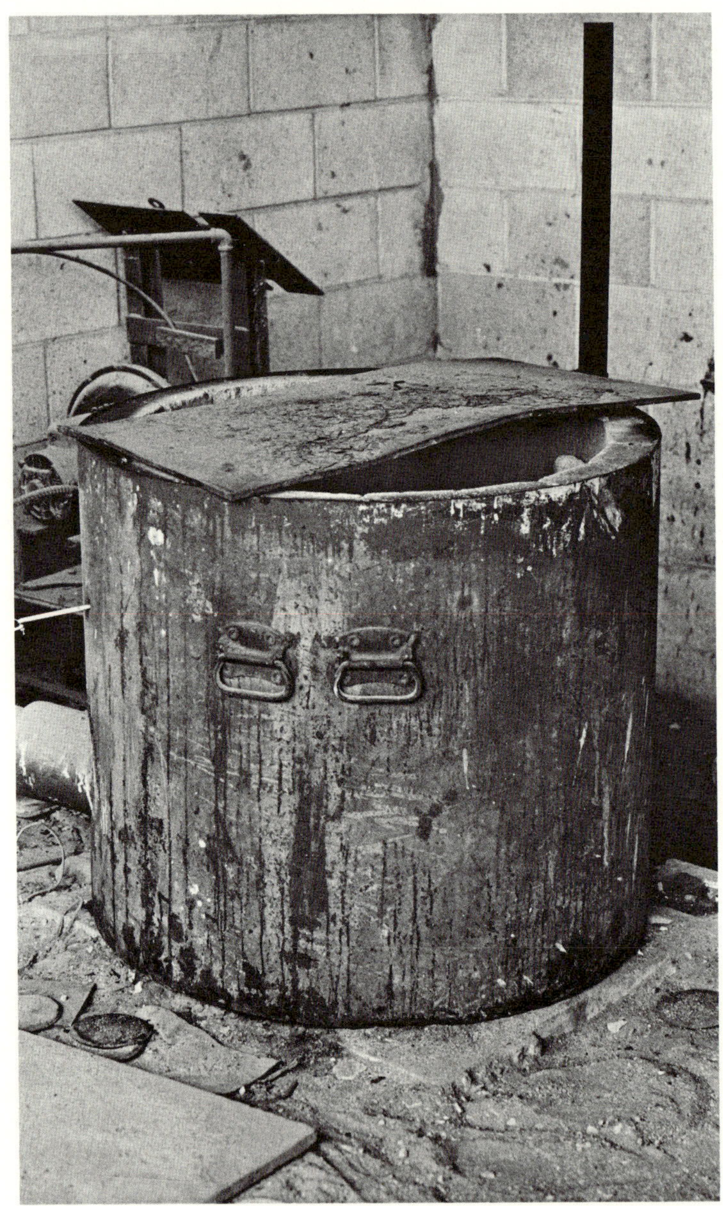

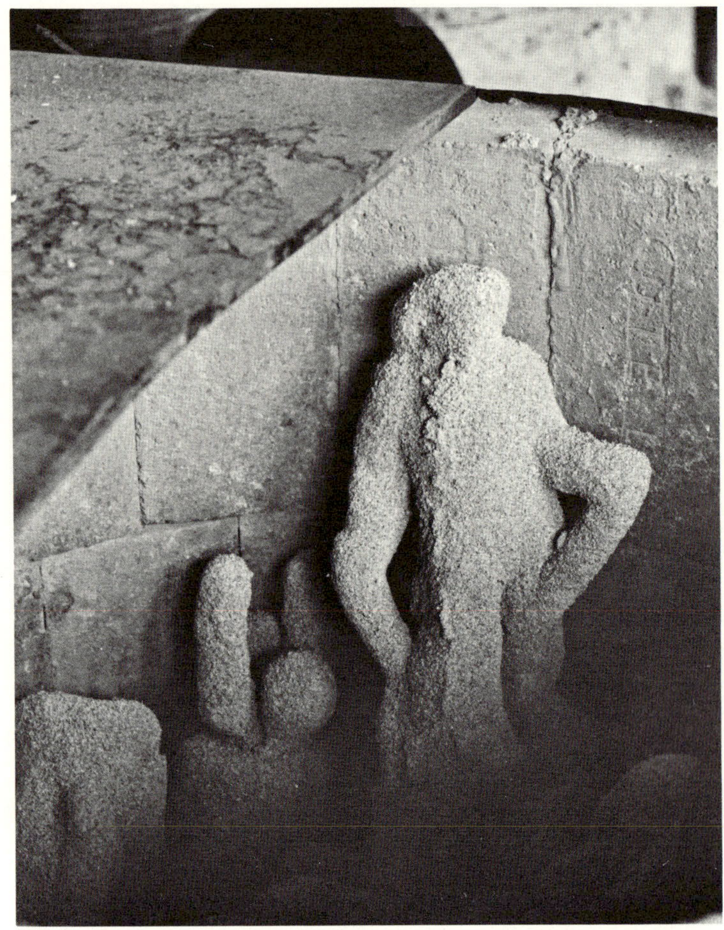

The ceramic-coated assembly is then placed into a furnace. This step is called burning out the mold. The wax shell melts and drains out through the system of gates and sprues. The heating of the furnace is also critically important at this stage.

Molten bronze is then poured into the cup and goes into the ceramic shell where the impressions of the wax have been retained in the initial slurry layers. Success at this stage depends on the careful and correct execution of each step that has led up to this point.

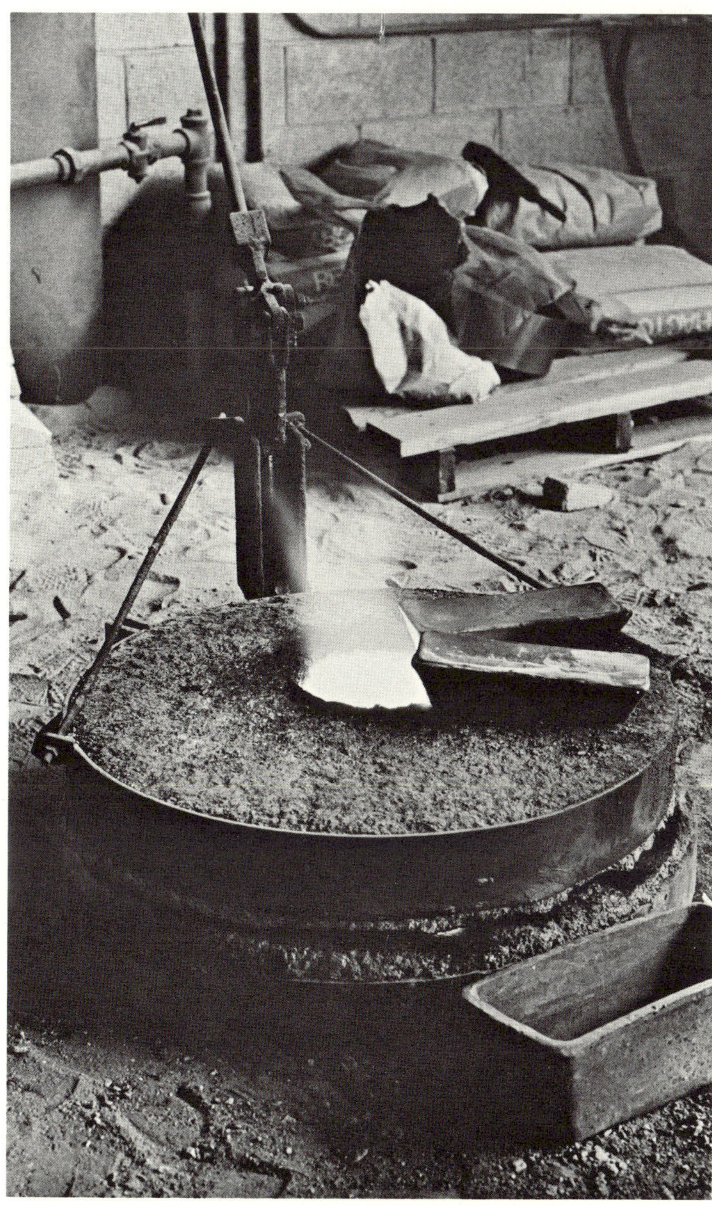

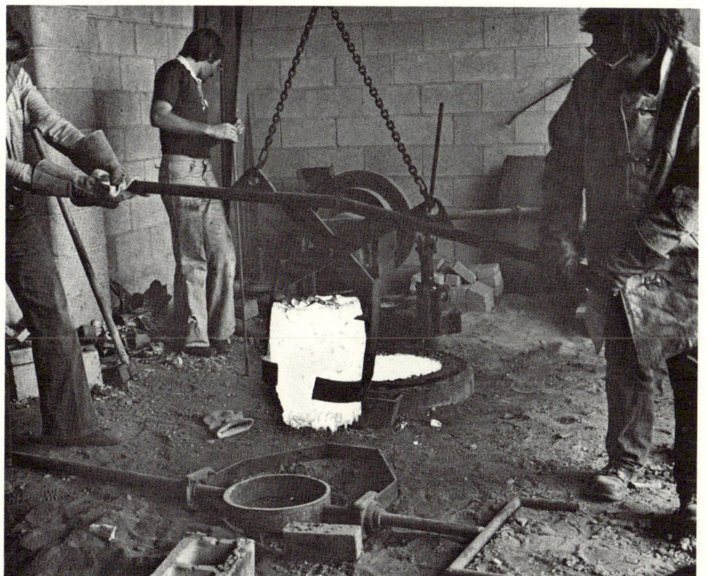

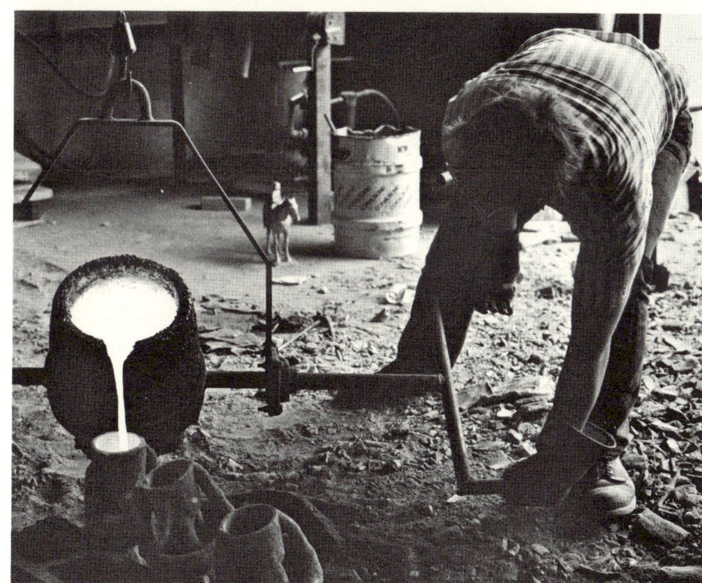

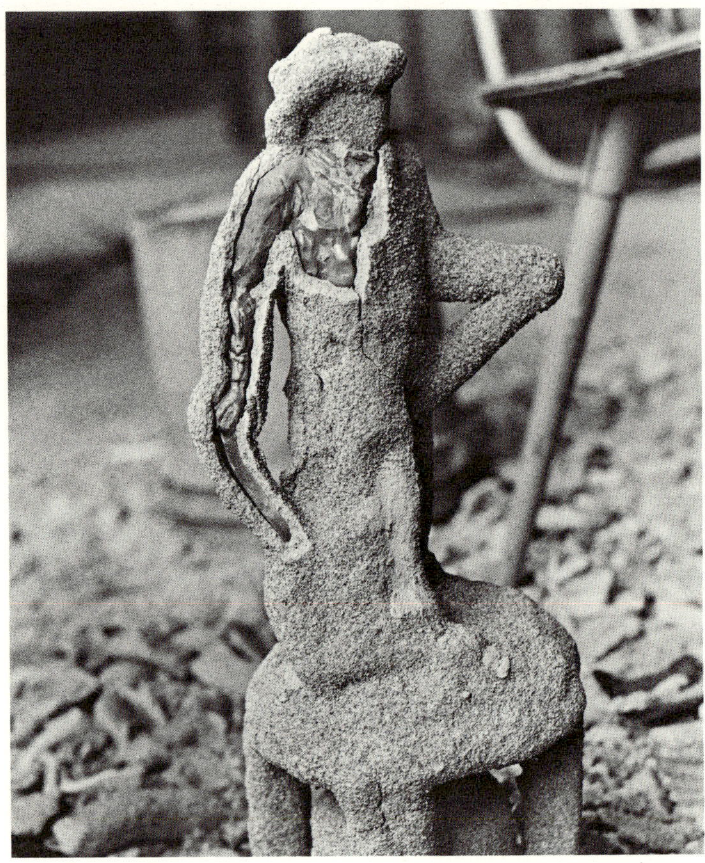

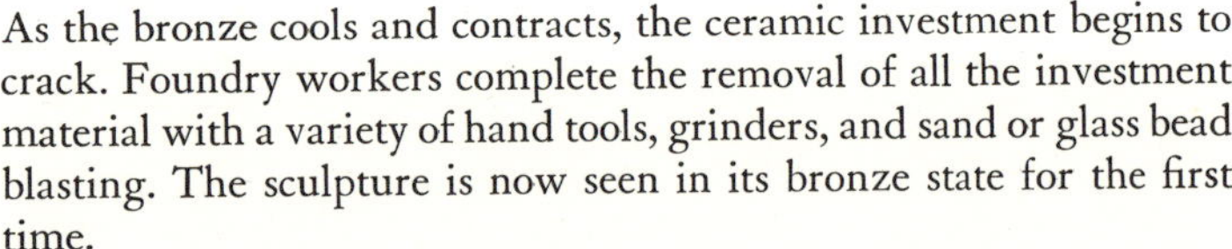

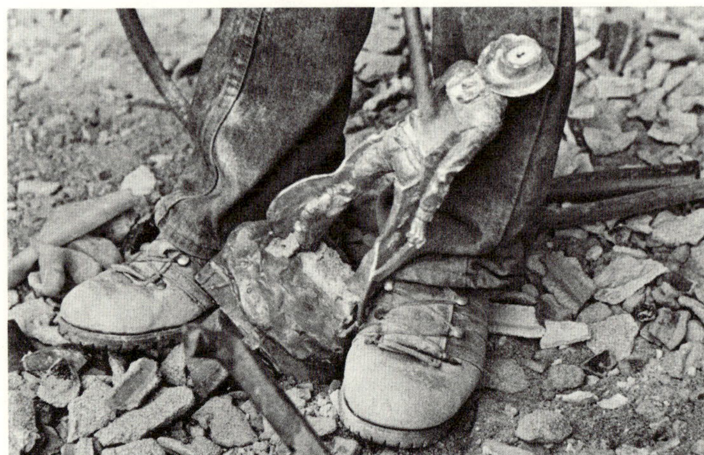

As the bronze cools and contracts, the ceramic investment begins to crack. Foundry workers complete the removal of all the investment material with a variety of hand tools, grinders, and sand or glass bead blasting. The sculpture is now seen in its bronze state for the first time.
Pits and other flaws in the bronze are filled with a heli-arc welder. The foundry workers then use a variety of metal tools to "chase" or file down the beads from the welding to match the texture and configuration of the cast bronze. This is an important part of the total process and calls for expert foundrymen.

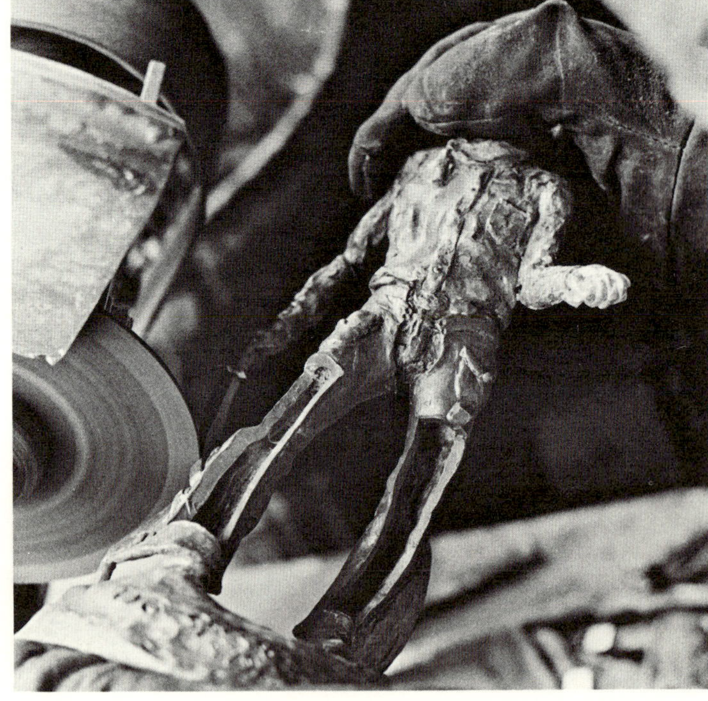

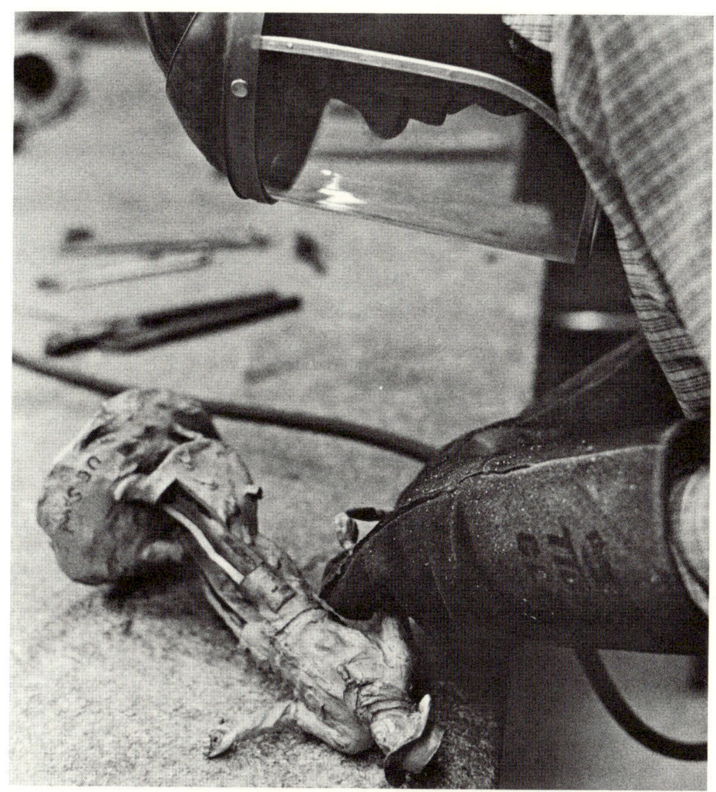

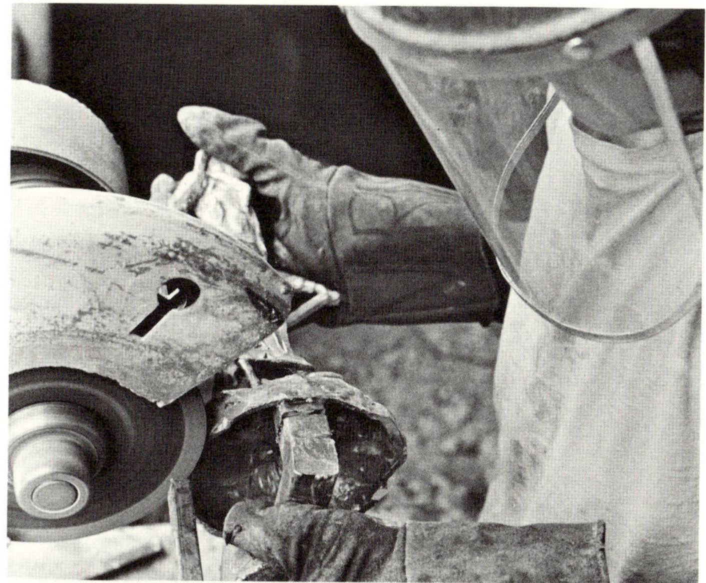

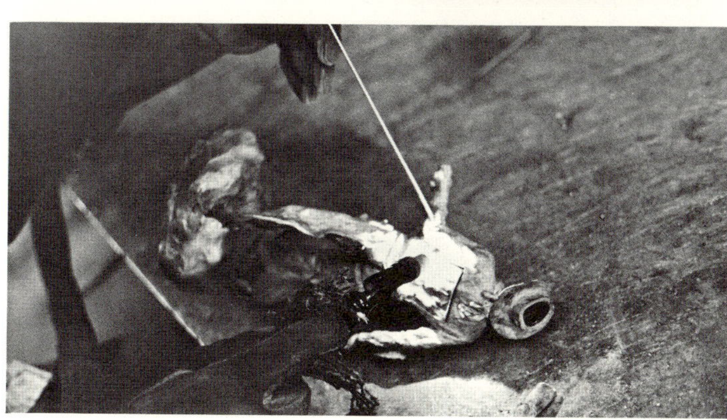

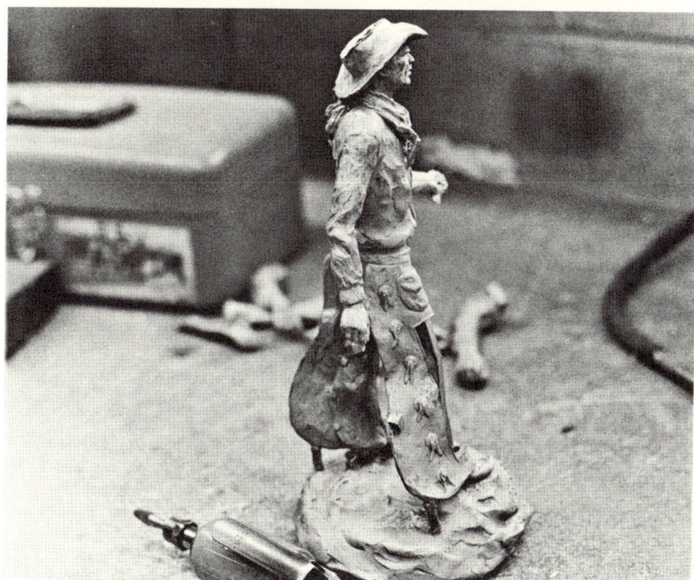

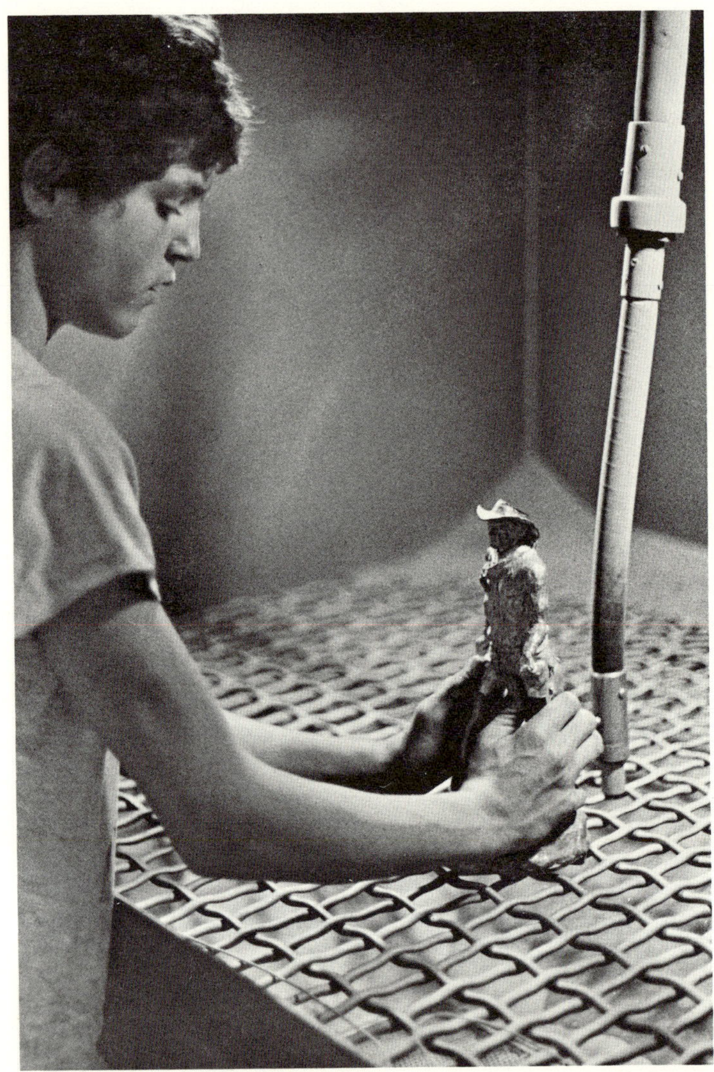

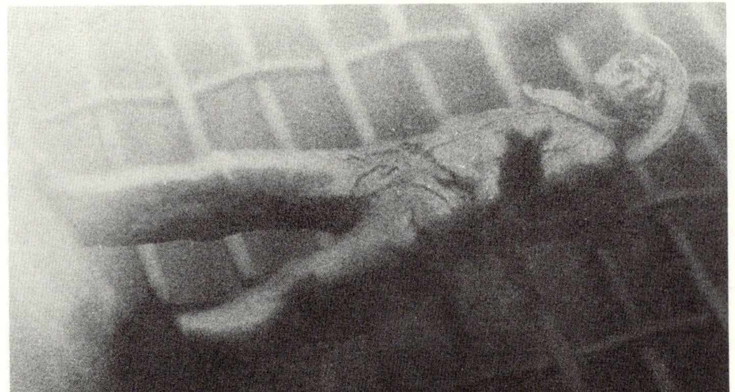

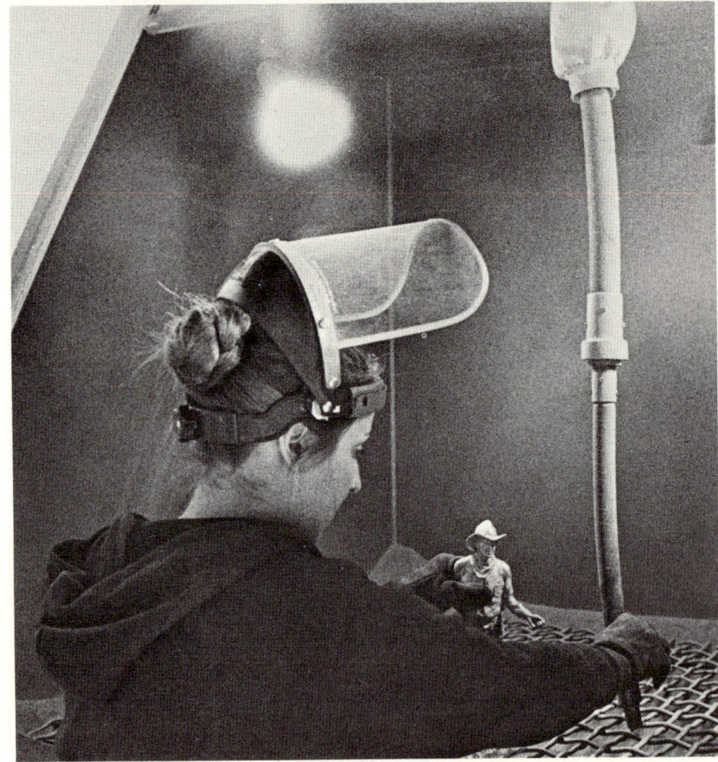

After the metal chasing is completed, the bronze is returned to the sand or glass bead blaster to remove all foreign material and discoloration from the surface of the bronze.

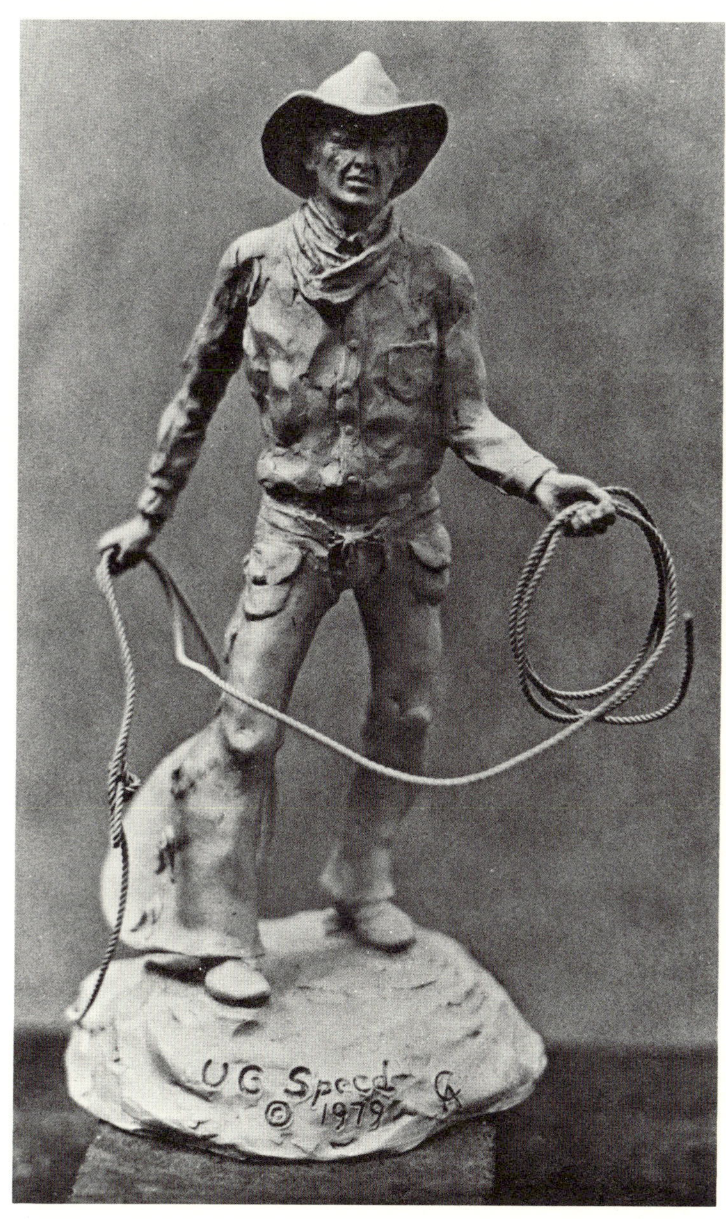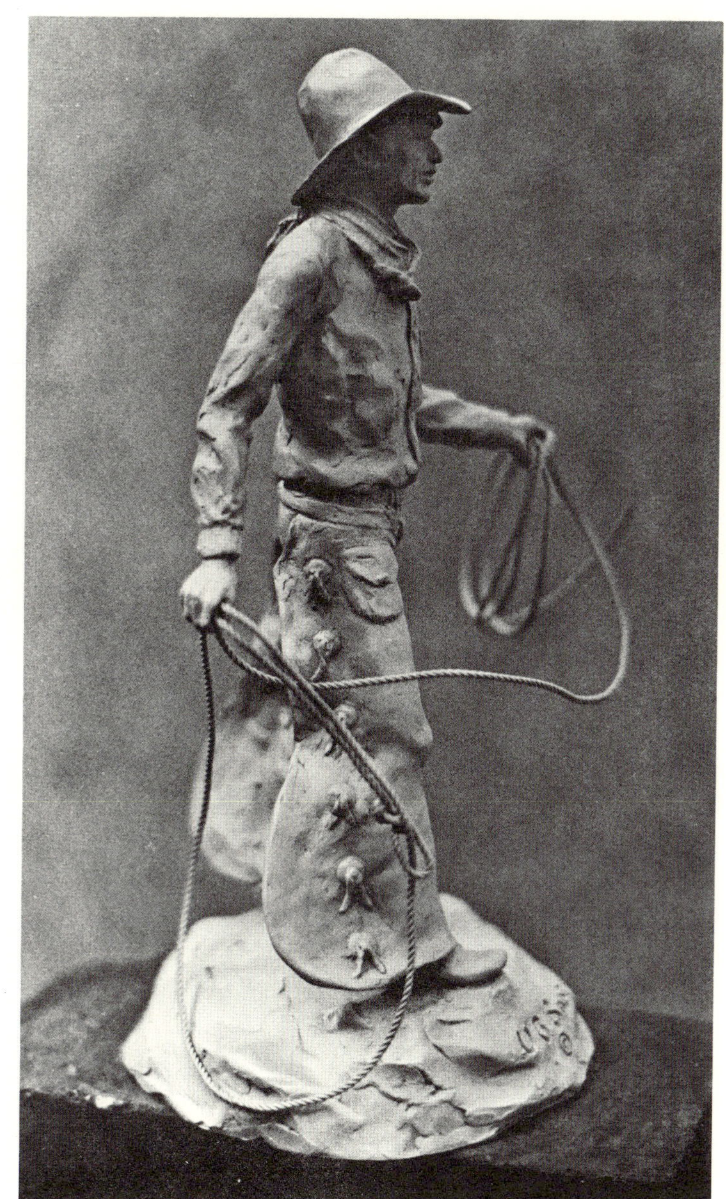

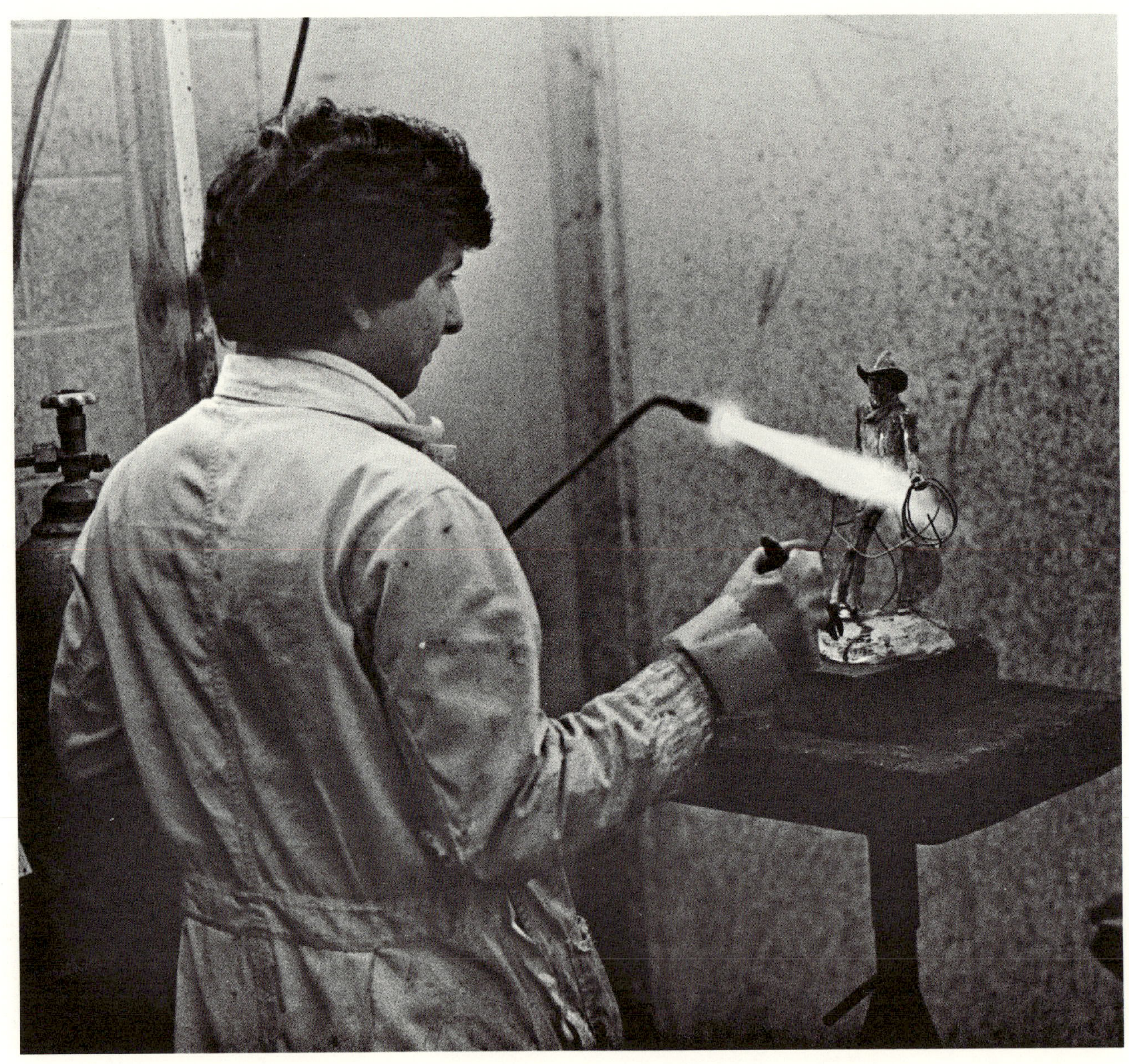

The patina or color is achieved through a controlled chemical application.

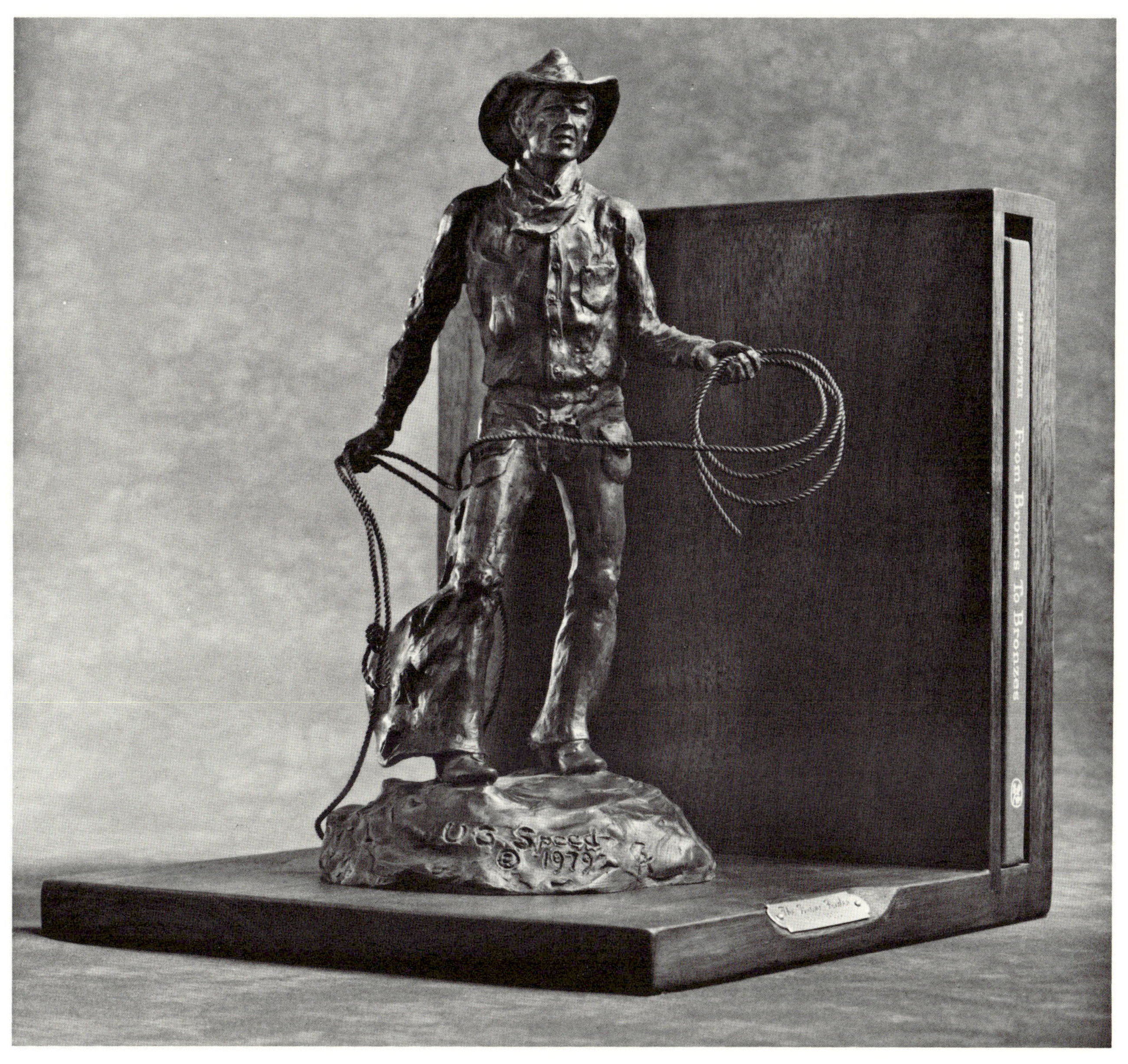

Here is the finished piece, *The Bronc Rider,* which was conceived
and executed in an edition of one hundred to accompany the limited
edition of this book.

CHAPTER FIVE

The Portfolio

Grant Speed is a sculptor, a fine artist, whose work deals with western subject matter. He is something more than what is generally implied by the term "western artist." That term puts the emphasis on subject matter rather than the principles of fine art. Somehow "western artist" is too limiting when one considers Grant's artistic accomplishments. His work is artistically mature and distinguished beyond the considerations of subject matter.

Grant's style ranges from the straightforward honesty of realism to a more recent, refreshing trend toward impressionism. The merit of his work is greater than can be accounted for by historical fidelity. Aside from being executed with the level of technical accomplishment called for in fine art, most of Grant's bronzes also evoke in the viewer impressions and emotions that go beyond an understanding of literal subject matter. The flavor and originality of Grant's work enhances the appeal of each piece individually and becomes, as in all fine art, as important as the idea that he is seeking to communicate.

Sculpture like this has the artistic substance that will appeal to knowledgeable critics without any need for interpretations of western history. Anyone who appreciates and understands the principles of fine representational art can be comfortable with work such as this.

Nevertheless, it is a fact that a large measure of Grant's appeal has been to those who are drawn to his artistic storytelling. This is a more traditional role for western art — representing a visual insight into the West.

From this perspective, Grant's bronzes present a broad and dramatic collection of western themes, both historical and contemporary. The era of the mountain man, episodes and characters in the history of the North American Indian, the golden age of the range cattle industry and the old time cowboy, the contemporary figure of the cowboy, and modern ranch life are all a part of the art of Grant Speed. All of his bronzes involve a temperate blend of Grant's own personal impressions of subjects and a skillful handling of the elements of sculpture.

Biography almost always intrudes into critical considerations of contemporary western art. If one reads a sampling of exhibit catalogs, magazine articles, and books dealing with this subject, it appears that the background of the artist is of more importance than is the art work itself. But biography is only one aspect of art appreciation.

The fact that Grant was raised as a west Texas ranch country kid and became a working cowhand and a good bronc rider offers little that is meaningful to enhance our appreciation of such outstanding artistic achievements as his bronze *The Half-Breed*. This piece, as an example, is independent of the artist's own life. It, like others, was created whole; it does not need the sculptor's own life story to support its artistic value or to compensate for the lack of it. It is not necessary that we know about and approve of the artist's life in order to evaluate the artistic substance of his work.

The only biographical considerations genuinely worth noting in regard to a particular artist's work are those that may predispose him to a particular subject matter. Grant Speed, as a westerner, was drawn to western subject matter in his sculpture. And, as a sensitive westerner, he had sympathy and feeling for the heritage of his own land.

Grant became a real force in western art at the 1970 Cowboy Artists of America show when he exhibited *Ridin' Point*. This was the first in what would eventually be a series of six busts. It is a widely-held opinion that these six pieces are a singular and distinguished contribution to the entire realm of western art. They are evidence enough to support the often-repeated claim of contemporary collectors that Grant Speed is one of a very, very small handful of contemporary sculptors who have lent artistic depth and substance to contemporary western art.

Four of the six pieces, *Ridin' Point, The Free Spirit, One Who Lived to Tell It,* and *Almost Home from the War,* incorporate a unique feature. To the strength of these traditional busts, Grant has added a sculptured vignette in reduced scale that gives new and exciting dimensions to the monotony of traditional forms of western sculpture.

This original concept represented the freshest, most creative innovation in the present generation of western art. But because it was different, it involved an initial risk for the artist. It represented a marked departure from not only what Grant had been doing, but what collectors had come to expect in western sculpture. It is a matter of no small significance that Grant was willing to accept the risk of doing something new.

Ridin' Point was displayed along with his more traditional pieces at the 1970 Cowboy Artists show. The entire edition sold out immediately. This was a new experience for a contemporary sculptor, and it was abundantly clear that the collectors were ready to accept something new. Since that time, the other three "bust-vignette" bronzes, as well as *The Half-Breed,* have received instant acclaim to the extent that the total editions of each have been sold out simultaneously with their premier showing.

This is something of a marketing phenomenon in contemporary western sculpture. It is just a fact that bronzes do not sell as well, or as quickly, as do paintings at western shows.

These six bronzes established the fact that Grant was a genuinely creative and talented artist. The accomplishment represented by this series can be considered from both the technical and the aesthetic perspective.

Technically, they are evidence of the degree of Grant's mastery of the physical skills involved in sculpture. The execution of each of these pieces shows that Grant understands and is able to bring to his work all of the necessary technical elements of the medium. Additionally, he has met the difficult challenge of dealing with two scales of size within the same sculpture and the associated problems of composition and design.

There are several aspects that figure in to the aesthetic success of the series. First, they represent a new, fresh concept, which is rare in contemporary western art. Contemporary western artists have, for the most part, been content to endlessly rework the ideas of Russell, Remington, and other earlier western artists. Grant's series of the six busts are uniquely his own, in concept and in execution.

There is also a universality to the individual bronzes that is characteristic of all truly fine art, western or otherwise. One does not have to understand the culture or the history of the old West to appreciate the beauty of such bronzes as these. There are no subtle meanings that only an in-depth knowledge of the West can unlock. This is not always the case with western art, however, where the artist is frequently more concerned with history than with art.

The universality of the bronzes says something about Grant's special capacity for hitting on sensitive ideas that evoke thoughtful consideration of his work by those who see it. The subjects of the six busts are something more than particular individuals. They are representations of frontier types and of the spirit and character of whole segments of life on the American frontier. On the four bronzes that include the sculpted vignette, the communication of the artist's concept is further enhanced.

There is a common denominator evident when the entire body of Grant's work is considered. In the series of busts, as well as in all of his other bronzes, there is a clean and basic honesty of concept and execution. This is a characteristic that Grant continually strives for with conscious effort. It is the artistic ingredient that made Russell's bronzes so vital in their appeal to Grant. He does not try for complexity in the design of his sculpture but is content to concentrate on simplicity.

The idea for a bronze is of major importance to Grant. Once he has conceived of a worthwhile idea, he executes it in the most straightforward manner he can. This results in a subtlety in most of his bronzes that allows viewers to bring their own feelings into play.

Bronzes such as *End of the Open Range* represent much more than a literal scene of the West. They constitute symbols and attitudes. Grant gives those who see his work the freedom to interpret the art in light of their own feelings and experiences. He does not particularize his pieces into narrow, restrictive representations. Instead, he offers us a chance to "read between the lines" whatever we choose.

We can use the bronze *End of the Open Range* to illustrate this feature of Grant's method. This bronze is a straightforward representation of a cowboy on horseback leading a pack horse. The cowboy has stopped and is looking at some rolls of barbed wire. On one level, it is merely a visual image of an old-time cowboy and his horses. The cowboy's clothes, the saddle, and the other details are historically accurate. On another level, the barbed wire can become a significant element in the piece. On this level of interpretation, the cowboy could be thinking of the work of building fence which the wire implies. But at the deepest, most profound level, Grant has given us an emotional statement about the time in range history when the coming of barbed wire sounded the death knell for the open range and the cattle trail. Barbed wire changed the cowboy from a free-roaming spirit who rode as he chose, from Texas to Montana, to a hired man restricted to the well-defined boundaries of barbed wire fences. *End of the Open Range* makes a simple yet eloquent statement, the kind of statement that makes great art.

And *End of the Open Range* is but a single example of the eloquence of Grant's bronzes. There are many more such statements made in pieces like *During the Chilly Hours of Dawn, Bought 'Em for Two and Sold 'Em for One, On to a Better Range, Openin' Up New Country, In Between Jobs, In the Wake of the Mountain Men,* and many others.

Grant's bronzes have something more for us than just a visual experience. They also communicate an idea, an impression, or an attitude, and they invite us to become involved within our own thoughts. Grant's work appeals to the eye as well as to the mind. This is something rare in contemporary western art. As Grant has matured in his art, he has developed his sensitivity for new and meaningful ideas for subject matter. Long-time observers of the western art scene put Grant at the top of the list among contemporary sculptors. Collectors eagerly anticipate each new bronze. There can be little doubt that he will create even more significant work in the years to come.

One indicator of the confidence in Grant's work is that it has been displayed and even included in the permanent collections of such major western museums as the Whitney Gallery of Western Art. This is an achievement that few contemporary artists can claim. Such an accomplishment strengthens Grant's professional credentials and enhances the feelings of those who believe that Grant's work has attained a distinguished and lasting place in the context of western art.

A large measure of Grant's success is accounted for by his command of the physical elements involved in sculpture. He has a comprehensive knowledge of the entire process, from the modeling right on through the casting processes. But there are plenty of "good" sculptors who are as well prepared in this area. What makes Grant's work something more than just "good" goes beyond the physical aspects of sculpture. Through his work Grant not only shares his talent with us, but more importantly, he shares intimate, personal feelings about the culture, the heritage, and the life of which he is a product — that of the West.

There will always be an obvious measure of sincerity and of passion in Grant's work because he is a legitimate heir to western heritage. This gives his art a dimension that will continue to elude those artists who portray the West from the perspective of an observer rather than that of a participant.

A natural talent that has been refined through study and discipline, and a genuine empathy for the subject matter, come together in Grant's work and strike just the proper artistic balance. It can be said with confidence that he has made lasting contributions to the present generation of western art. His bronzes will be recognized and respected to an increasing degree as we grow in our awareness of western art as fine art and not just historical illustration.

The Portfolio

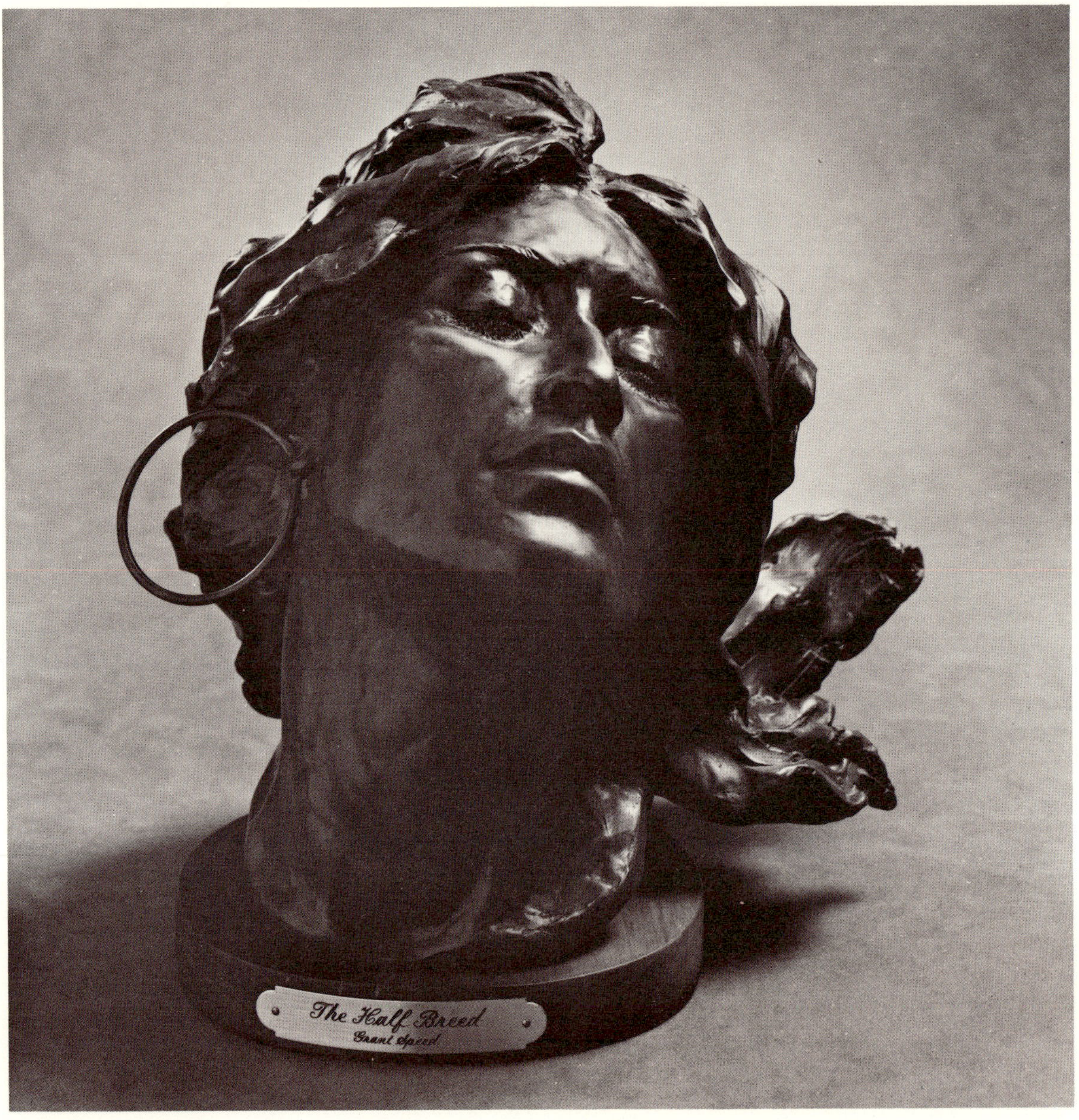

THE HALF-BREED

This is generally acknowledged to be the most artistically significant bronze in the series of six western busts created by Grant. It is also considered to be one of the two or three finest examples of contemporary western sculpture ever produced.

At the 1976 exhibition of the Cowboy Artists of America it was awarded the coveted Gold Medal for sculpture. The entire edition of thirty was sold out during the first night of the show.

The delicately sculpted face and the sensitive posturing of the head give *The Half-Breed* an aura of classic art.

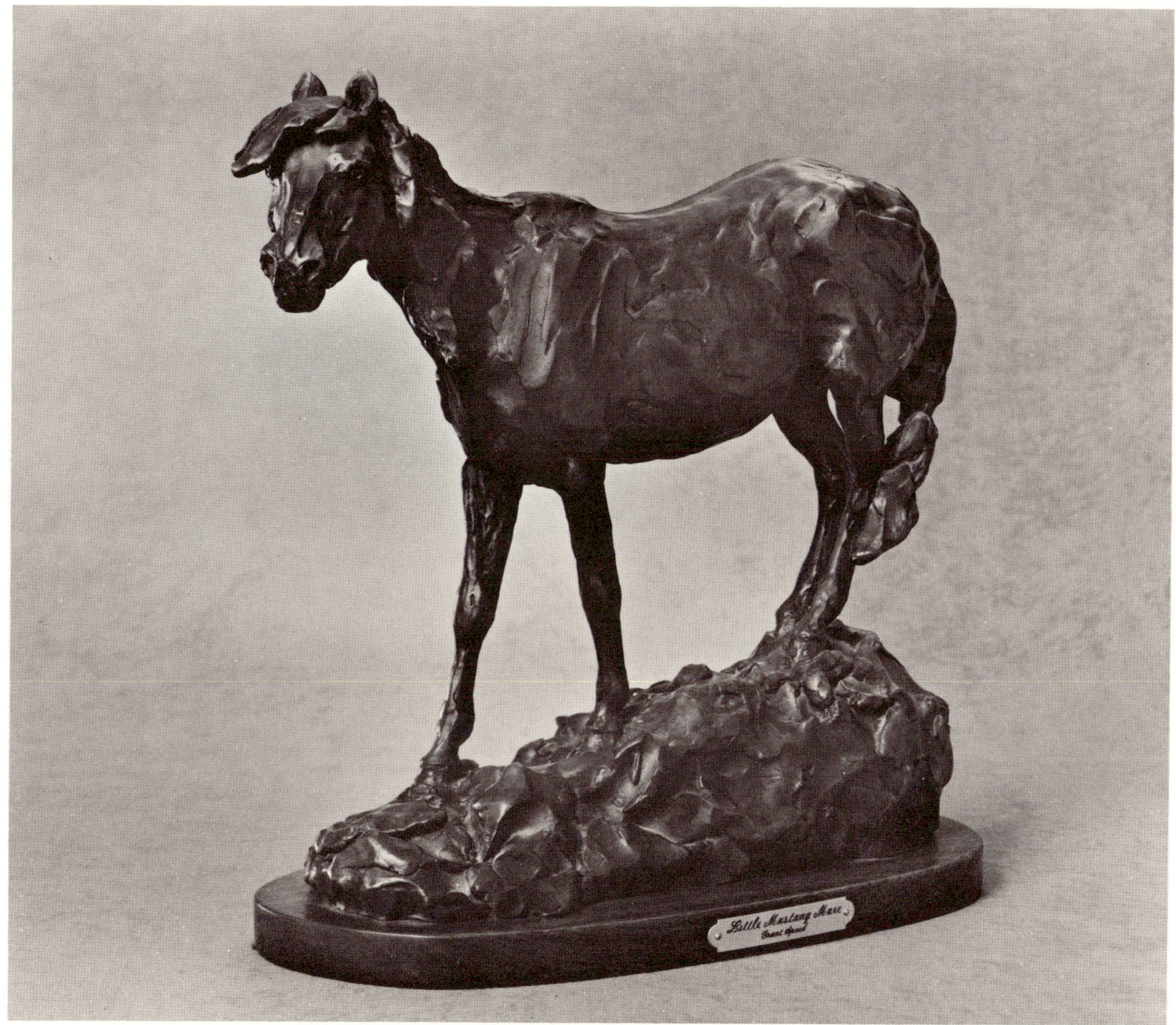

LITTLE MUSTANG MARE

Grant's work first began to take on a loose, impressionistic touch with this piece, which was in the 1974 Cowboy Artists exhibition. The concentration on artistic form rather than historical storytelling in bronzes such as this indicates Grant's maturity as a fine artist.

There is something meaningful, too, in the subject of the bronze.

The mustang is perhaps the finest symbol of the original nature of the West. It was a wild and free country, and so were the mustangs. They, like the buffalo and the longhorn, symbolize an earlier time when men had not yet gained the upper hand on the West.

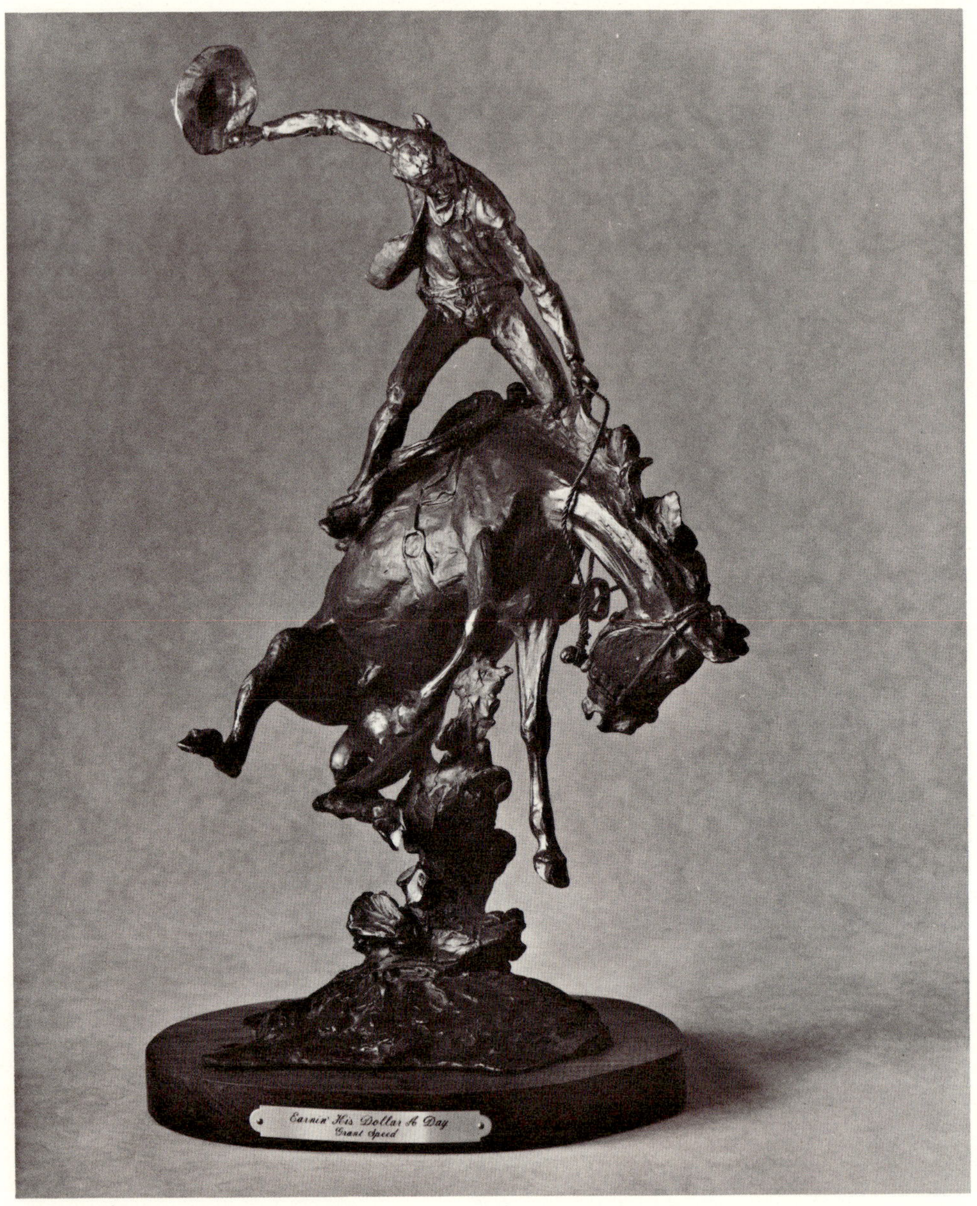

EARNIN' HIS DOLLAR A DAY

This is Grant's best bucking horse bronze to date. It combines all of the power and strength inherent in such man-against-horse confrontations. The bronze was designed in such a way as to create a sense of thrusting motion.

The title of the piece says something about Grant's knowledge of the reality of cowboy life. Rather than the implication that this is an extraordinary event, it is presented as just another cowboy doing a routine part of his job. The high degree of drama was commonplace as the cowboy went about his daily work.

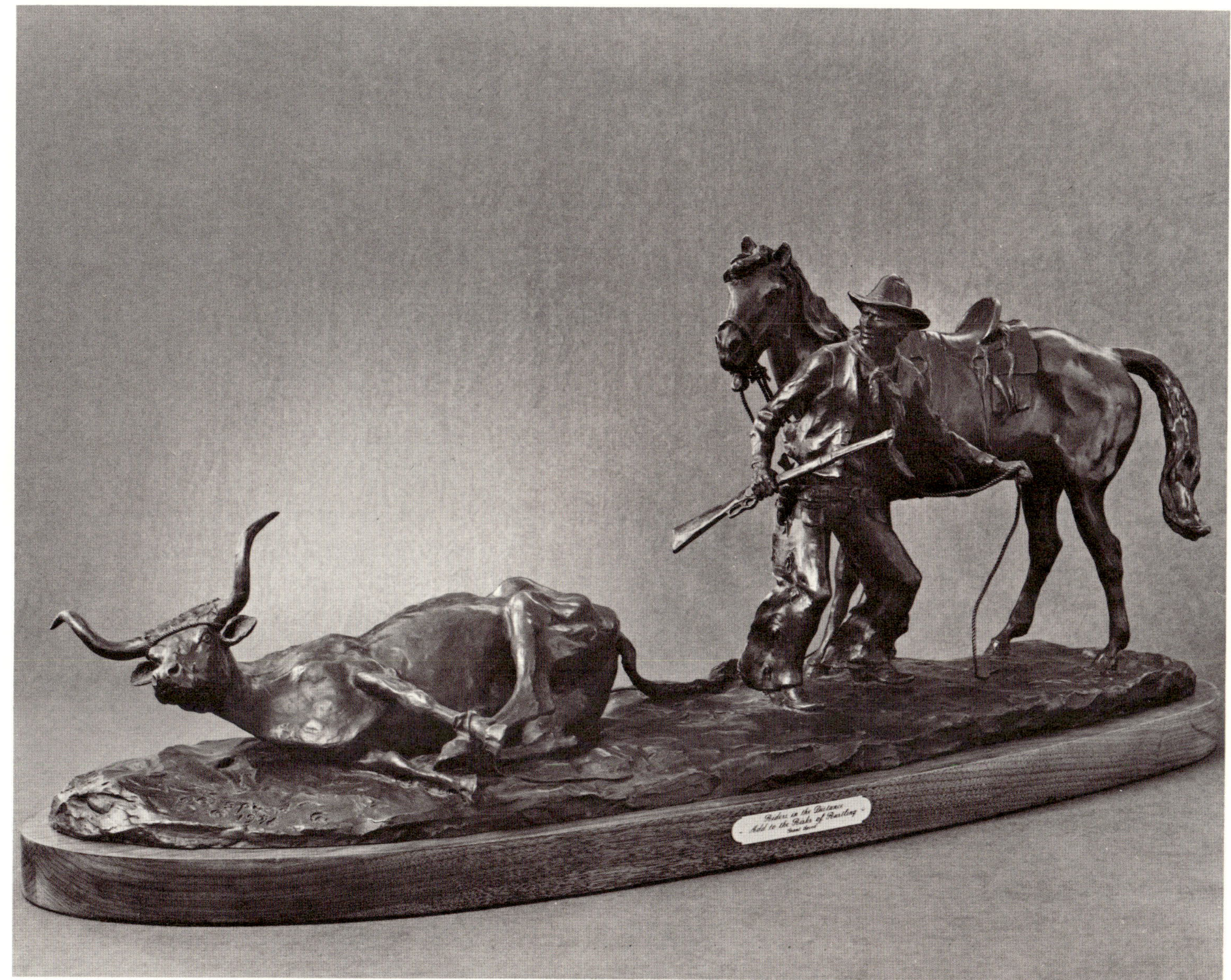

RIDERS IN THE DISTANCE ADD TO THE RISK OF RUSTLING

Here, as with *Quick Tied by the Texas Ranger,* Grant has made a piece in which unseen elements are a significant part of the sculpture.

Something has clearly disturbed the cattle thief in his work. He has gotten his Winchester from the saddle boot and is preparing for trouble, but he is not trying to get away.

Grant leaves it to us to finish the story however we choose — a delightful experience beyond our appreciation for the physical aspects of the sculpture.

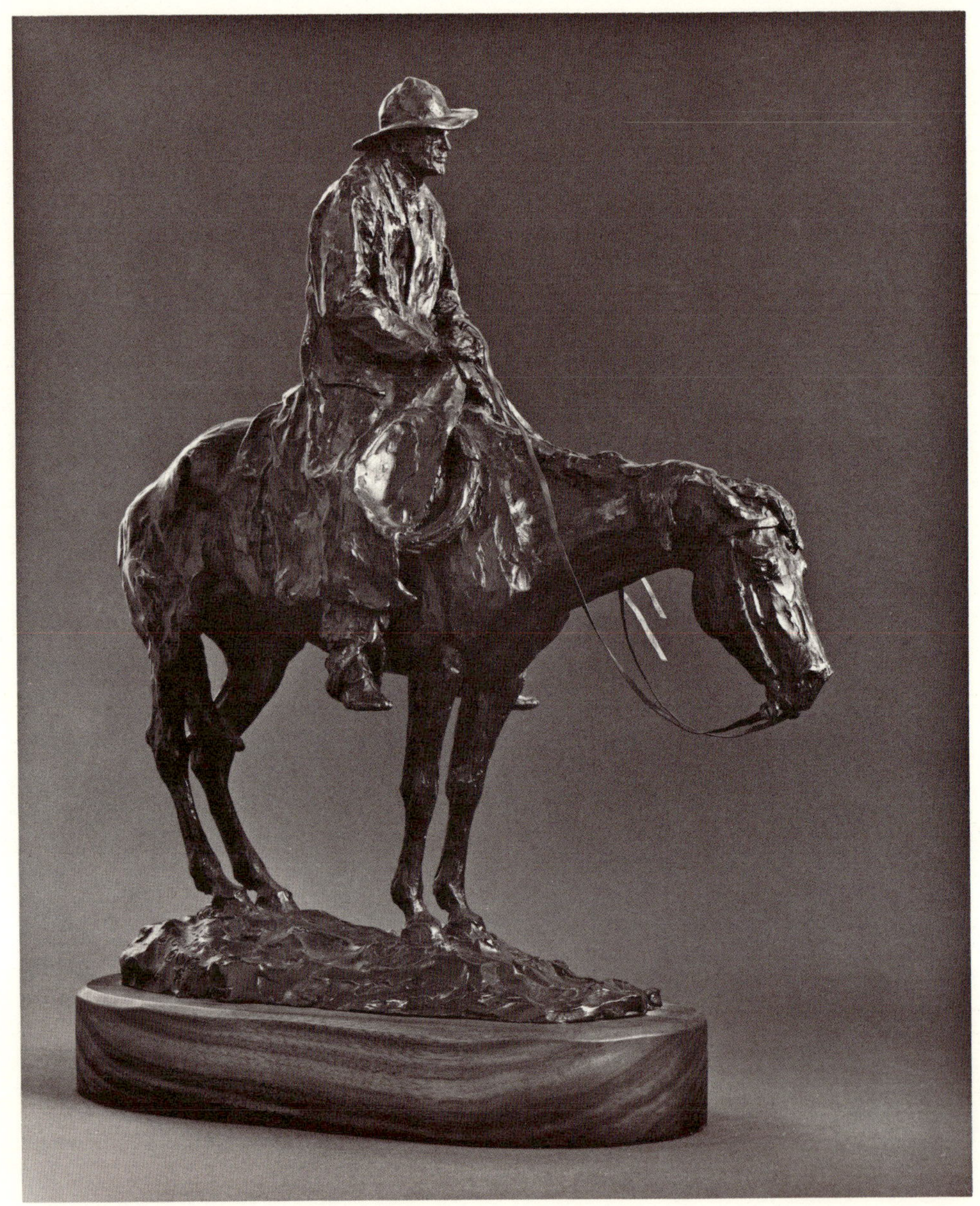

NIGHTHERDIN' IN A RAINSTORM

The movies would have us believe that cowboying was a colorful, heroic, and glamorous endeavor. But they rarely show the other side — the reality of life in the saddle.

This bronze presents one of the most dismal situations in an old-time cowboy's life. "Pitch Dark and Soakin' Wet" would be another appropriate title for the piece. It was times like this, when the cowboy was wet, cold, tired, hungry, and just generally miserable, that made him seriously reconsider his calling in life.

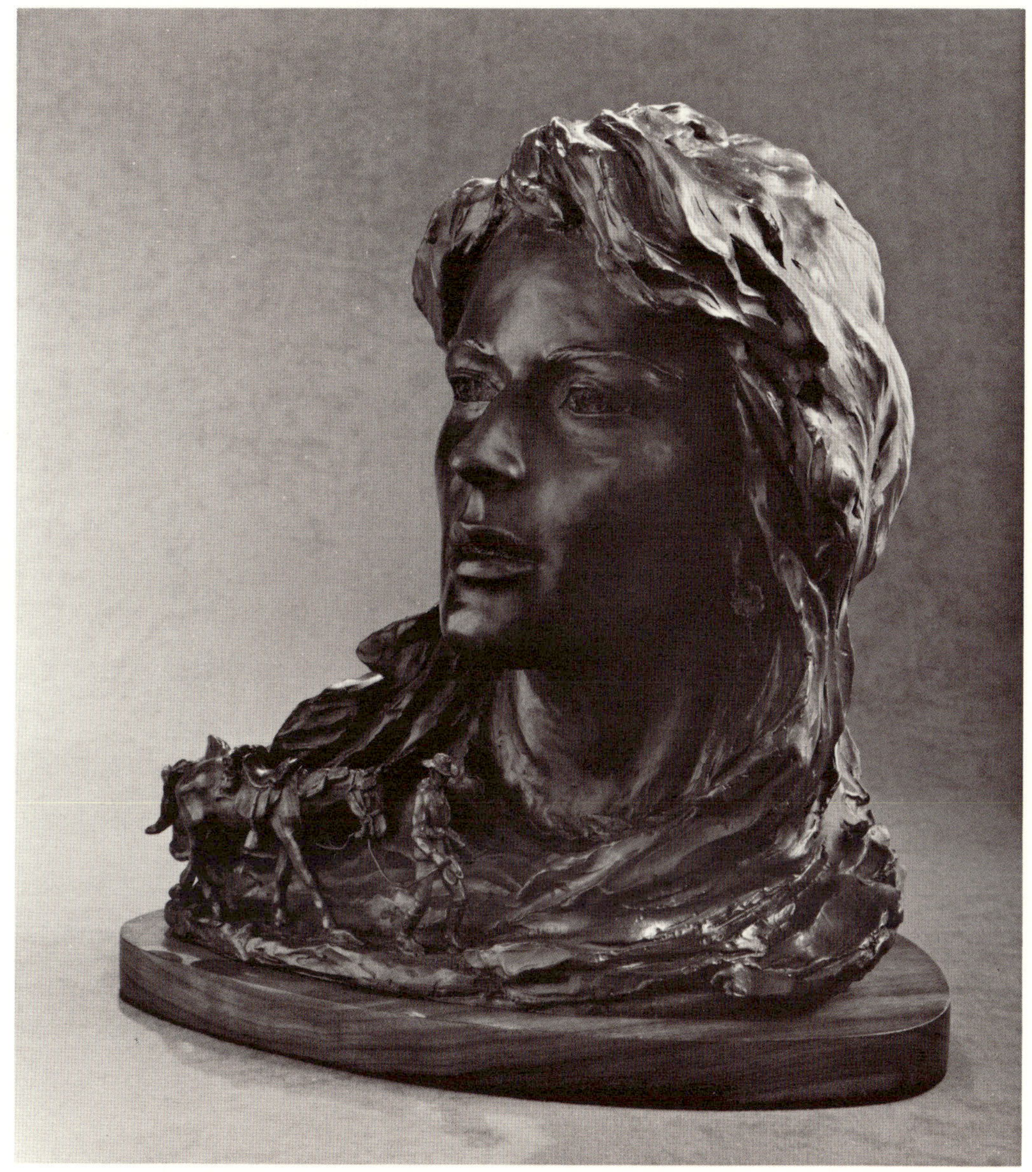

ALMOST HOME FROM THE WAR

This is the final important piece in the western busts series. It incorporates the popular miniature vignette feature, as well as the subject of a woman, which was so well received in *The Half-Breed*.

Collectors and dealers encouraged Grant to continue the series after this bronze was cast and sold out. He did do a few less-signifi-cant variations but decided he had achieved his purpose and went on to develop other original concepts.

The idea of this bronze captures a mood that is rarely seen in contemporary western art. The returning Civil War veteran and his loved one are presented in a unique and touching composition.

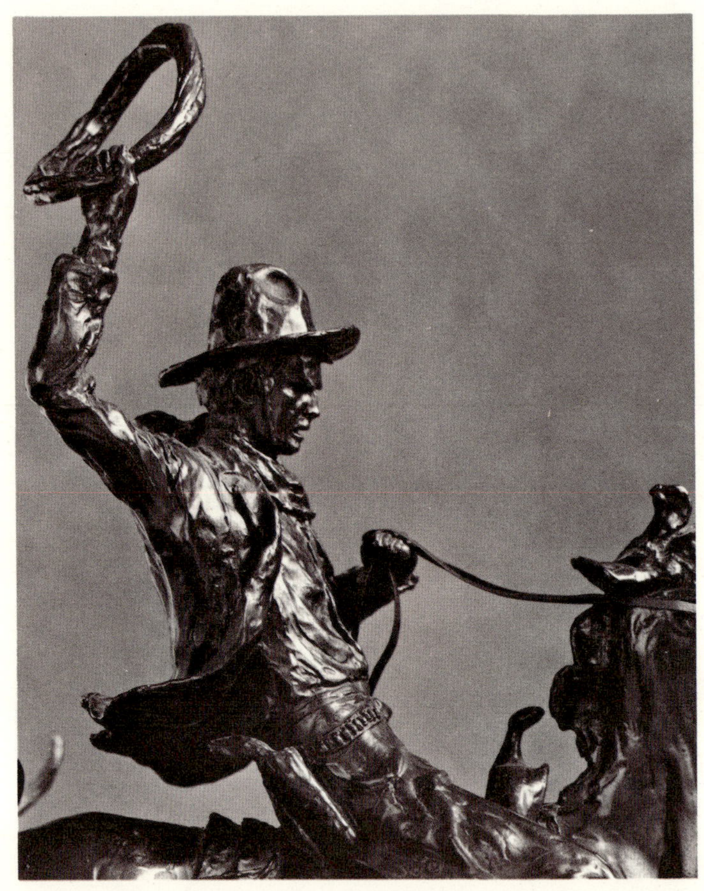

Detail of "Stampeding Over A Cutbank"

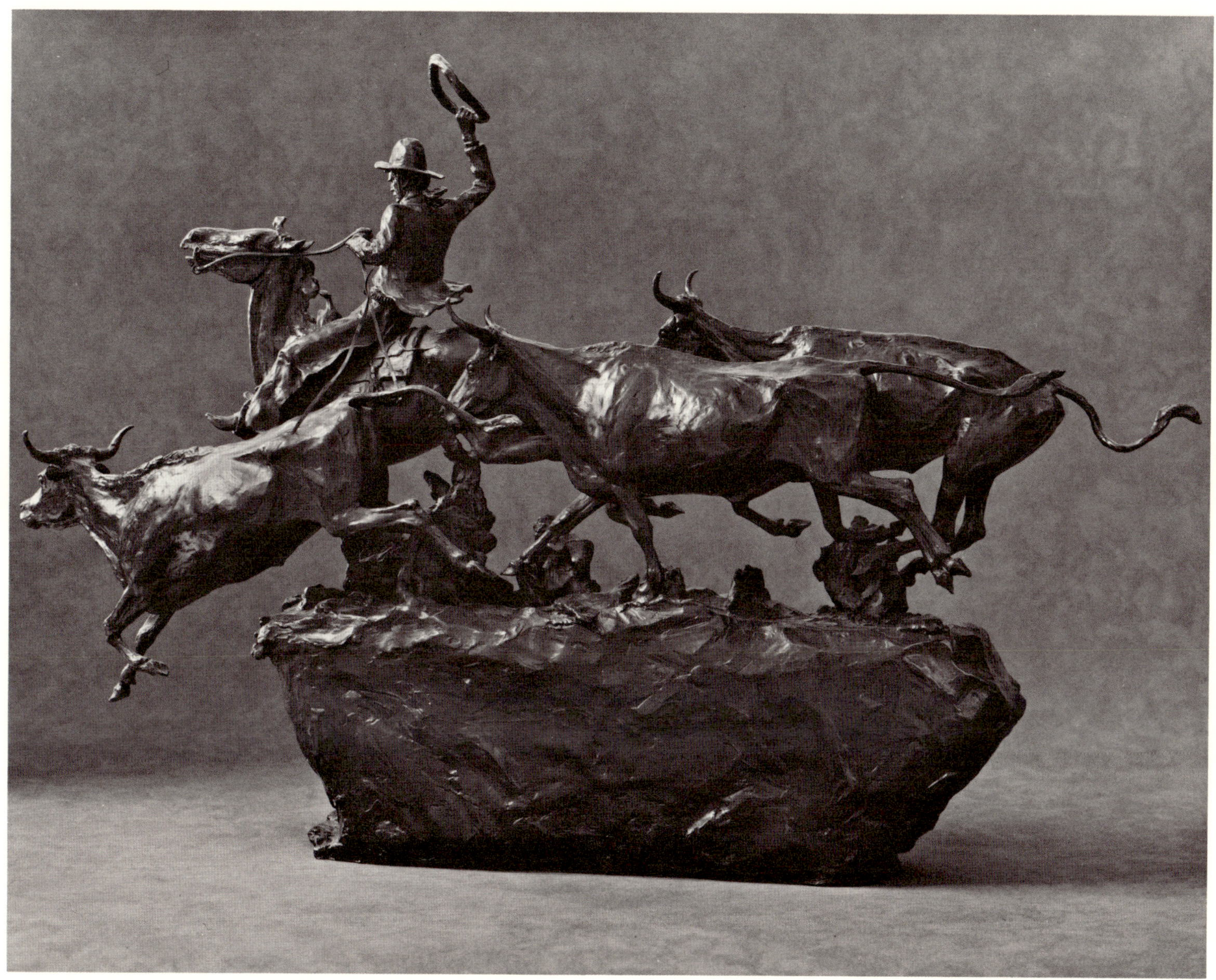

STAMPEDING OVER A CUTBANK

Unlike what the movies would have us believe, cowboys were seldom killed in Indian raids or in gunfights on the dusty streets of cow-towns. The most constant danger during the trail driving period was the threat of a stampede. The cattle were more than half wild, and it took very little to "spook" them. Once a stampede got started, every cowboy was in the middle of things, trying to stop the herd. The potential for fatal situations was clearly present. In this bronze the danger is magnified as the cattle run off the cutbank.

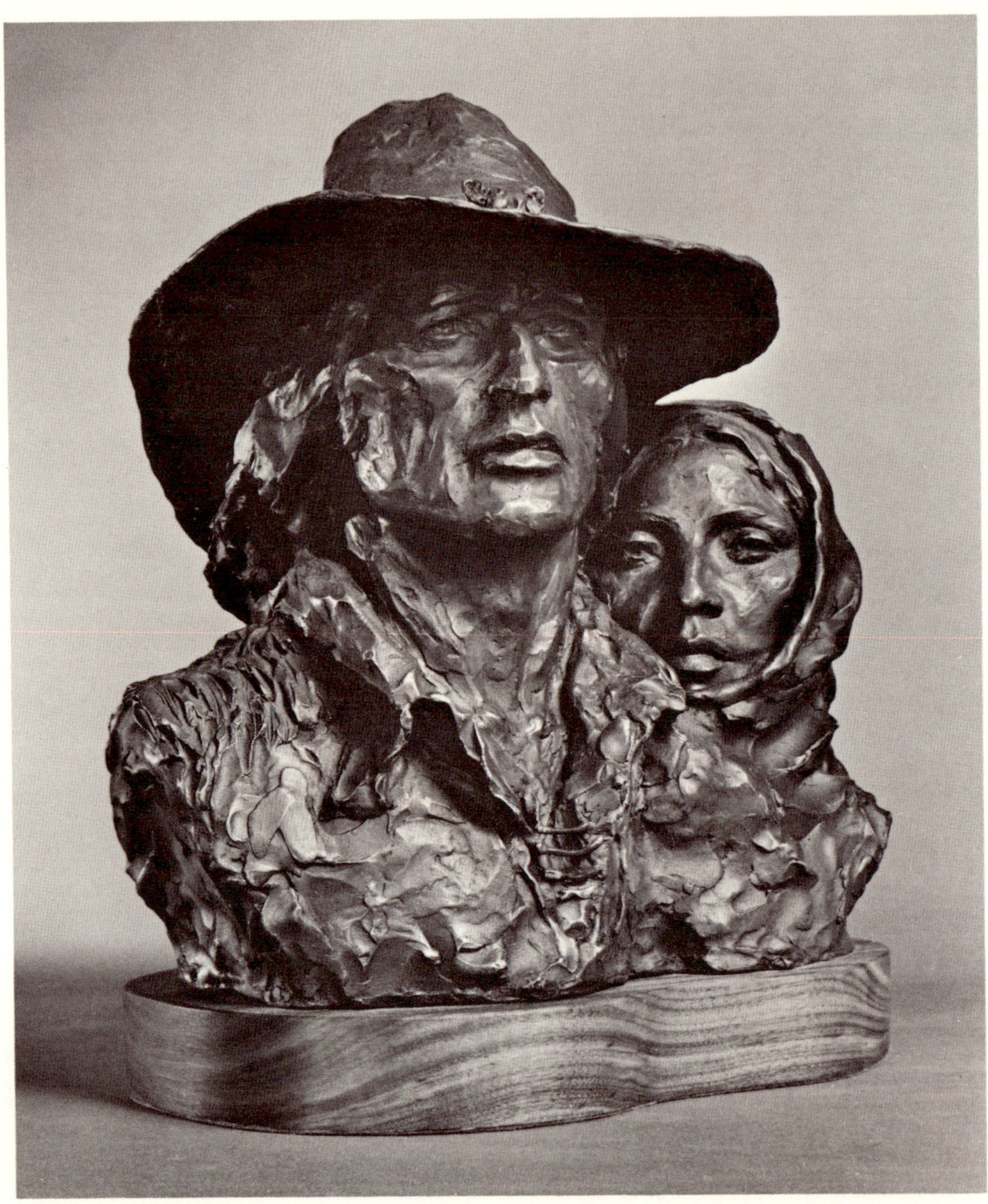

THE SQUAW MAN

In this bronze, the sculptor developed and expanded upon his concept for the western busts series. This was the third in the series. Here, Grant omitted the miniature figures at the base and added an additional bust at full scale.

This innovation enhances the overall artistic accomplishment when considered together with the two previous busts, *Ridin' Point* and *Free Spirit*. The composition of the two heads, the frontiersman and his Indian bride, is an appealing idea, and the manner in which it was executed is excellent.

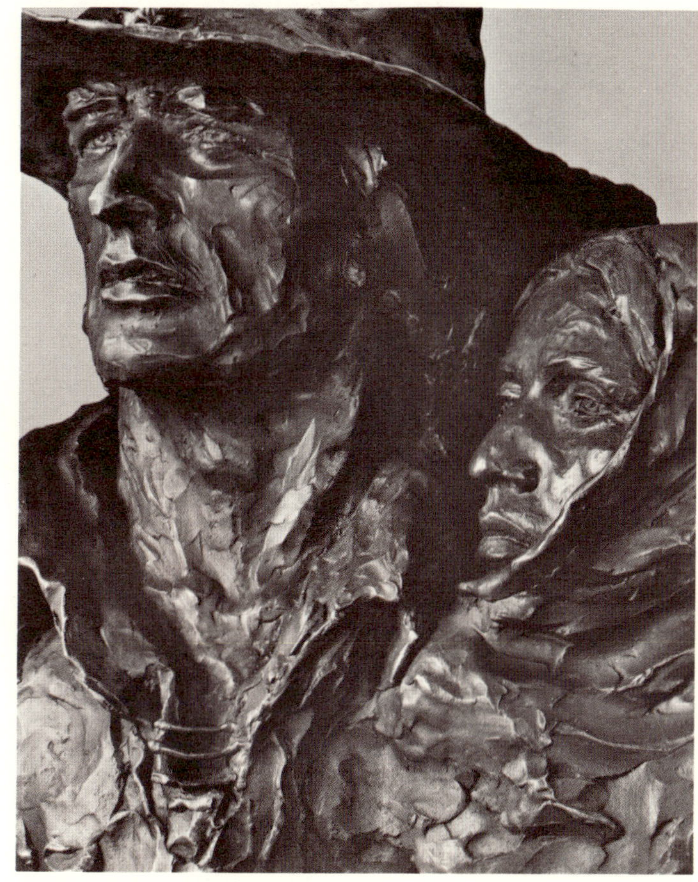
Detail of "The Squaw Man"

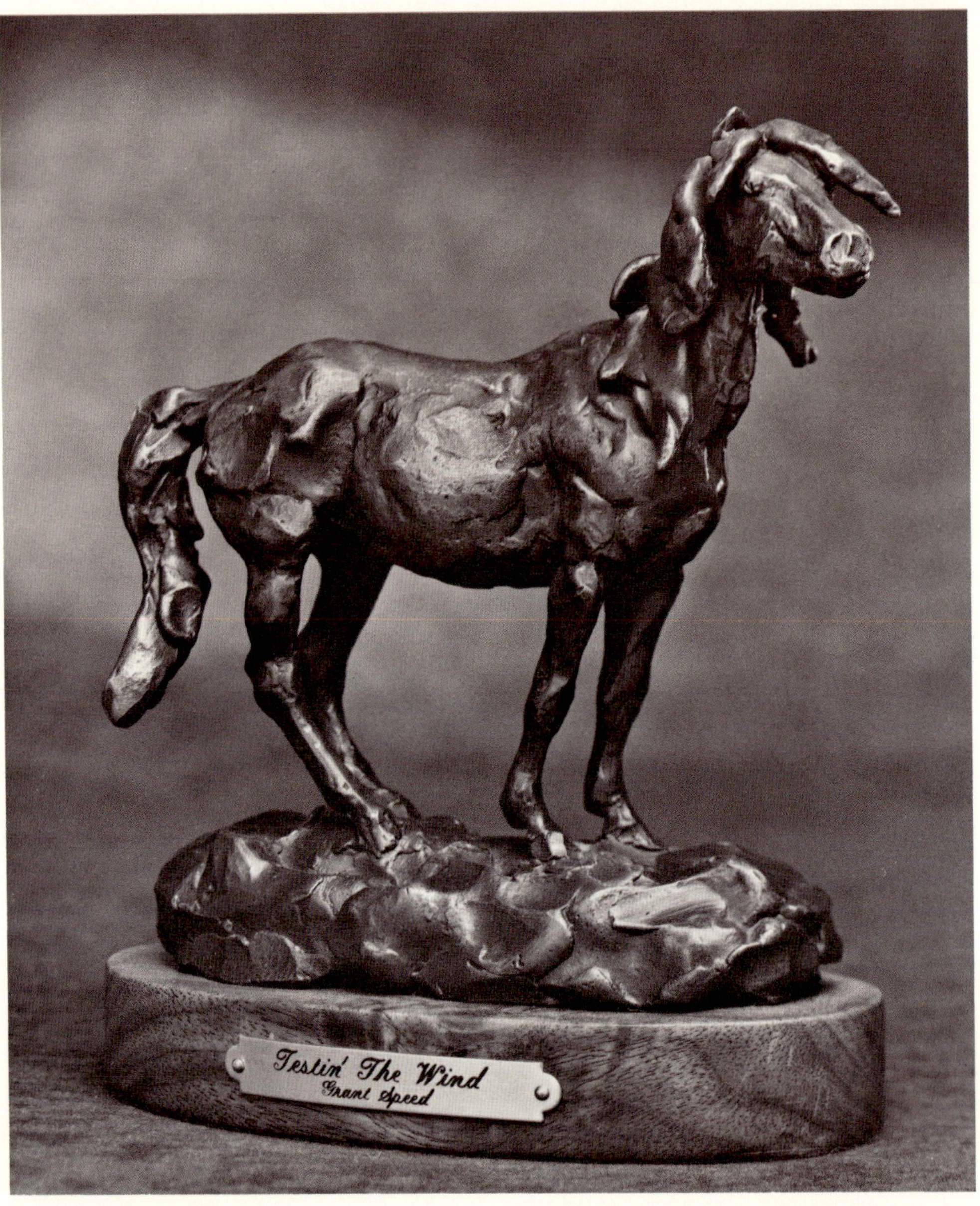

TESTIN' THE WIND

This bronze is similar to Grant's *Little Mustang Mare*. It, too, is executed in an impressionistic manner that enhances the subject's attitude of high-spirited freedom.

The posture of the head and neck communicates both power and tension as the horse searches for scents that might mean danger.

Grant's own ranch background provided him with a knowledge of range horses beyond just anatomical considerations. By being around all kinds of horses in a variety of situations, Grant gained an insight into horse nature that could never come from casual observation.

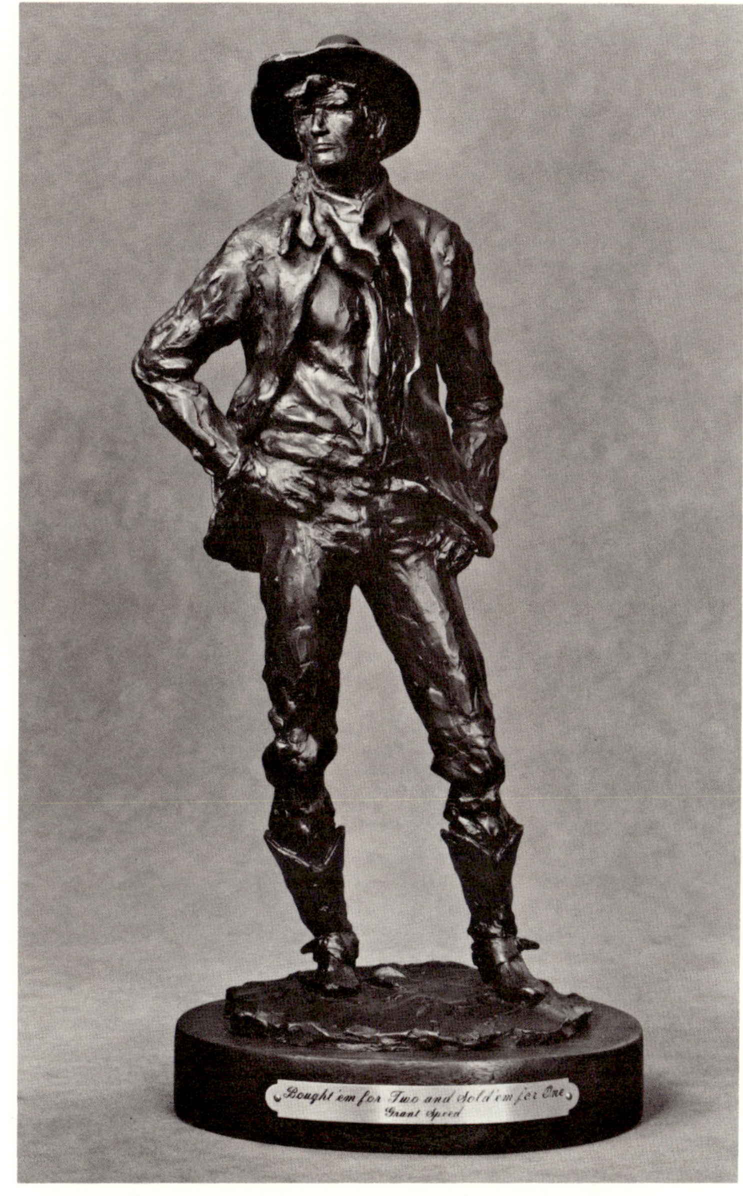

BOUGHT 'EM FOR TWO AND SOLD 'EM FOR ONE

There is nothing heroic or noble about the subject of this fine bronze. The cowman gives a revealing impression of the emotion frequently experienced by the rancher who has bought cattle when the market was high and sold when it was low — helpless resignation.

There is a subtlety in this bronze that comes closer to capturing the real essence of the cowboy personality than any of the bucking horse pieces. The bronze is quiet and reflective; it evokes our personal response in a manner that wild action subjects cannot. It is an honest and accurate representation of the genuine cowman.

77

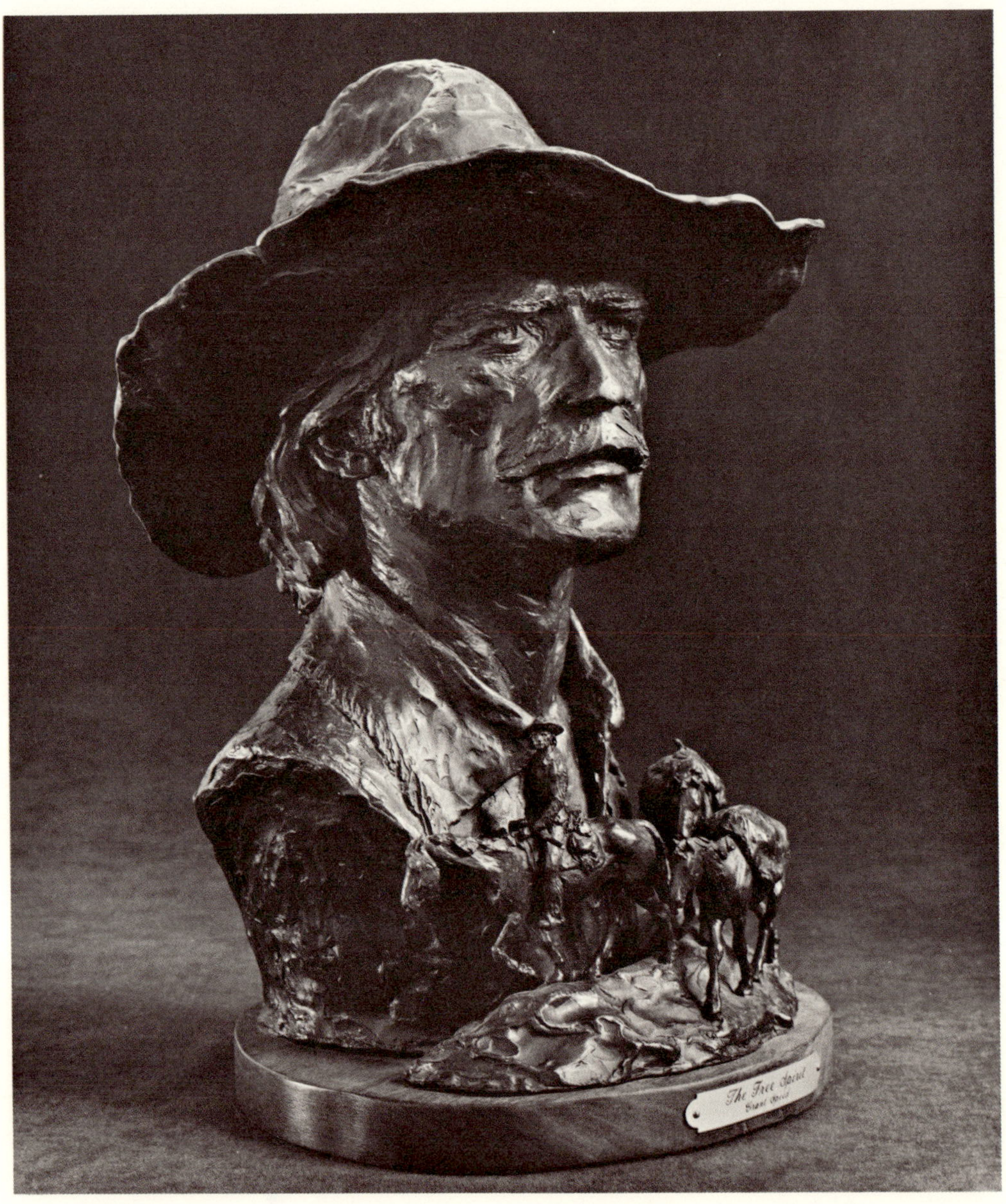

THE FREE SPIRIT

This was the second in the series of western busts created by Grant. Like the earlier *Ridin' Point*, it sold out immediately at the Cowboy Artists of America exhibition in Oklahoma City.

The small vignette at the base was a totally unique concept in western art. This originality is one of the features that accounts for the tremendous response to the piece from long-time collectors.

The subject is a mountain man from the era before any significant number of white men had begun to penetrate the western mountain wilderness.

78

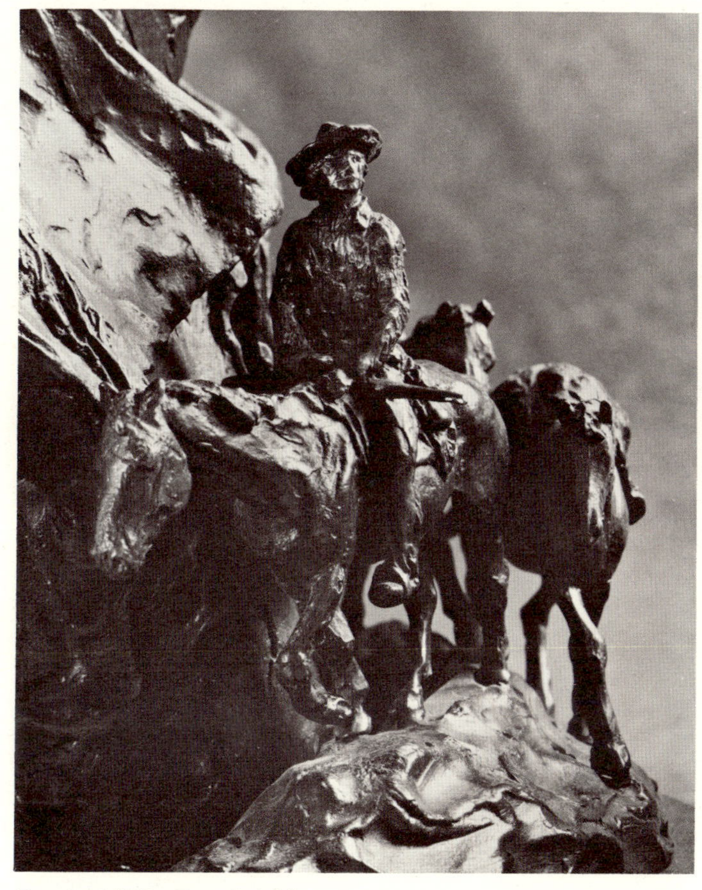

Detail of "The Free Spirit"

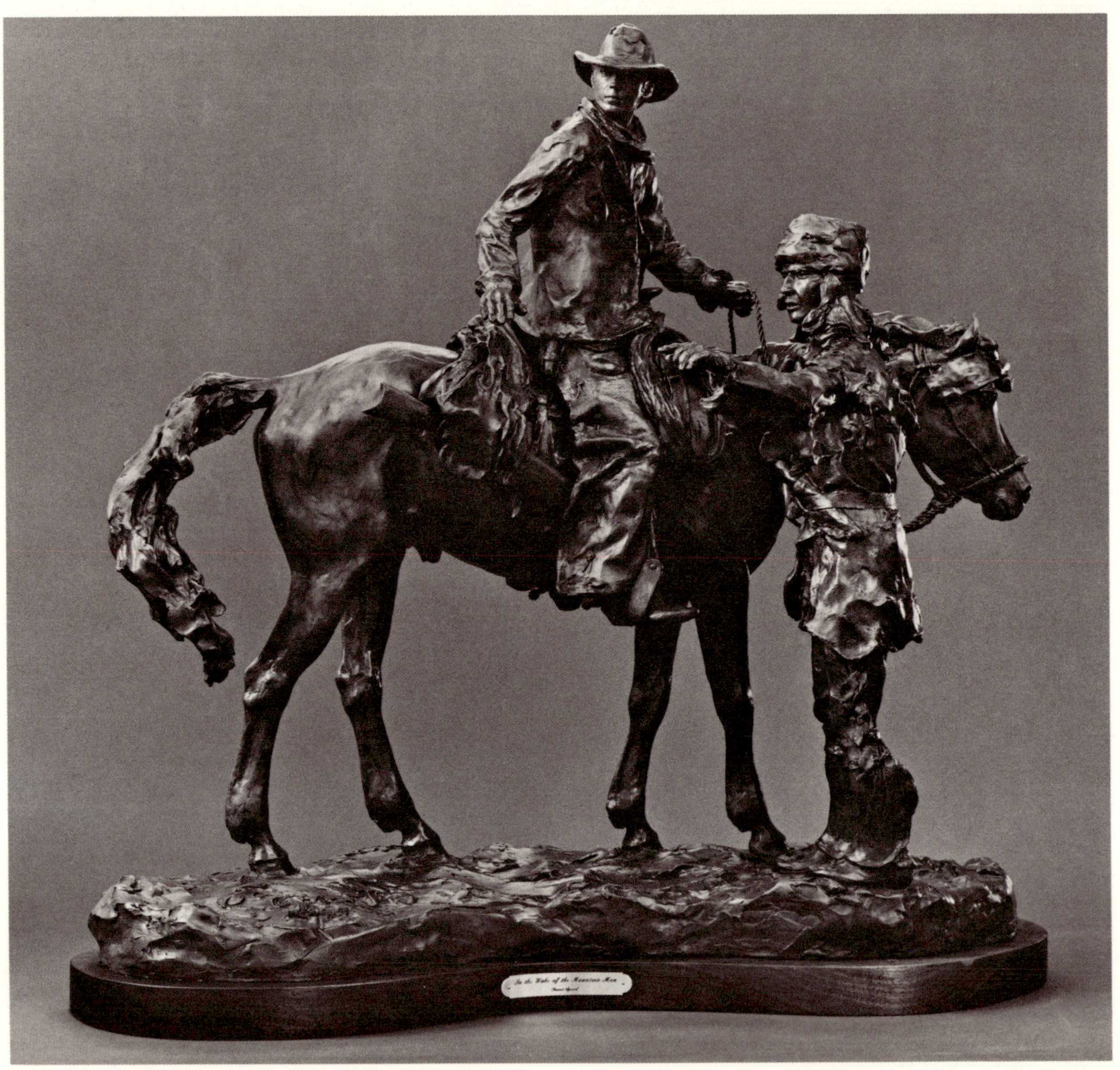

IN THE WAKE OF THE MOUNTAIN MEN

This sculpture from the 1977 Cowboy Artists exhibition is the largest and most ambitious bronze Grant has produced. It indicates a continuing maturity on Grant's part and further evidence of his ability to develop new and meaningful ideas in his work.

It is also another example of Grant's choice of symbolic subjects.

This bronze represents one of the transition periods in western history: the end of the fur trade era and the dawn of the range cattle industry on the northern plains. This same kind of historical turning-point is dealt with in *End of the Open Range* and *Red Men's Grave Markers*.

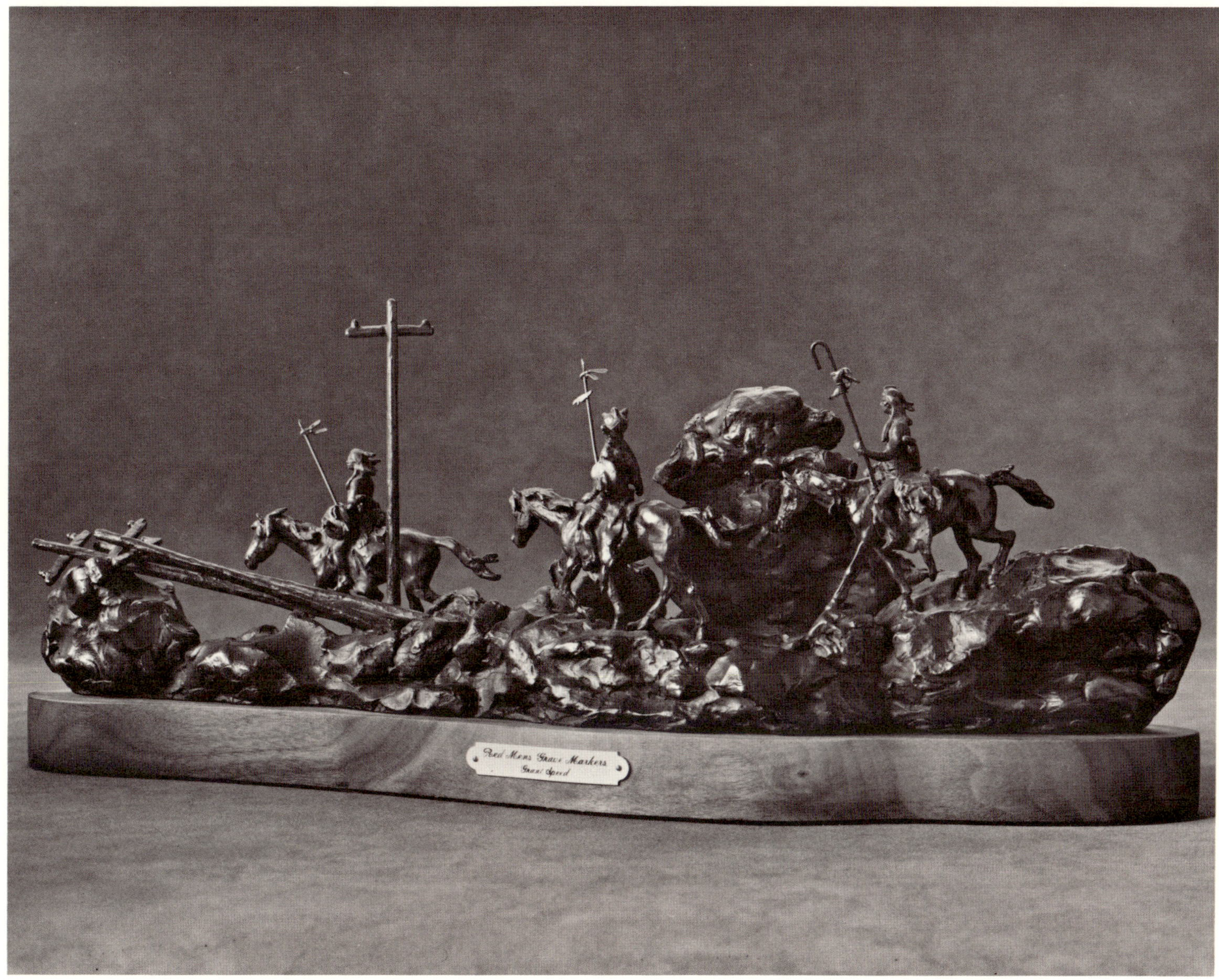

RED MEN'S GRAVE MARKERS

The statement in this bronze resembles that of *End of the Open Range*. Just as barbed wire signaled the end of the free grass era for the cowboy, so the telegraph poles were harbingers of disaster for the Indian's way of life.

Such an idea for a western sculpture is rare. This is the kind of heroic theme that not only tells us something about the artist's empathy for the West but is also a genuine challenge to his talent. It is one thing to conceive such an idea, but it is something much more difficult to translate it into actual form and space.

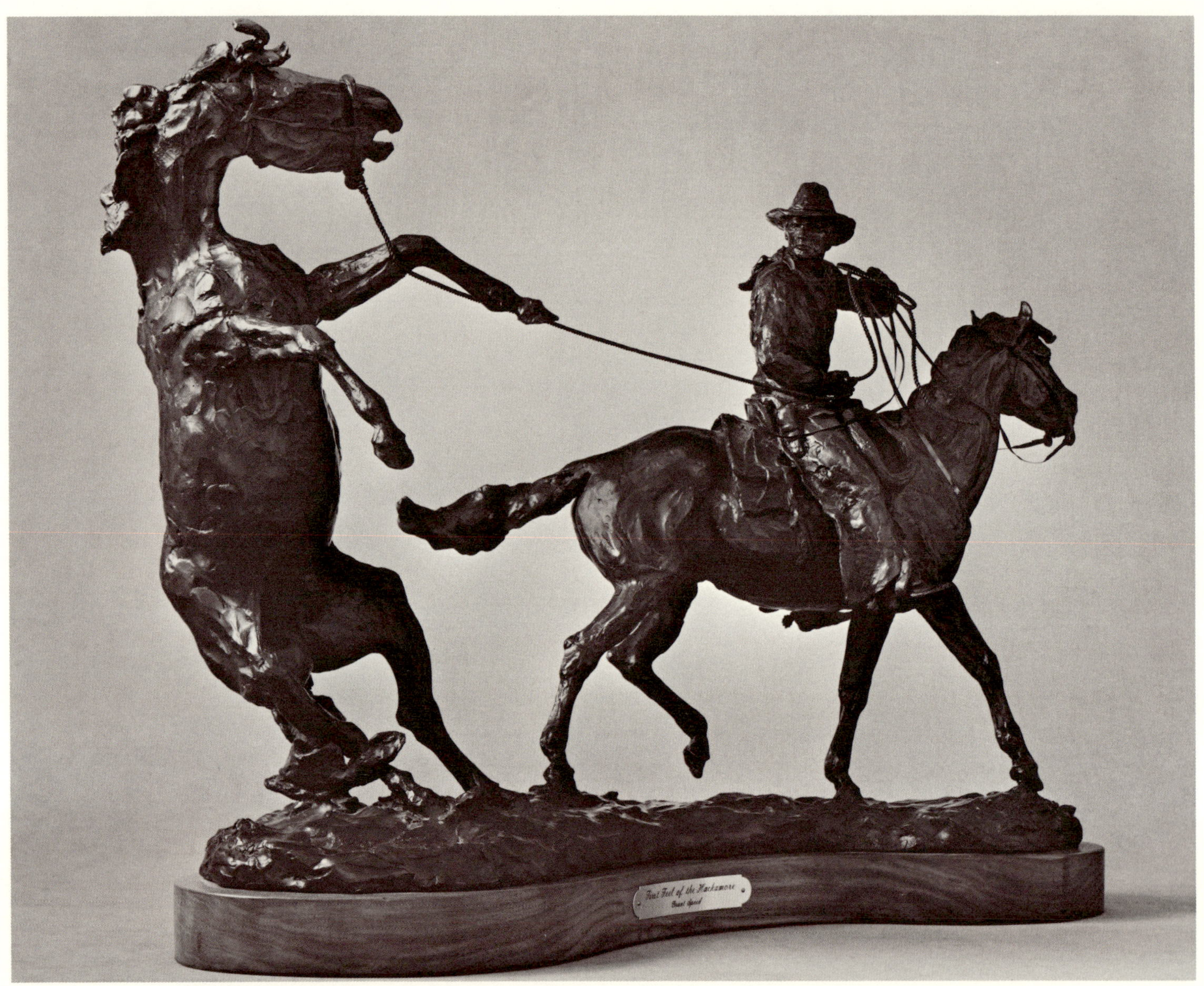

FIRST FEEL OF THE HACKAMORE

The inspiration for this bronze came out of Grant's own experience, as with many of his sculptures that involve horses.

A hackamore is a bridle without a bit and is used in the earliest stages of breaking a ranch horse to ride. A rawhide noseband, or "bosal," is used to control the horse. Here the bronc is fighting against the hackamore as the cowboy attempts to lead him around. There will be another "storm" when a saddle is cinched on for the first time.

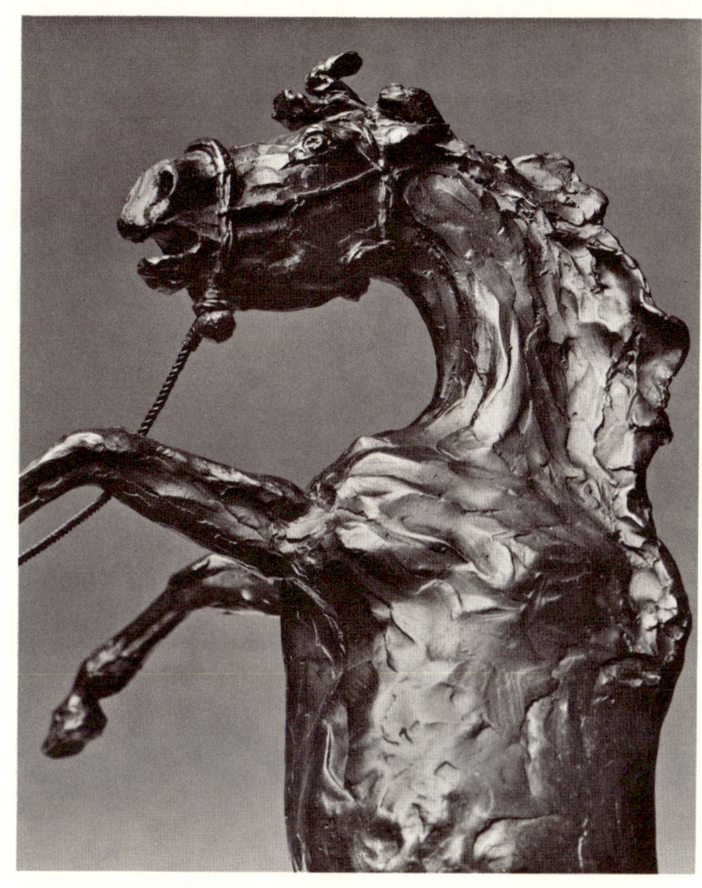

Detail of "First Feel of the Hackamore"

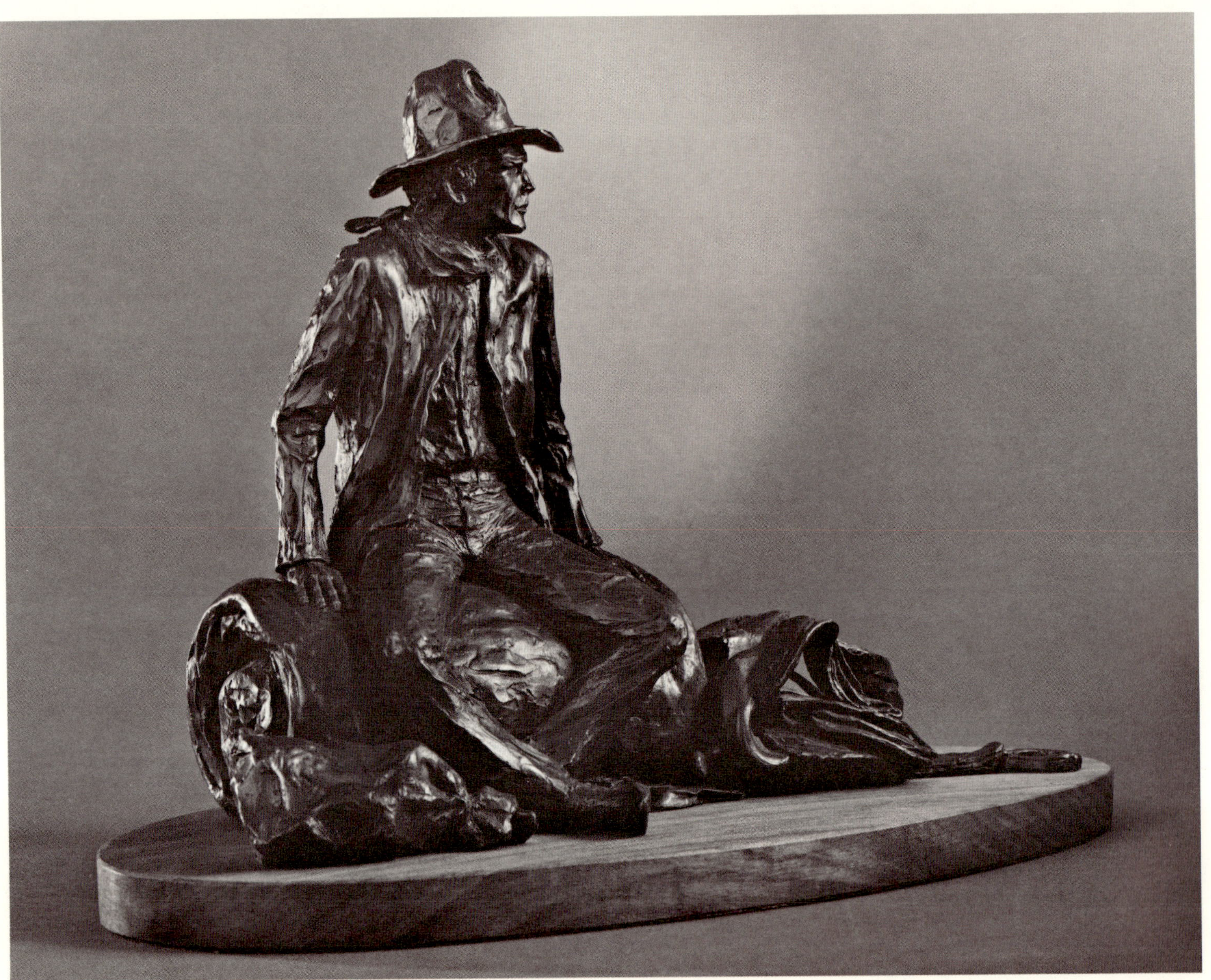

IN BETWEEN JOBS

No one was ever better able to take care of himself than a cowboy. It was a matter of pride that he would "do for himself" and ask no one for anything that he didn't earn.

Here is a cowboy who has probably just finished seasonal roundup work and is out of a job. Rather than being troubled by uncertainty about where his next meal is coming from, he anticipates new adventures and new ranges. All of his gear is in his bedroll. This, his saddle, and the clothes he wears are his only possessions. He is not tied down and will always be free to come and go as he pleases.

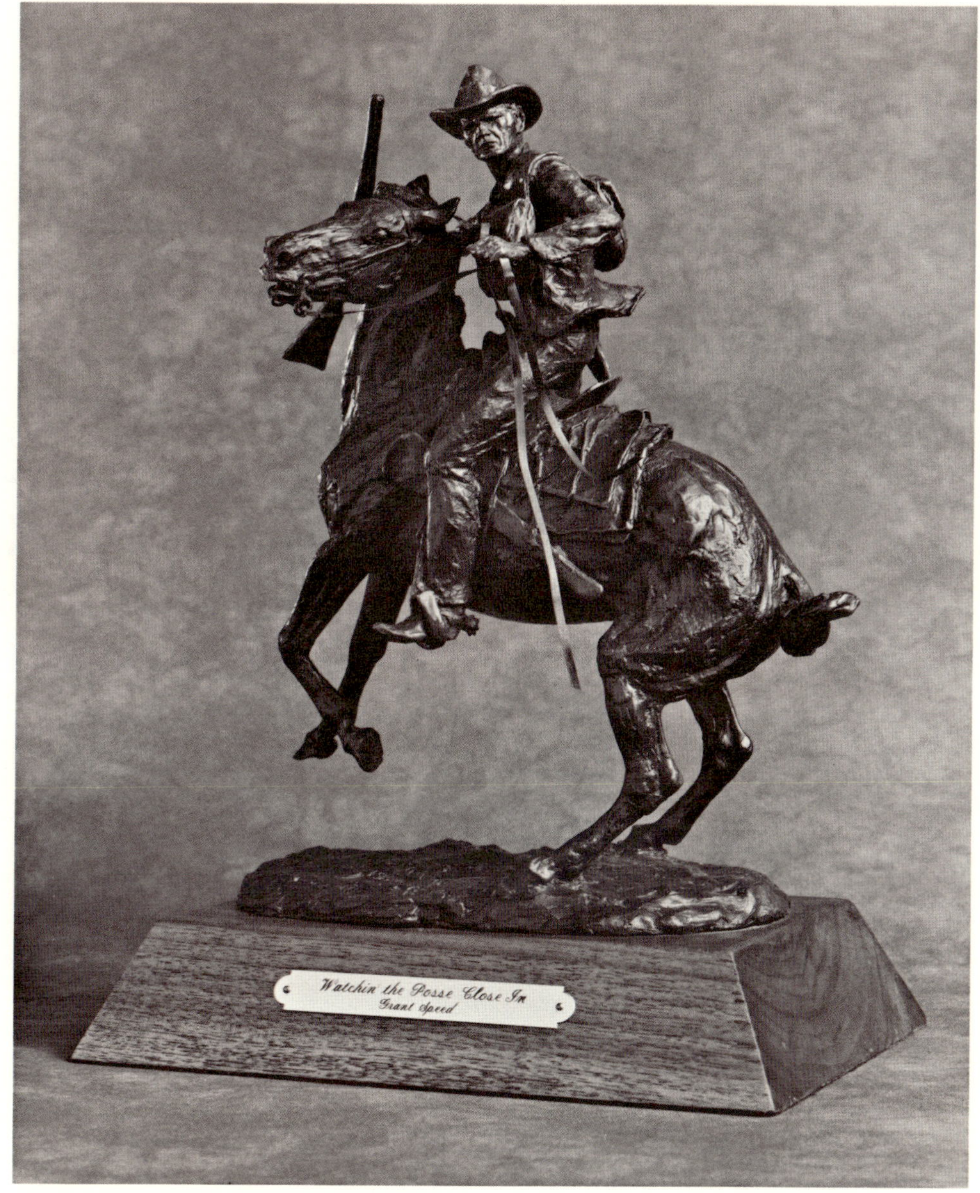

WATCHIN' THE POSSE CLOSE IN

This is yet another in Grant's series of pieces that deal with "gun-totin'" cowboys. The title of this bronze tells us that this man is being pursued by lawmen. But again, Grant lets us make up our own story to account for the situation. He simply supplies the dra-matic image and the implication of gun smoke.

This piece also points out one of the truest of all cowboy traits: even though the posse is closing in, there is no hint that the man intends to surrender.

85

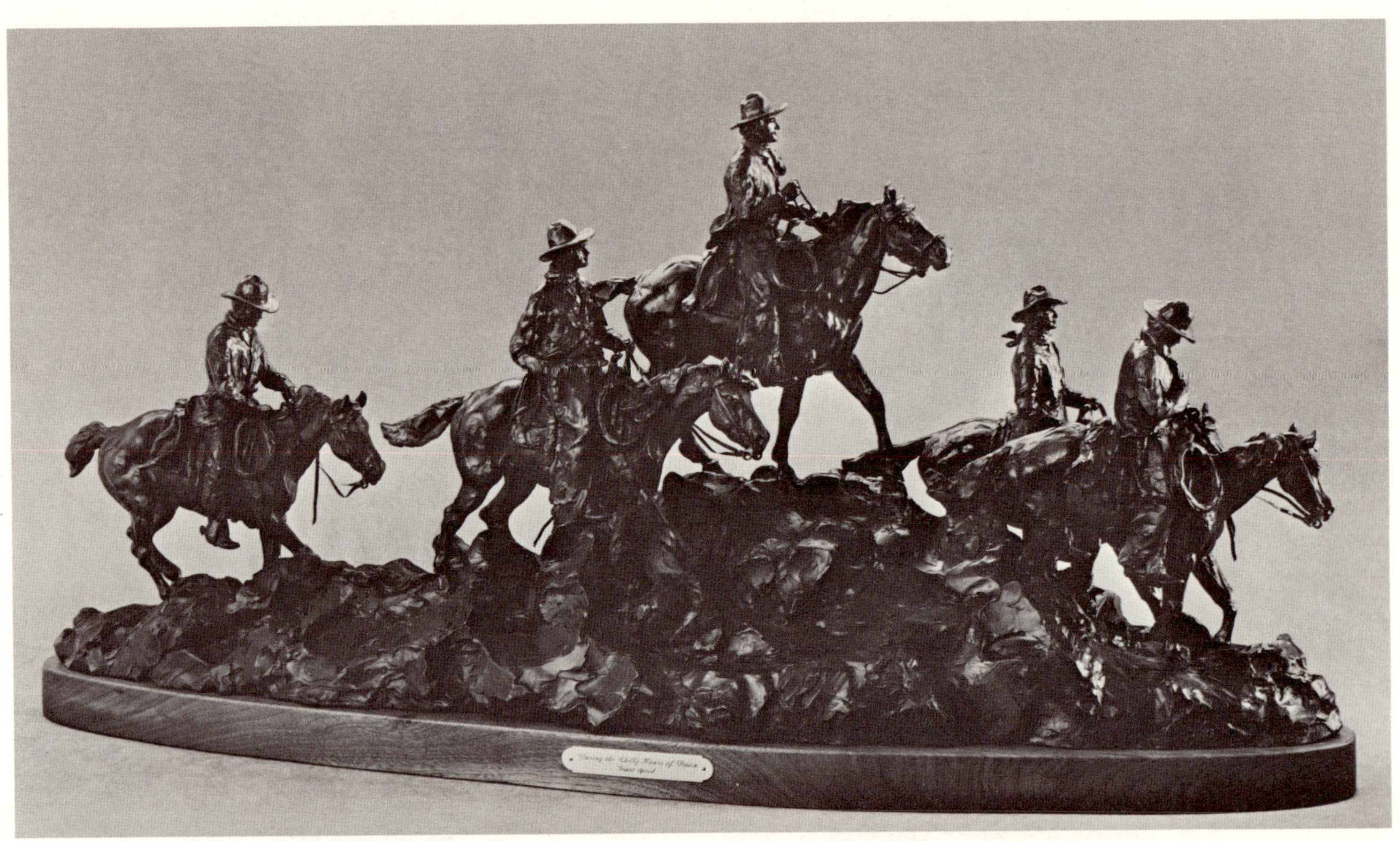

DURING THE CHILLY HOURS OF DAWN

Many discriminating collectors were disappointed when this bronze did not win the Gold Medal for sculpture at the 1975 Cowboy Artists exhibition. It is a magnificent work, both in idea and in execution. It is the kind of piece that will find its way into museum collections, representative of the present generation of contemporary western sculpture.

The scope of this piece is broader than most of Grant's work. Here is a roundup outfit starting out for a day's work. The cowboys, the horses they ride, and the cattle they seek are the entire cast and crew of the "Golden Age" of the range.

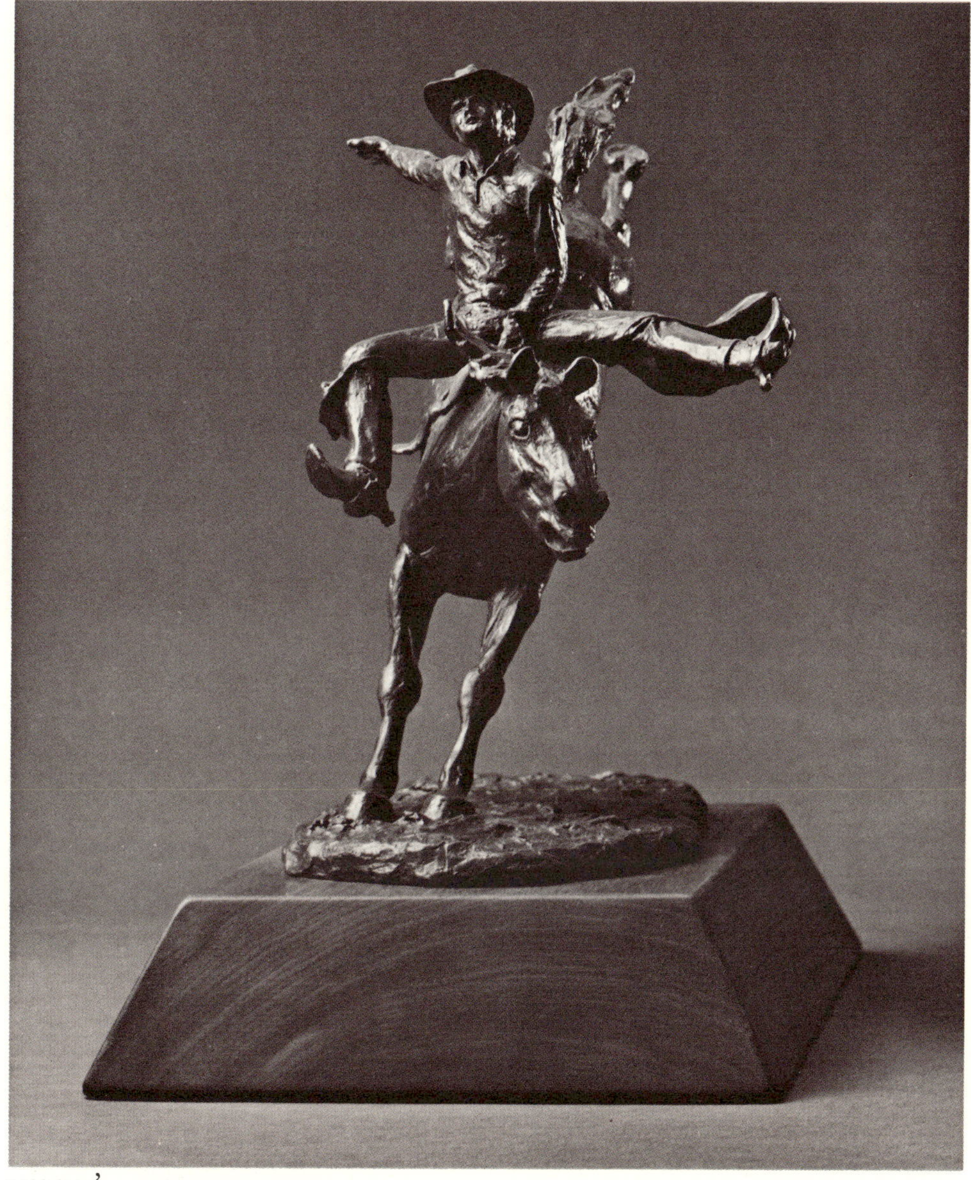

FITTIN' A HUNGRY RIDE

The title of this piece is straight out of a cowboy's vocabulary. It is generally held that a man will sit a little tighter, and spur a little wilder, when he needs to win the money. No cowboy ever wants to buck off, but there are times when economic realities give him added incentive.

Grant fitted plenty of hungry rides during his rodeo days. Some-times cowboys use all their money just to get up the entry fee; then they've got to win so they can buy gas to get home, not to mention eating until the next rodeo.

This bronze is an example of a cowboy talking to cowboys and about cowboys through the medium of fine art.

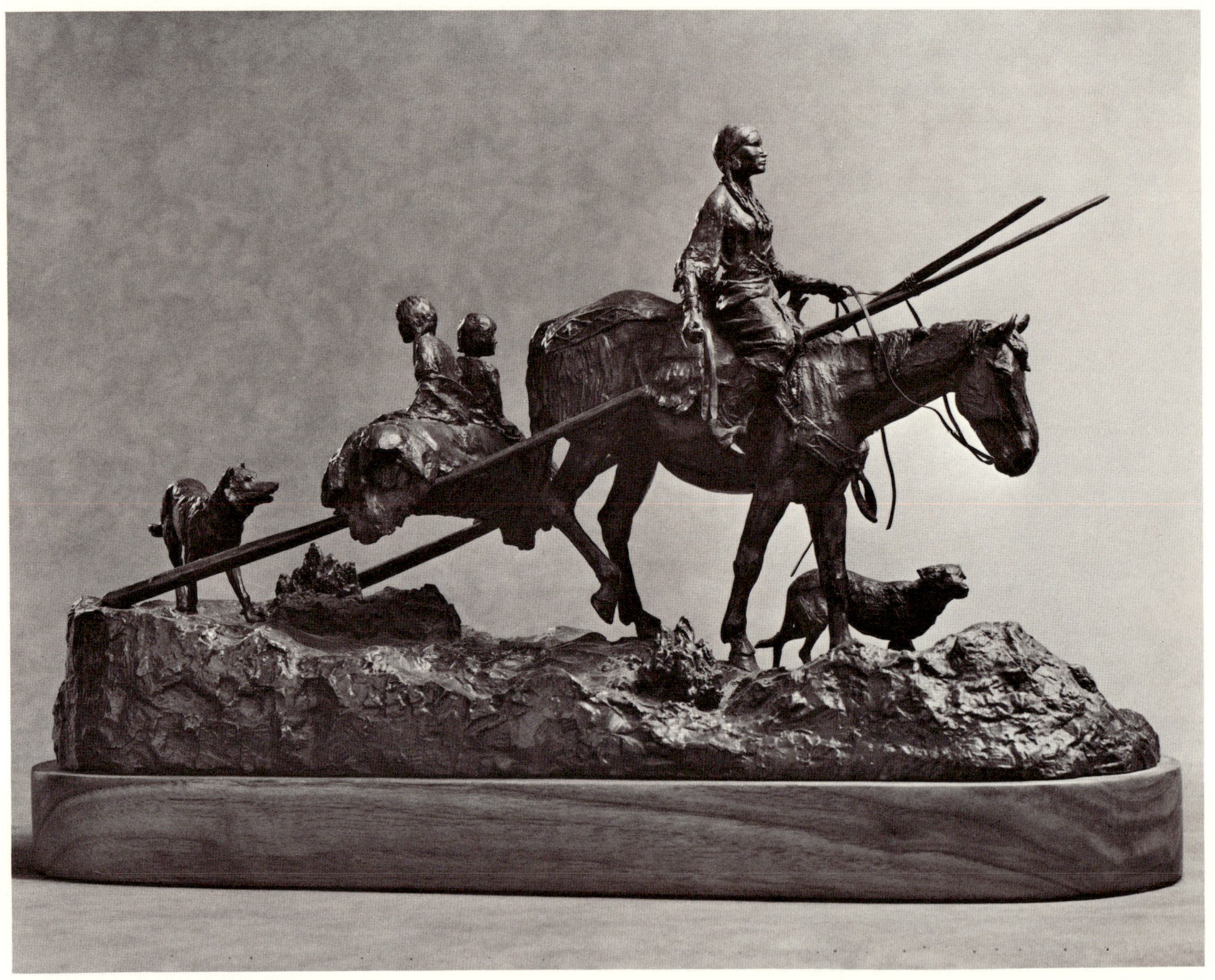

ON TO A BETTER RANGE

Grant has seldom used Indian subjects for his bronzes, although Indians and their stories are of continuing interest to him. Grant is a student of western history, and the Plains Indian is a major part of western heritage.

Here Grant has developed an interesting composition and a fresh, original idea for a bronze. The Indian family is moving their camp to a new location, perhaps following a migrating buffalo herd.

The *travois* was an important device in this kind of operation. It hauled the tipi, family possessions, and children as well. There is a happy feeling in this bronze.

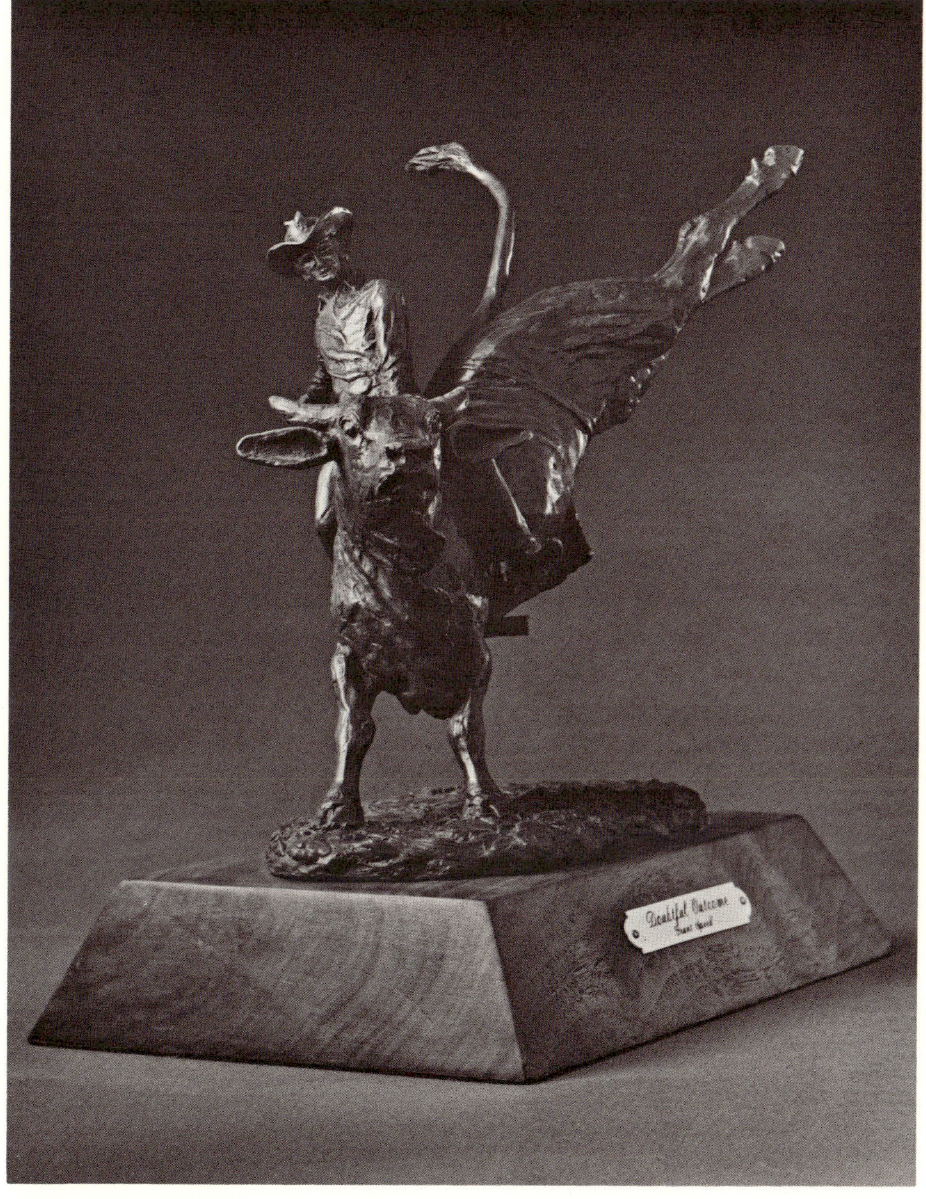

THE BULL RIDER

Rodeo was an important part of Grant's life before he ever even thought about a career in art. His own experiences in the arena give added depth and strength to his bronzes that deal with rodeo subjects.

This bronze was included in the very first Cowboy Artists show.

It was selected as a trophy by the Rodeo Cowboys' Association to be presented to the All-Around World's Champion Cowboy.

The fact that it was one of the very first pieces Grant had cast, and that it was of a subject that he felt close to, made this a high point in Grant's early career — one he still remembers fondly.

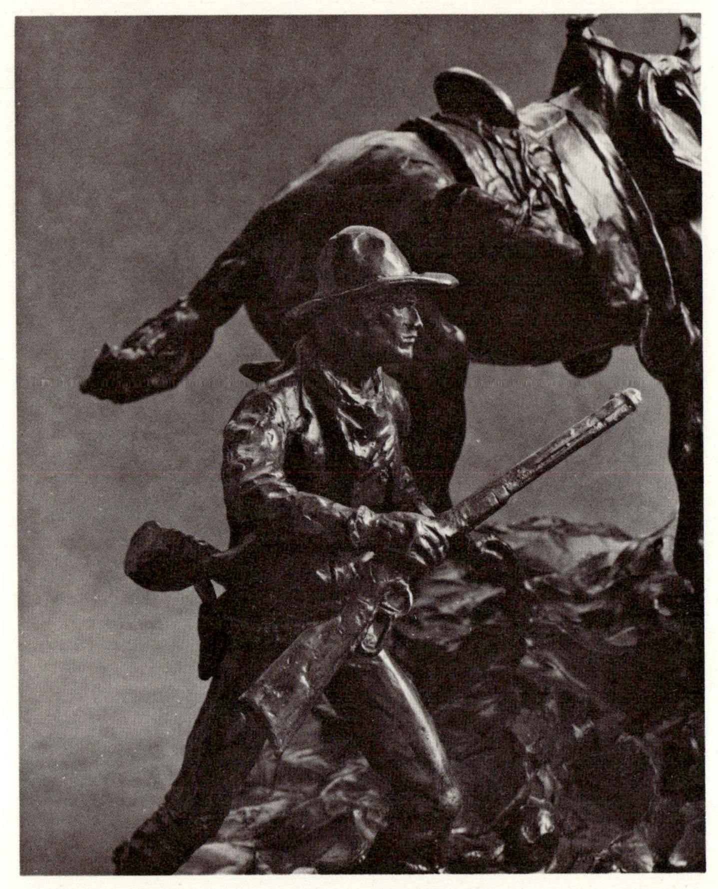

Detail of "Quick Tied by the Texas Ranger"

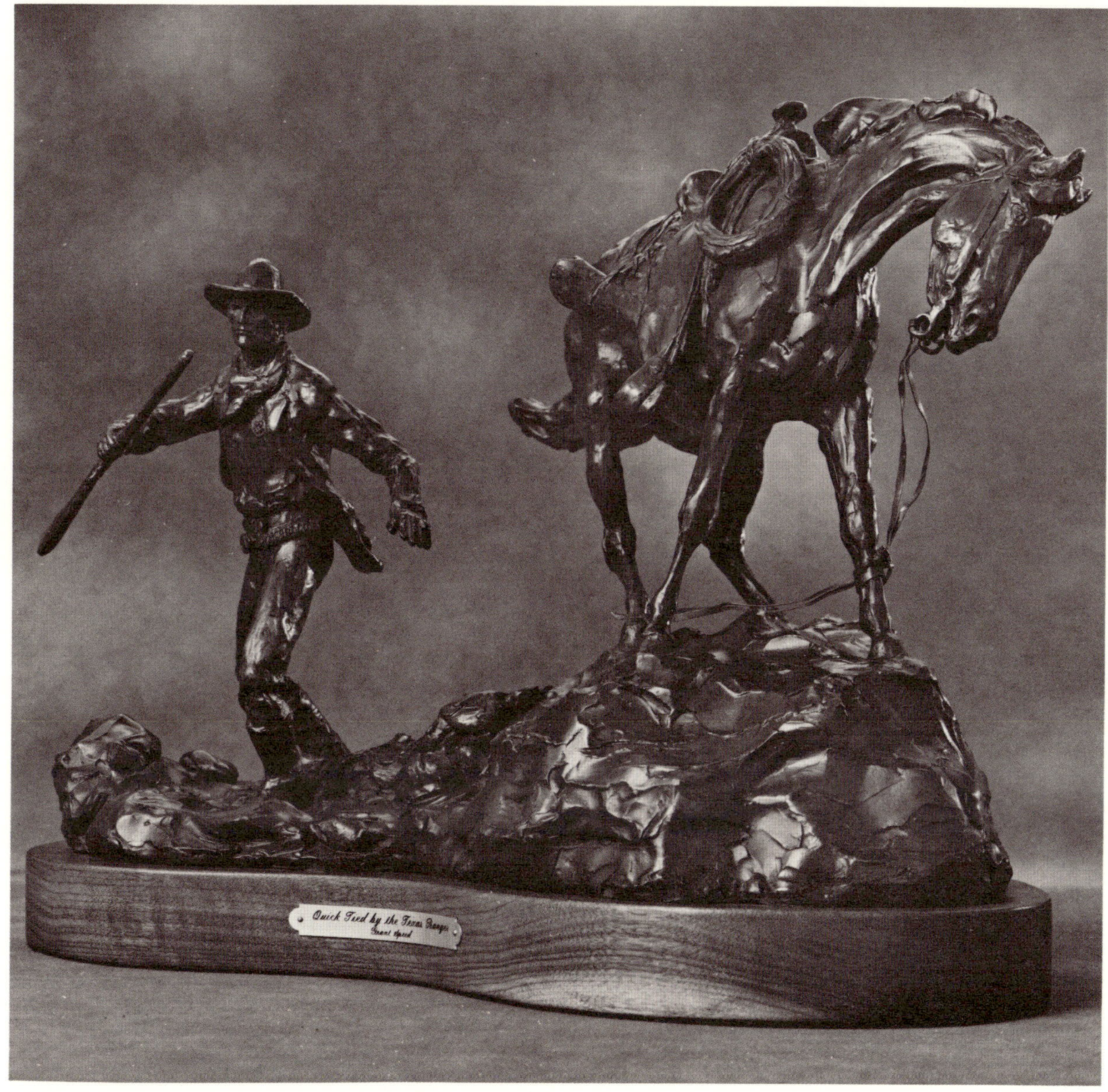

QUICK TIED BY THE TEXAS RANGER

This bronze uses an element of implied, rather than obvious, drama. It is clear that the ranger has dismounted in a hurry and is ready for trouble with gun in hand.

But rather than restricting the viewer to a specific interpretation, Grant leaves it up to each of us to become involved in the creative process as we consider the things not seen in the bronze itself.

This is a mark of a mature artist. He allows his audience to bring their own feelings into his work.

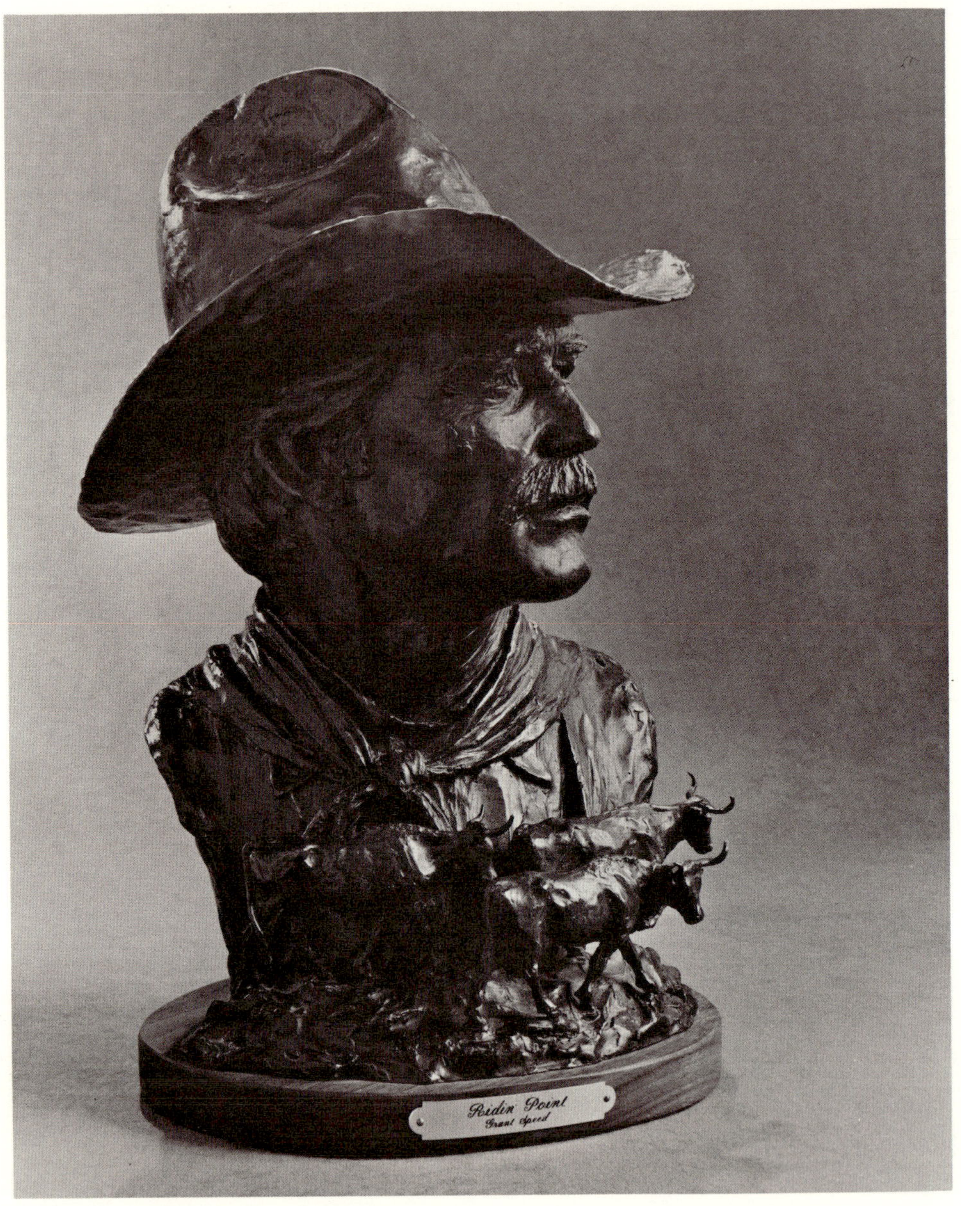

RIDIN' POINT

This was the first in what would eventually constitute a series of western busts using a vignette in reduced scale at the base. The bronze received immediate acclaim by collectors at the Cowboy Artists of America show in 1970. The entire edition sold out on the preview evening of the exhibition, the first time this had happened at any contemporary western art show.

The widespread acceptance of this piece created a demand that led Grant to expand the concept to finally include six pieces over the next eight years. The series as a whole represents one of the major landmarks in contemporary western art.

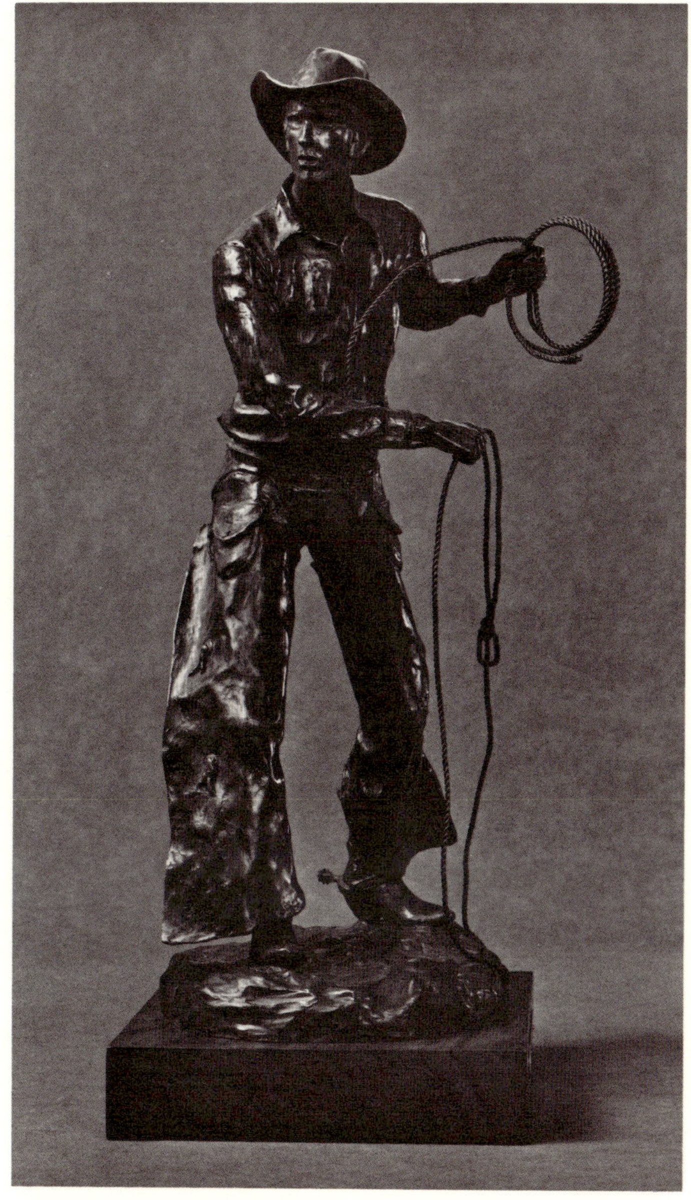

A young cowboy makes slow, sure movements as he prepares to rope a horse for the day's work. Instead of twirling the loop around his head and spooking the horses, he is ready to throw the rope backhanded. The loop will turn over in the air and settle around the horse's neck. Old-timers called this loop the "hoolihan."

This is another autobiographical subject for Grant. He has roped horses in corrals from Texas to Wyoming. And like every man who ever cowboyed, Grant still enjoys playing with a rope.

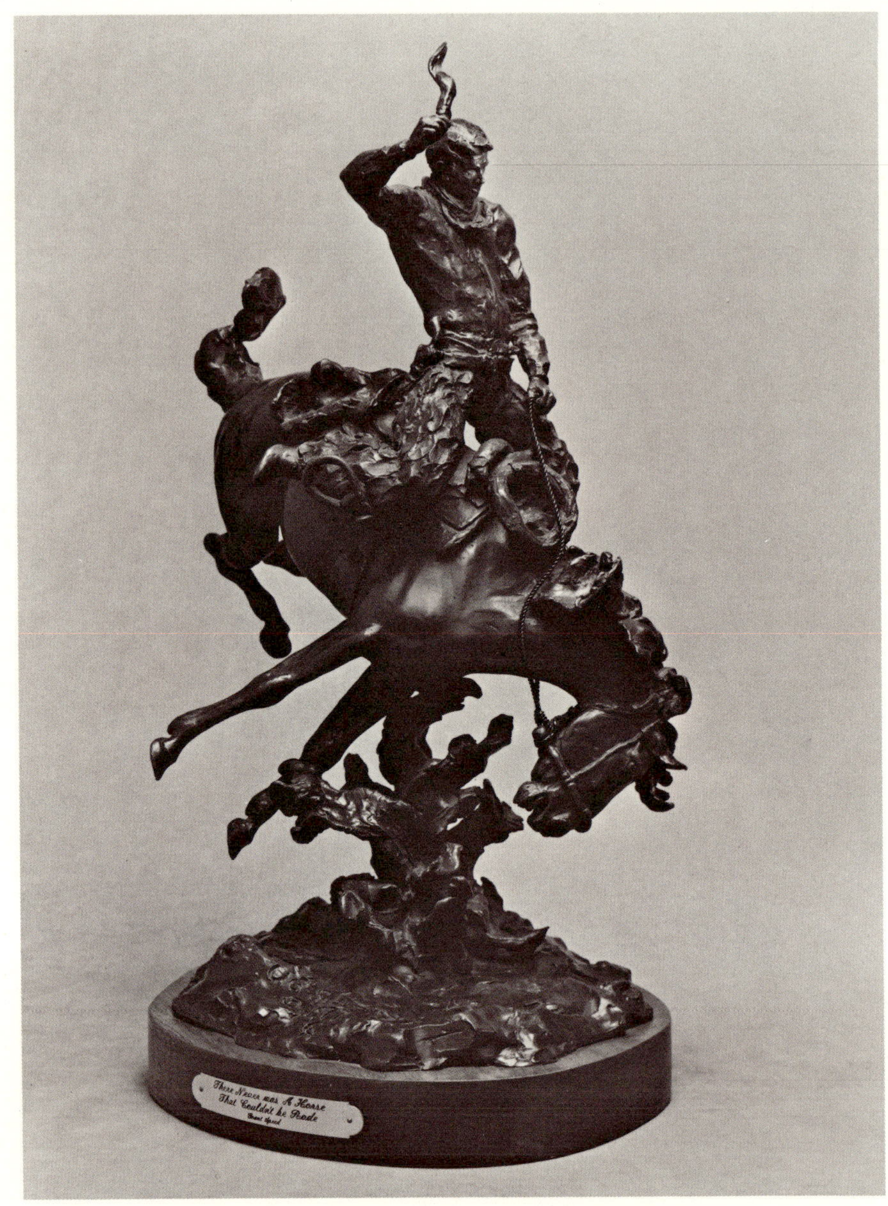

THERE NEVER WAS A HORSE THAT COULDN'T BE RODE

This is one of the bucking horse pieces, a favorite theme in Grant's earlier work. This stems from his own background with outlaw ranch horses and rodeo broncs. The title and the idea are fundamental to western life. The statement implied by the cowboy staying aboard a bad horse reflects a basic cowboy belief that a man can do whatever he sets out to do.

For Grant, this bronze represents something more than a particular horse and a particular bronc rider. It is a tribute to the style and determination of all cowboys.

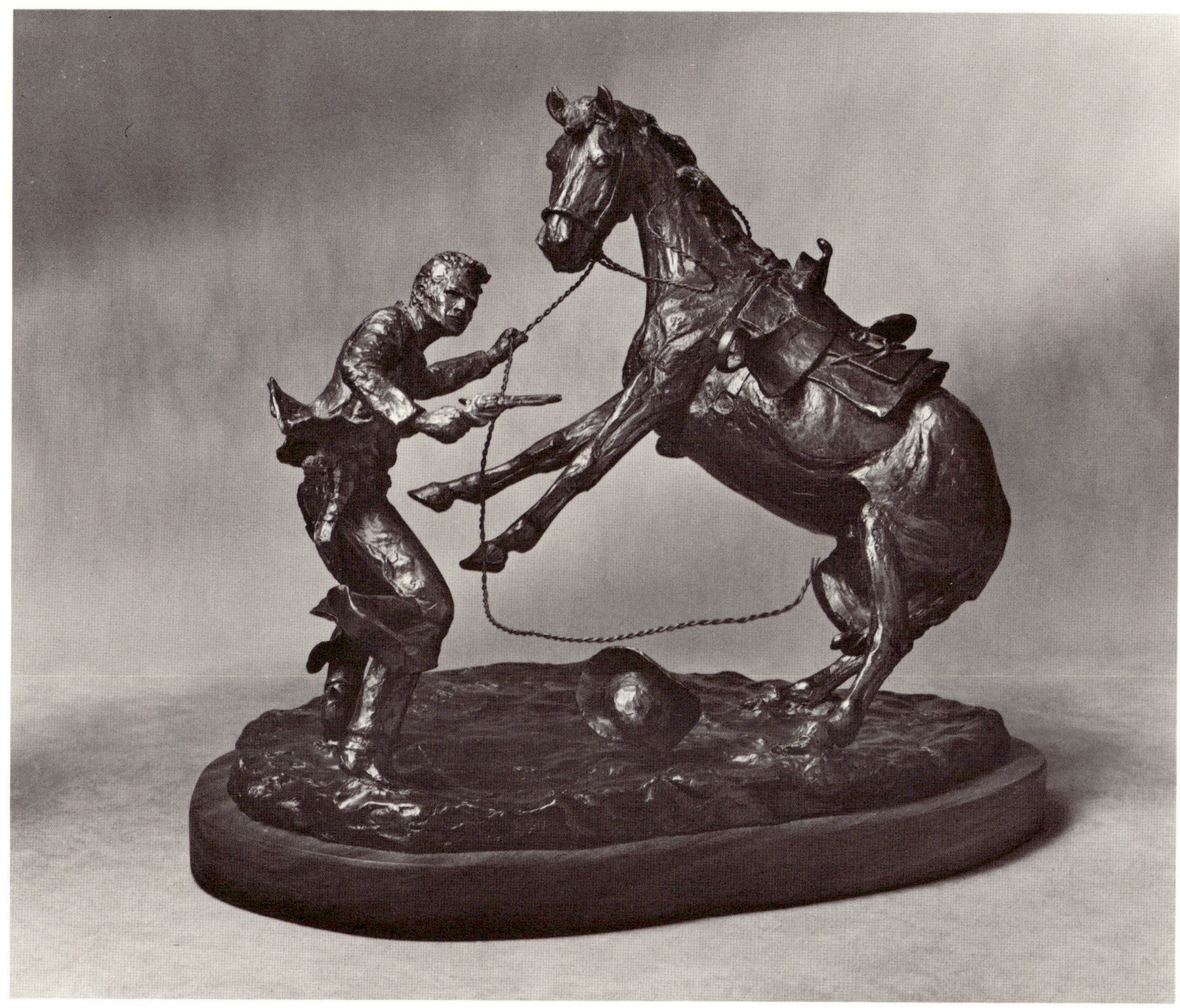

FAST GETAWAY

There are several recognizable themes in Grant's work; among them are bucking horses and gunfighters.

This bronze, along with *Quick Tied by the Texas Ranger, Watchin' the Posse Close In,* and *Riders in the Distance Add to the Risk of Rustling,* exemplifies Grant's use of the gunfighter theme.

It is important to note, however, that Grant portrays the six-shooter, or the saddle carbine, as only another part of the life, just like saddles and ropes. He does not over-dramatize the gunfighter concept in the contrived manner of a Hollywood movie.

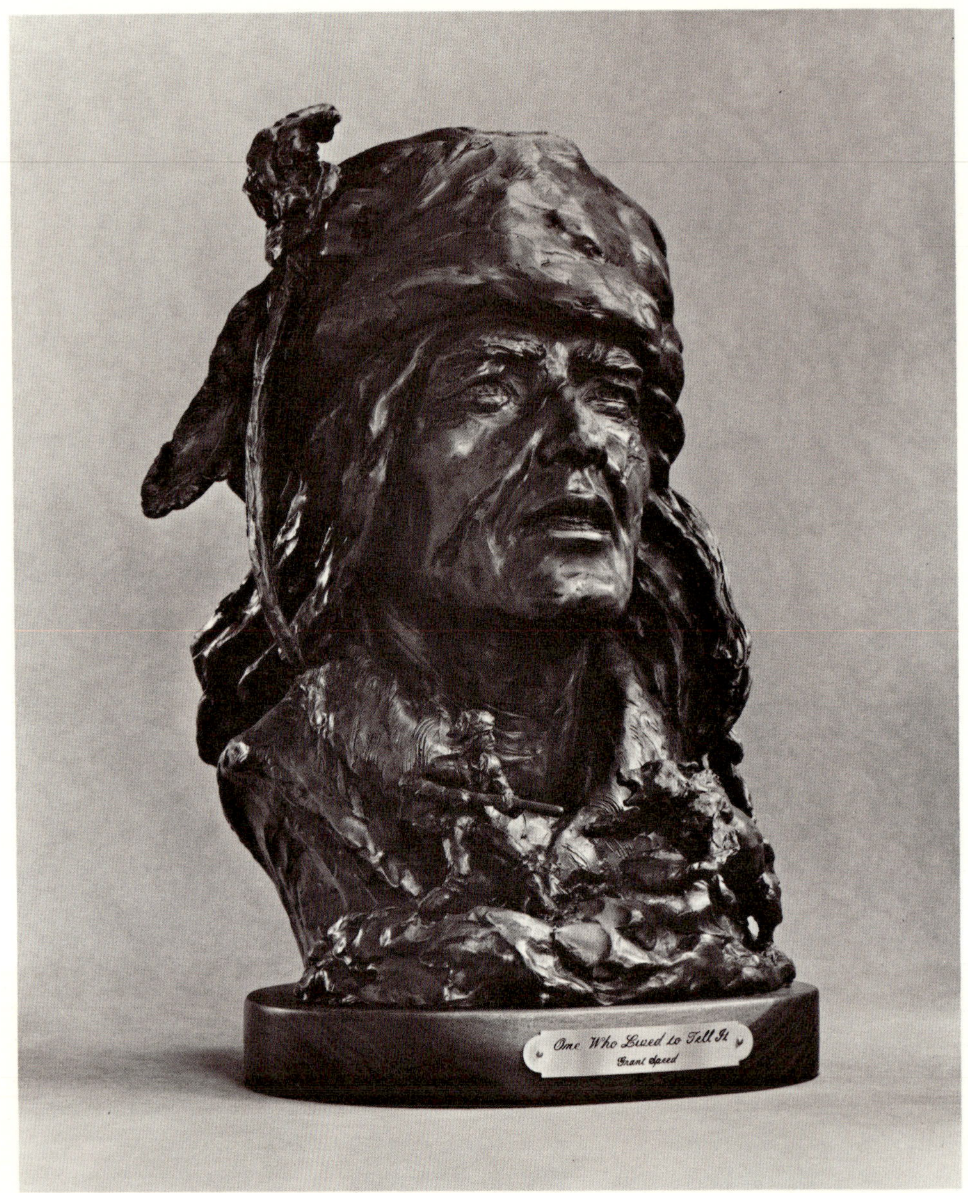

ONE WHO LIVED TO TELL IT

In this, the fifth piece in the series of western busts, Grant returned to the original design with the inclusion of the miniature vignette at the base.

By the time this bronze was first shown, in 1977, the collectors were aware of the significance of Grant's series concept, and once again the entire edition was sold out in short order.

This bronze is reminiscent of the story of the early mountain man, Hugh Glass, who tangled with a grizzly bear and lived to tell about it. It is a story and a bronze with the flavor of high adventure.

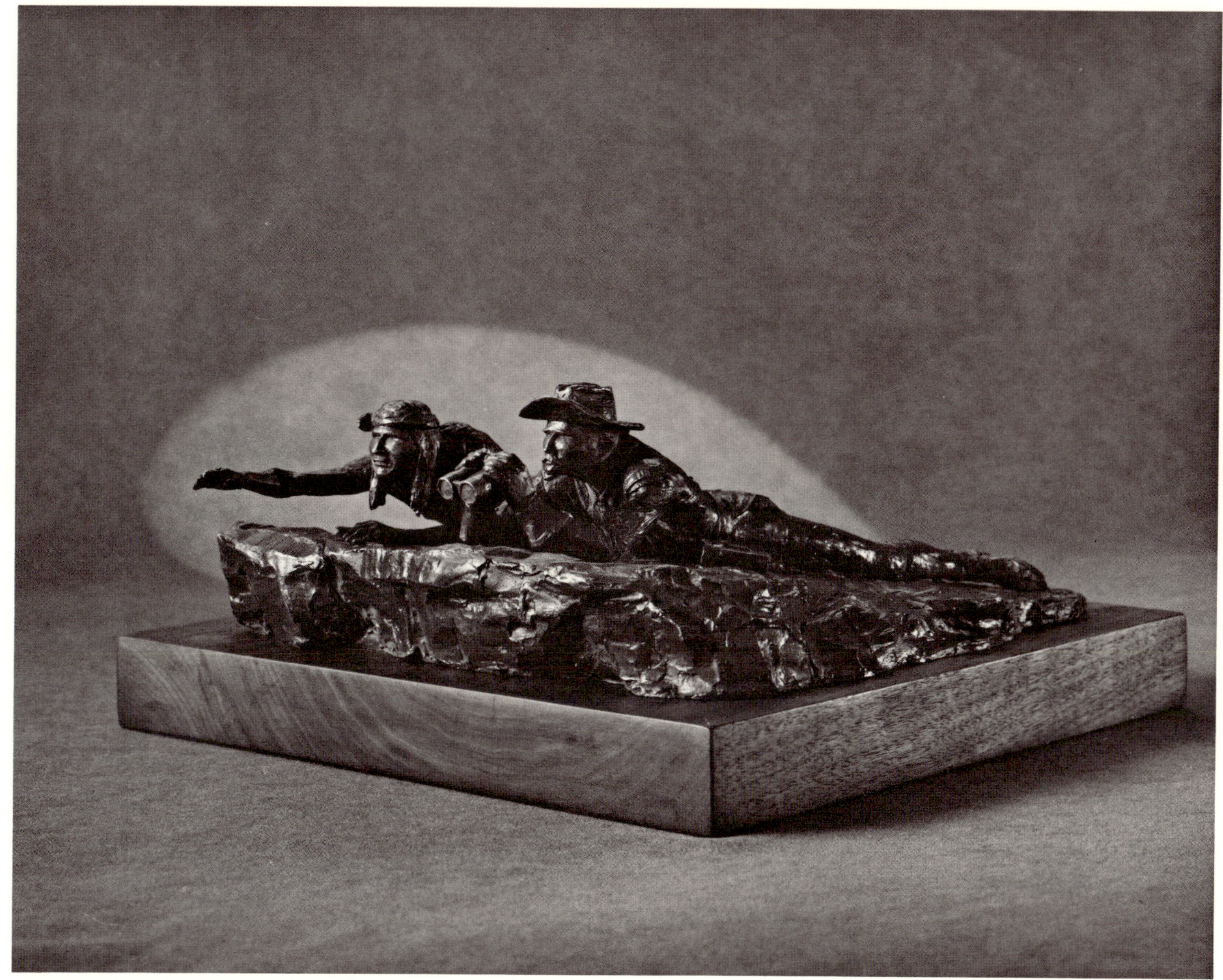

SCOUTING A WAR PARTY

The design of this bronze is another example of the originality with which Grant approaches his work. Sculpture usually has a strong element of vertical line, but here Grant has emphasized the horizontal. The strength of the piece is in the upper bodies of the cavalry trooper and his Indian scout. The subtlety of the lower bodies dramatizes the concentration of the two men as, once again, an unseen element becomes an essential part of the story.

The sculptor's magic has created an impression of a high cliff, and we can easily sense the war party in the canyon below.

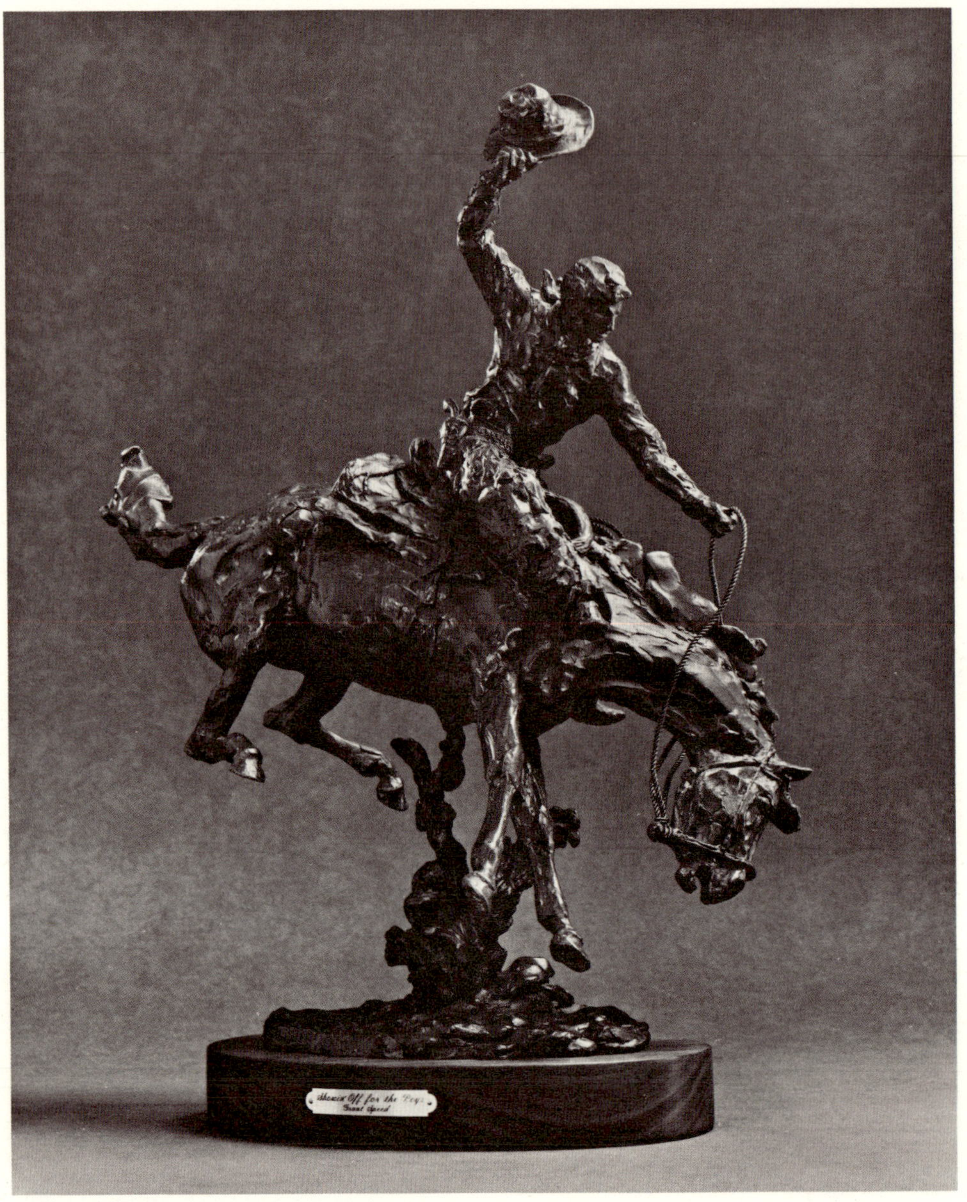

SHOWIN' OFF FOR THE BOYS

It is hard for Grant to ever get away entirely from the subject of bucking horses. They were a part of his experiences as a ranch hand and as a bronc rider, and they have become a part of his art. Grant sculpts bucking horses and bronc riders for the same reasons you would expect a sailor-turned-artist to deal with boats and seamen.

Given an artistic talent for his medium, who could do a better job with this subject than a man who knows how it actually feels to be on the back of a bad horse? No comprehensive selection of Grant's work could fail to include one of his bucking horse bronzes.

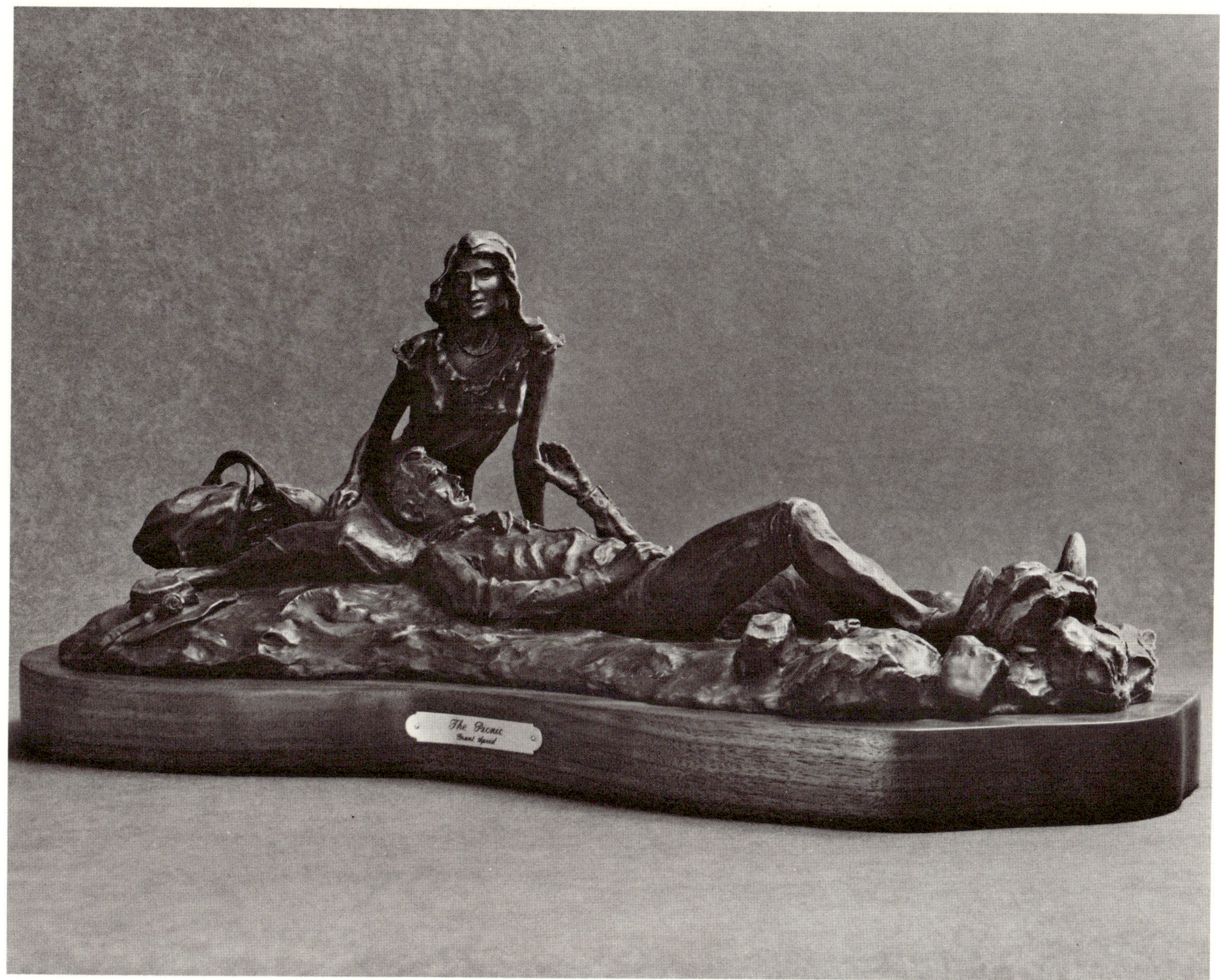

THE PICNIC

Very few western artists have used women in their paintings or sculpture. This probably has something to do with the heavily masculine nature of the frontier experience. But women actually figured into practically every phase of the development of the West.

Grant has used women in several of his works: *The Squaw Man,* *The Half-Breed, Almost Home from the War,* and *On to a Better Range.*

The Picnic is a pleasant bronze. It makes us consider the fact that the West was not all gunfights, trail driving, and bucking horses.

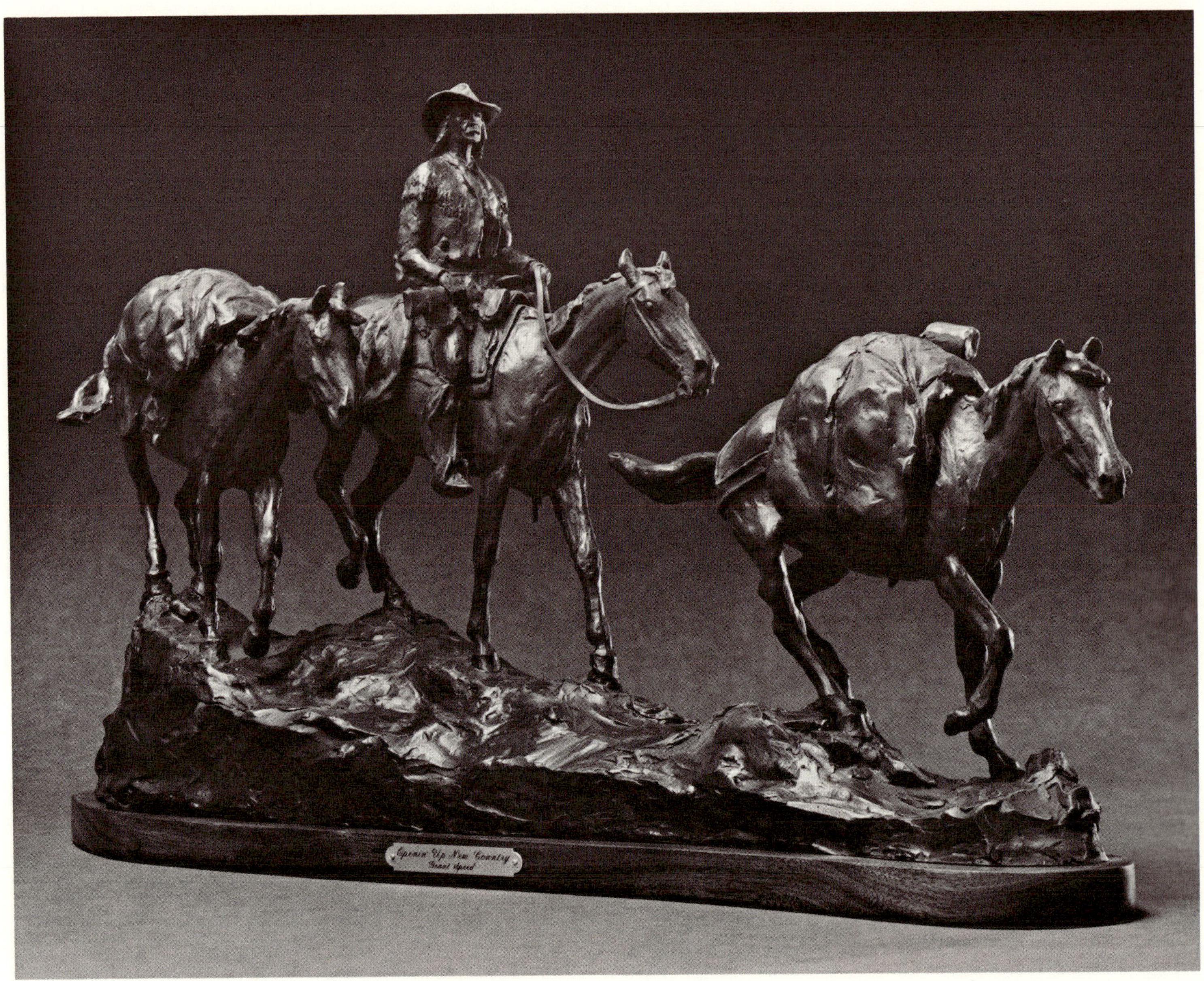

OPENIN' UP NEW COUNTRY

This is a full-blown representation of the type of frontier character shown in Grant's head, *Free Spirit*. These were the men who rode into the Trans-Mississippi West when it still belonged to the Indian. They were explorers, fur trappers, and hunters: a type known as mountain men. They were the essence of independence and resource-fulness. The West was a hostile land and these were the men who blazed the trails along which civilization would follow. Grant has a special feeling for these men. He identifies with their grit and their determination to persevere.

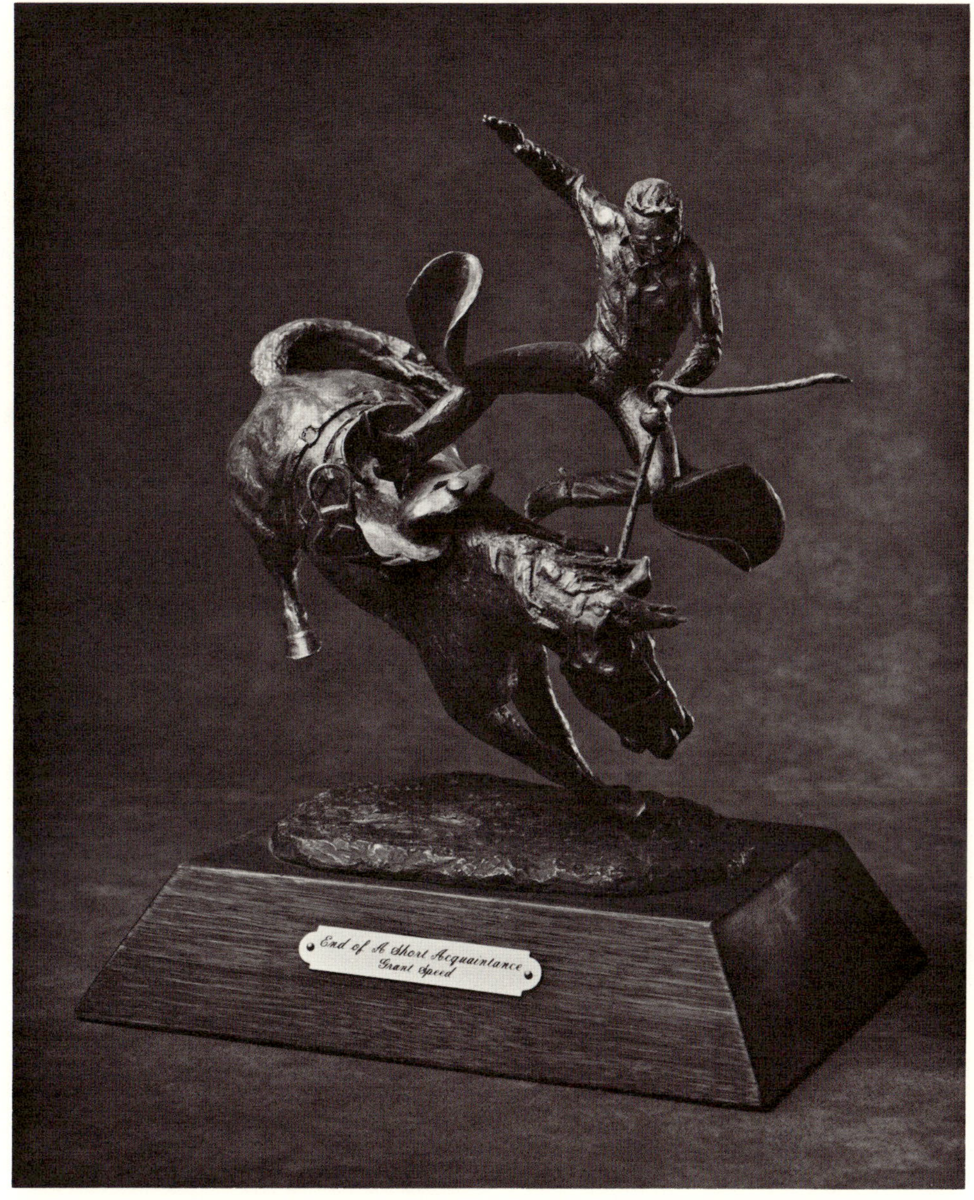

END OF A SHORT ACQUAINTANCE

Here is a bronze that could be called, "What Grant Speed Did Best in College." Saddle bronc riding was Grant's best event when he was rodeoing. It just so happens that it is also the rodeo event that lends itself most suitably to sculpture.

There is obvious power and strength in the wild action of the horse, and just as obvious is the helplessness of the cowboy, who is past the point of no return. It is an episode that is purely western — one that has been repeated thousands of times on ranches and at rodeos all over the West. And Grant has been there plenty of times.

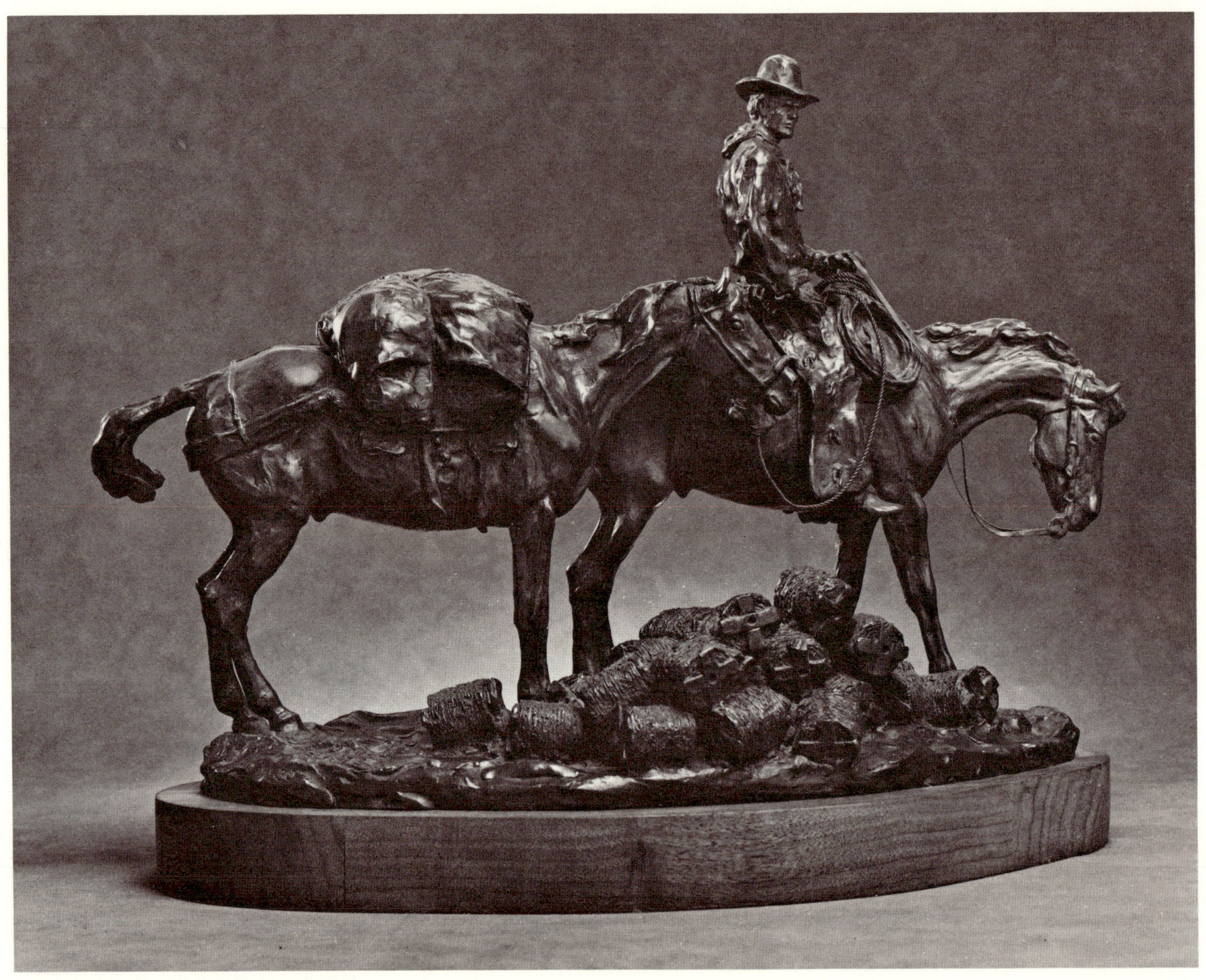

THE END OF THE OPEN RANGE

Here is an excellent example of the ability Grant has for making a profound statement with ordinary symbols. The cowboy in this sculpture represents the open range era, when men could ride from Mexico to Canada as they chose. In the bronze, the cowboy is looking at rolls of barbed wire. We are not sure if the cowboy realizes it, but Grant knows that the wire is going to change the range country forever. Once the ranges were fenced, the cowboy was restricted to specific ranch areas, and the mood of unrestrained freedom was no more.

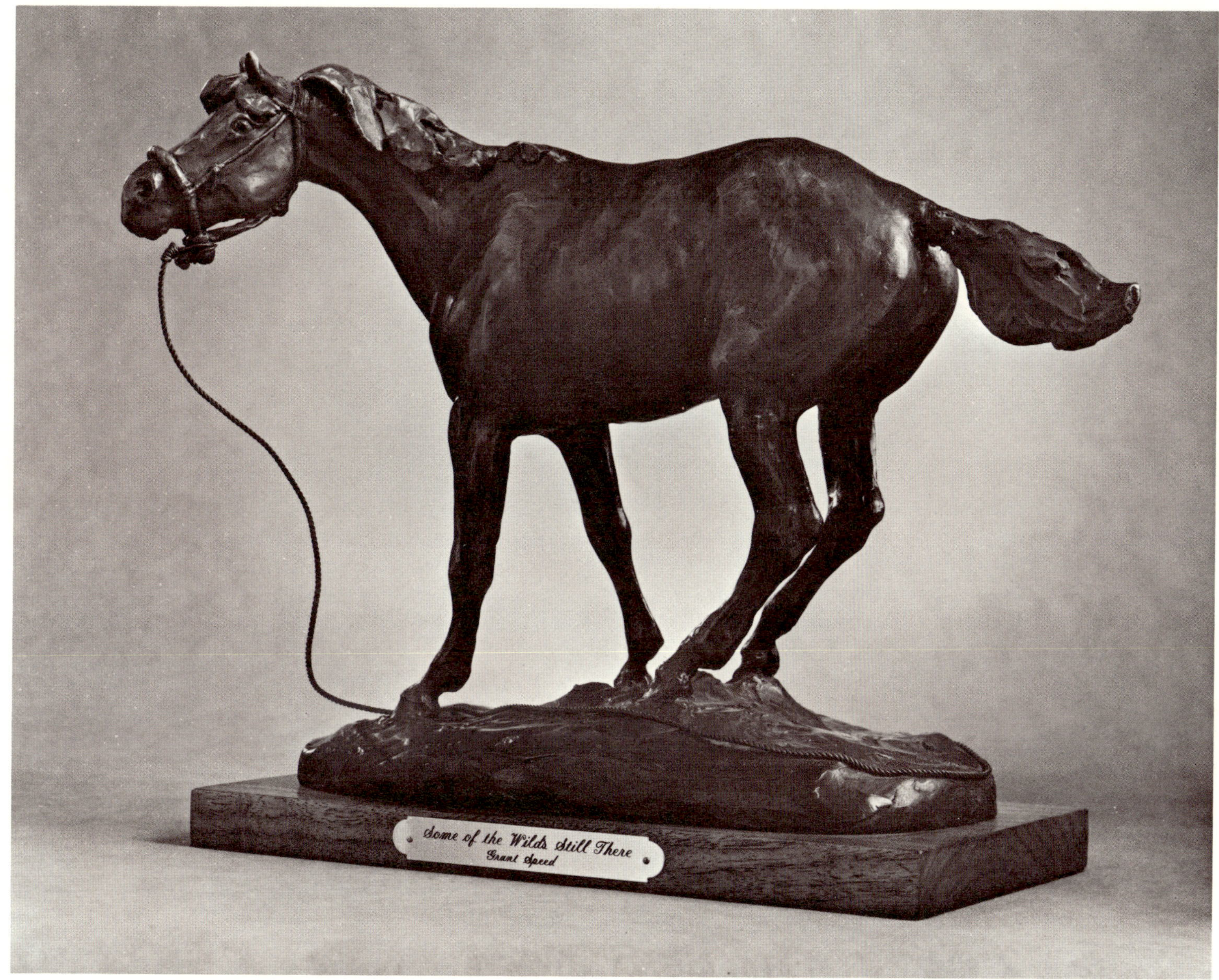

SOME OF THE WILD'S STILL THERE

This is another of Grant's sensitive horse studies. Again, the posture and attitude of the horse create a personality and mood for the piece. The horse is probably a good cowpony, but it is also evident by his bearing that he still knows how to buck. He just does not have the air about him of a docile old plow horse.

Grant learned about such things when he was earning a cowboy's wages, and they are not easily forgotten.

Work in Progress

It is a dream of every sculptor to see one of his own creations cast in life- or heroic-size for public display. This mark of accomplishment in American sculpture is associated with such names as St. Gaudens, Proctor, the Frasers, and the Borglums. But this opportunity has not been afforded to many contemporary sculptors, and even more rarely to those who deal with western subjects.

Recently, Grant has received a commission to do such a sculpture of the most famous of all Texas cowmen, Charles Goodnight. The commission came from the Mesa Petroleum Company, and the finished piece will be installed at their company headquarters in Amarillo, Texas. It is appropriate that a native Texan with strong roots in the traditions of the cowboy will make this lasting tribute in bronze to Goodnight, the man who was a cornerstone of the Texas range cattle industry. This project involves more for Grant than just his work and his talent; it also involves his heart and his feelings about his own life. The finished piece will stand for all time as a commemoration of cow country heritage; that same heritage that Grant embraced the summer when he was twelve years old and started learning to be a cowboy on the Pecos River ranch of his Uncle Boone.

Shown here is the 24-inch study for the bronze, and the larger bronze itself.

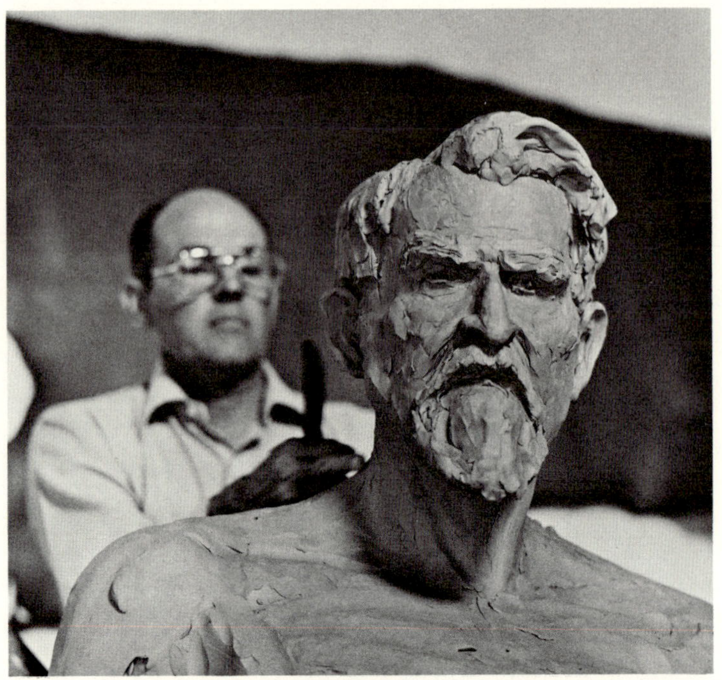

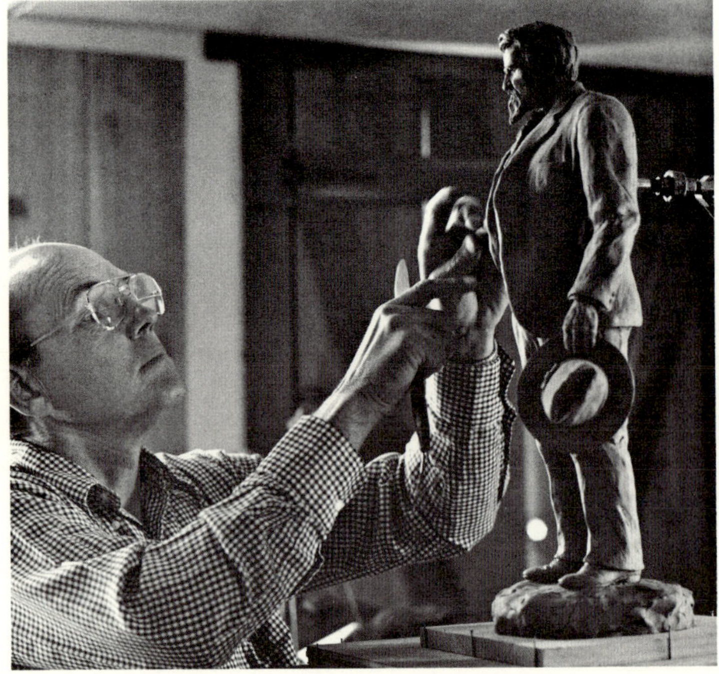

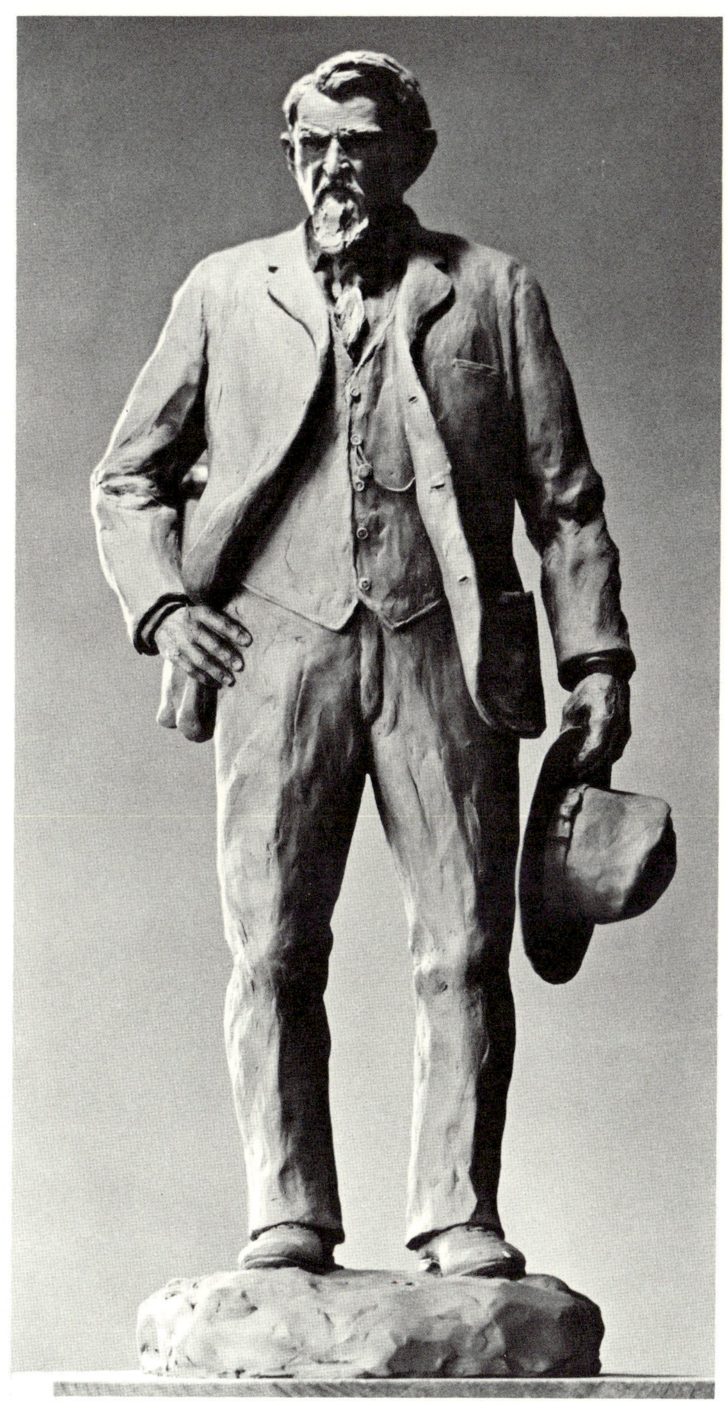

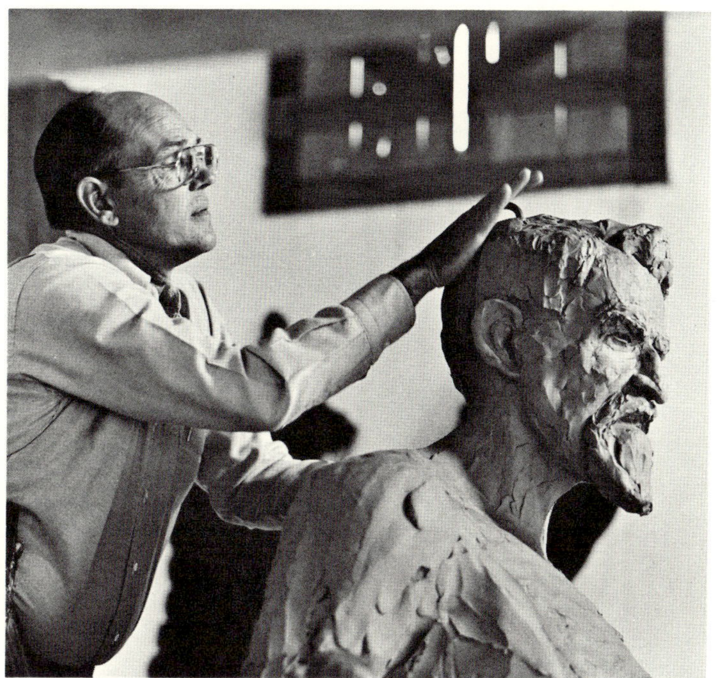

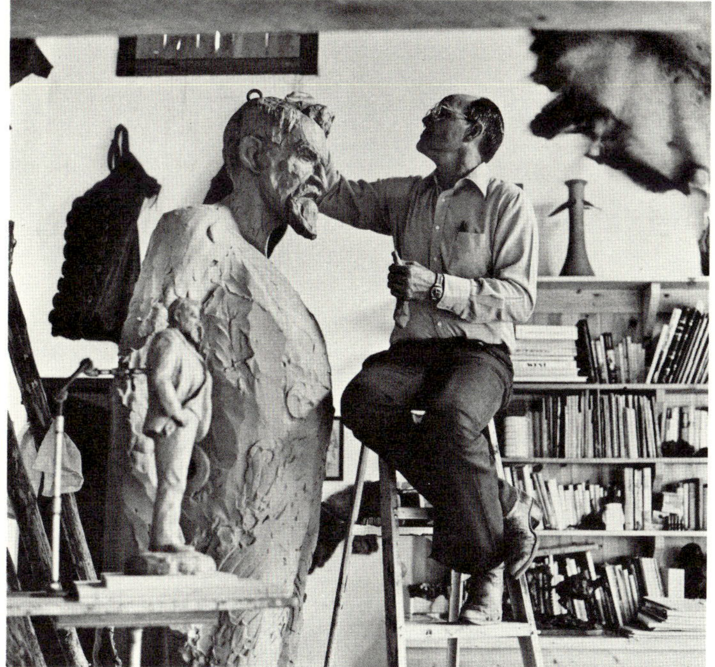

Casting Information

BRONZE	YEAR	FOUNDRY	EDITIONS	SIZE
A Stop at the Line Camp	1979	Wasatch	30	12 ″ high x 17½″ long
Almost Home from the War	1977	Wasatch	30	12 ″ high
Bought 'Em for Two and Sold 'Em for One	1975	Wasatch	30	14 ″ high
The Bronc Rider	1979	Wasatch	100	12½″ high
Charles Goodnight	1979	Wasatch	7	23 ″ high
Distant Riders Add to the Risk of Rustlin'	1976	Wasatch	30	36 ″ long
Doubtful Outcome	1966	Speed and Curtis	10	10¼″ high
During the Chilly Hours of Dawn	1975	Wasatch	30	42 ″ long
Earnin' His Dollar a Day	1971	Classic	25	17½″ high
End of the Open Range	1973	Wasatch	30	15 ″ high x 18½″ long
End of a Short Acquaintance	1965	Speed	10	8¾″ high
The Fast Getaway	1969	Speed and Curtis	15	9 ″ high x 10½″ long
First Feel of the Hackamore	1974	Wasatch	30	19 ″ high x 25 ″ long
Fittin' a Hungry Ride	1966	Speed and Curtis	10	8¼″ high
Followin' the Bell Mare	1979	Wasatch	30	21 ″ high x 40 ″ long
The Free Spirit	1971	Speed and Curtis	25	14 ″ high
The Half-Breed	1976	Wasatch	30	9½″ high
In Between Jobs	1972	Wasatch	25	10 ″ high
In the Wake of the Mountain Men	1977	Wasatch	30	32 ″ high x 34 ″ long

BRONZE	YEAR	FOUNDRY	EDITIONS	SIZE
The Law Man	1979	Wasatch	30	16 " high
Little Mustang Mare	1974	Wasatch	30	12½" high
Night Herdin' in a Rainstorm	1973	Wasatch	30	15 " high
On to a Better Range	1968	Speed and Curtis	15	11¼" high
One Who Lived to Tell It	1977	Wasatch	30	15 " high
Openin' Up New Country	1971	Speed and Curtis	25	14½" high x 24 " long
The Picnic	1978	Wasatch	30	12 " high x 26 " long
The Powder Monkey	1978	Wasatch	30	14½" high
Quick Tied by the Texas Ranger	1975	Wasatch	30	18 " long
The Rattle of the Feed Bucket	1979	Wasatch	30	18 " high
Red Men's Grave Markers	1975	Wasatch	30	20 " long
Ridin' Point	1970	Speed and Curtis	15	14 " high
Ropin' Saddle Horses	1978	Wasatch	30	21 " high
Scoutin' the War Party	1967	Speed and Curtis	10	4¼" high
Showin' Off for the Boys	1974	Wasatch	30	18½" high
Some of the Wild's Still There	1978	Wasatch	30	12 " high
The Squaw Man	1974	Wasatch	30	15 " high
Testin' the Wind	1975	Wasatch	50	6 " high
There Never Was a Horse That Couldn't Be Rode	1977	Wasatch	30	21 " high
Stampedin' over a Cutbank	1972	Wasatch	20	22 " high x 33 " long
Watchin' the Posse Close In	1970	Speed and Curtis	15	12 " high

Acknowledgments

THE AUTHOR AND ARTIST wish to specially thank the following individuals and galleries: Candy Bedner, Mr. and Mrs. David Blue, Mr. and Mrs. Jack Brotherson, Mr. and Mrs. Bill Burford, Mayor and Mrs. Bobby Folsom, Mr. and Mrs. Neil Hadlock, Dr. and Mrs. Richard M. Hebertson, Mr. and Mrs. Bobby Hillin, Mr. and Mrs. Bill Jorgensen, Mr. and Mrs. John Long, Main Trail Art Gallery, Mr. and Mrs. Irvin Pernikoff, Mr. and Mrs. Dennis Sabin, Mr. and Mrs. George Sontag, the Texas Art Gallery, the Tivoli Art Gallery, Mr. and Mrs. Royal Tribe, Mr. and Mrs. Herb Ware, Dr. and Mrs. Gary Watts, Mr. and Mrs. Sidney Wolfe, the staff at Northland Press, and the artist's family — Sue, Peggy, Boone, and Samantha.

DESIGNED BY MARK SANDERS
COMPOSED IN LINOTYPE GRANJON
WITH DISPLAY LINES
IN GARAMOND LIGHT
PRINTED ON WARREN'S OLDE STYLE
AT THE PRESS IN THE PINES

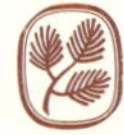

NORTHLAND PRESS

BOUND BY ROSWELL BOOKBINDING
PHOENIX